OBJECTIVITY AND THE NEWS

OBJECTIVITY AND THE NEWS

The Public and the Rise of
Commercial Journalism

DAN SCHILLER

UNIVERSITY OF PENNSYLVANIA PRESS
Philadelphia
1981

This work was published with the support of the Haney Foundation
Copyright © 1981 by Dan Schiller
Printed in the United States of America

Library of Congress Cataloging in Publication Data

Schiller, Dan, 1951–
  Objectivity and the news.
  Bibliography: p. 197
  Includes index.
  1. Journalism—Objectivity. I. Title.
PN4756.S3   070.4′3   80–52809
ISBN 0–8122–7793–7

To Sunie

I really look with commiseration over the
great body of my fellow citizens, who, reading
newspapers, live and die in the belief, that
they have known something of what has been
passing in the world in their time.

Jefferson to John Norvell

11 June 1807

CONTENTS

ILLUSTRATIONS

TABLES

ACKNOWLEDGMENTS

Friends and teachers contributed much to this effort. Robert Lewis Shayon and Thomas C. Cochran offered sound advice on many occasions. Larry Gross was helpful in numerous matters; his appreciation of photography as a historical practice has given me much to ponder. George Gerbner unstintingly proffered critical advice, analysis, support. David Chaney fired my initial interest in objectivity as a historical issue; Michael Schudson generously and critically responded to my formulations; David Kunzle helped me to trace culture into visual realms. Ted Peterson lent a hand early on, giving me access to his file on the *Police Gazette.* Marcus Rediker and Nancy Hewitt precipitated many of the thoughts below through continual discussion and questioning. Janet Wasko suffered through several outbursts generated by this work without complaint. Other new colleagues at Temple University have been supportive of my interests. I thank all of them.

Colleagues at the Centre for Mass Communication Research at the University of Leicester cheerfully forced me to confront a number of basic analytic issues. To James D. Halloran I owe thanks for taking a risk on a Yank. I am indebted to Philip Elliott for intercepting my harangues with incisive questions and comments. Graham Murdock helped me to think through important aspects of nineteenth-century criminality. Michael Pickering and Michael Tracey took time to read and comment on a chunk of this project. Other researchers at the Centre furnished assistance through their own ongoing work, which stimulated me to understand my own in different terms.

I am indebted to James W. Carey, who contributed a much-needed critique of this book; his suggestions improved it greatly.

Family members have not spurned me over the course of this project. Indeed, they helped materially to abet it. For discussion, interest, and warm support, I thank Anita, Herb, Zach, and Gramps; and Mary Ann, Dave, and KK.

Parts of chapter 3 have appeared in *Studies in the Anthropology of Visual Communication* (1977:86–98); a portion of the Conclusion has appeared in *Journal of Communication* (1979:46–57); and parts of chapters 5 and 6 have been published in *Media, Culture & Society* (1980). All are used by permission.

I must not neglect to mention John McGuigan, an editor who has steered me with good faith and good sense.

Finally, I thank Sunie Davis—for everything.

OBJECTIVITY AND THE NEWS

The Invisible Frame

There are no inherent limits to the reportability of events. If an occurrence is newsworthy, it will be made public—whether it takes place at Three Mile Island or in the Aleutians, in the Vatican or the Kremlin, on the top story of the Chase Manhattan Bank or in a basement in the Bronx. No aristocracy with formal title to coverage or fixed right of access should or does govern the practice of news reporting, although powerful private interests or designing politicians may, on occasion, manage to defraud the public by means of a cover-up. News may come from anywhere. Such, at least, is the belief.

The reality is different. News exemplifies values, and journalists work within increasingly well-researched, routine constraints. If a "news net" is indeed thrown virtually round the world, it is woven in such a way as to harvest only some species of fish (Tuchman 1978a). Writing news is telling stories (Darnton 1975): repetitive, even stylized narratives, bearing the stamp of a dominant social purpose.[1]

1. The knowledge that news exemplifies and animates values is, in part, a product of the research instituted by the Chicago School of urban sociologists and, most especially, by Helen Hughes (1940, 1942). According to this perspective, all news is selective, the result of a myriad of daily decisions, judgments, and routine organizational and institutional constraints. Research into news room practices has carried this valuable line of thought into the present (Breed 1955, 1958; Gans 1979; and Tuchman 1972, 1978a, are only the first references that come to mind). Only rarely, however, do such studies seek to explain the patterning of professional journalistic behavior as a *dependent,* rather than constitutive, series of practices. Hughes's key insight that the news "depends upon the point of view of the reporter who writes it, and the reporter's point of view emanates from the job itself, from the nature of his assignment, and from the character of his newspaper" (1942:11) has still not been properly appreciated as a *historical* dictum: for the newspaper, the beats it publishes, and the reporters who cover them are all subject to institutional changes outside, as well as within, the news room.

I

An invisible frame brackets news reports as a particular kind of public knowledge and a key category in popular epistemology. News reports repeatedly claim that, ideally at least, they recount events without the intrusion of value judgments or symbols. News is a map, a veridical representation, a report on reality, and hence not really a story at all, but merely the facts—this is the claim. But news—akin to any literary or cultural form—must rely upon conventions. Formally created and substantially embodied conventions alone can be used to contrive the illusion of objectivity. How else could we recognize news as a form of knowledge?[2]

The "objectivity assumption" is a paradoxical notion, which implies

> that there is indeed a world "out there" and that an account of a given event reflects that world, or a piece of it, with some degree of accuracy. The "objectivity assumption" states not that the media are objective, but that there is a world out there to be objective about. (Molotch and Lester 1974a:53)

Both within and outside the news room, objectivity undergirds the basic cultural role that the news media take as theirs: that of neutral or "unbiased" reporting of what often seem to be naturally occurring events. Objectivity facilitates the otherwise difficult belief that the newspaper "mirrors" or "reflects" reality. On the other hand, the claim to objectivity also enables the practices of news-story selection, treatment, context, and display to become a largely implicit foundation for the interpretation of public events (Gerbner 1973b:268; Chaney 1977:22). Invoked conventionally, objectivity ostensibly precludes the very presence of conventions and thus masks the patterned structure of news: it is an invisible frame.

Where did this notion of an objective report come from? Why did it arise? How did the journalistic commitment to rigorous separation of fact from value become publicly meaningful? How has objectivity been created and patterned by newspapers? What has it been possible to be objective about? If we do not attempt to answer these questions, we neglect a fundamental aspect of the history of journalism and, indeed, of modern communication theory.

Objectivity did not spring, fully developed, from the suddenly well-defined craft practices of professional journalists, and, for this reason, jour-

---

2. Tuchman (1972, 1978a) more than anyone else has contributed to our knowledge of these conventions, although she is less concerned with situating them within a relationship between public and news gatherers than with suggesting their importance as constraints in the production of culture.

nalistic professionalism can not constitute a sufficient explanation for the appearance of the convention. On the contrary, as Carey has asserted, objectivity and professionalism have long been intertwined, even perhaps mutually defined (1969:33). In helping to shape the institutional character of commercial journalism, indeed, objectivity may have furnished crucial ground for its own subsequent development as a canon of expertise among journalists. Professor Tuchman (1978a) has written perceptively of objectivity as a "web of facticity," which ensnares both professional news gatherers and members of the public. The lexical and visual conventions that evoke objectivity allow it to become, thus, a "strategic ritual," which may be used by journalists in warding off charges of bias or distortion, or other criticisms (Tuchman 1972). And such rituals, as Erving Goffman suggests, "are as needful of historical understanding as is the Ford car" (1976:71). It must be asked, How has news objectivity assumed this strategic importance, and why does it work in this way?

Researchers have sought to subordinate the tie between objectivity and professionalism to the all-encompassing need of the commercial newspaper "to serve politically heterogeneous audiences without alienating any significant segment of the audience" (Carey 1969:32). It was possible to use objectivity in this way, the argument goes, because news reports in the latter part of the nineteenth-century indexed "a secure world of politics, culture, social relations, and international alignments about which there was a rather broad consensus concerning values, purposes, and loyalties" (ibid.:35). Possibly the post-bellum world referred to was secure. But to characterize an era brimming with ethnic and class conflicts, wracked by depression, and ushered in by a civil war as consensual skips too lightly across this nation's history. As a keen-eyed business strategy, objectivity doubtless functioned to the commercial newspaper's advantage. Why, though, was the *public* convinced of its merits? What, after all, made the web of facticity *possible?* How was this even avenue of fact cut through the brambles of political faction, let alone traversed so confidently by the commercial press?

Some have been content to answer these questions by finding the roots of objectivity "in 19th-century technology and its concomitants, industrialization and urbanization" (Blankenburg and Walden 1977:591). The wire services, in particular, are often said to have developed objectivity, infusing it into newspapers in the form of "nonpartisan" or "unbiased" accounts (Siebert, Peterson, and Schramm 1963:60). Objectivity also reduced costs, it is argued, by permitting one news report to serve several clients (Bagdikian 1971:272; Sigal 1973:67; Gans 1979:186). The proper chronology of this development, however, is in dispute. Shaw (1967) isolates the decisive moment in the decline of news bias in the 1880s, when his sample of Wisconsin newspapers showed a large increase in reliance on wire-service news. Carey also opts for "the latter part of the 19th century" (1969:32). Bagdikian, however, locates the "commercial imperative" of news objectivity between 1914 and 1940—a period of "rapid growth" for the wire services (1971:272). Siebert, Peterson, and Schramm claim that "the theory of objective reporting" originated "sometime in the nineteenth century . . . and was widely acclaimed . . . during the first quarter of the twentieth century" (1963:60).

Yet there is evidence that objectivity was not a product of telegraphic transmission by the wire services. Soon after the onset of telegraphic service, the *National Police Gazette* proposed transforming the telegraph into a government-run operation as a means of remedying its evident "defects": "The public have no sufficient guarantee for the integrity of communications, which, if false, have the power of prostrating the hopes and fortunes of thousands at a breath" (19 December 1846). The telegraph, therefore, was superimposed on a news-gathering system that *already* placed a premium on apparent factual accuracy. Ingersoll describes an editorial council at the New York *Tribune* during the Civil War, where the managing editor, glancing at a news slip, exclaims:

> Now, this Associated Press dispatch is evidently a Rebel lie—two hundred armed negroes attack fifty unarmed whites, and two whites are wounded and fifty negroes are killed—what perfect nonsense! Reid, you write an article on this business . . . and have Dr. Wood look up the other cases in which the Associated Press dispatches are toned by the rebels. (1873:470–73)

An unusual case, stemming from the unprecedented social strains and dysfunctions brought on by the Civil War? Perhaps. Nonetheless, objectivity was not synonymous with news-agency routine but instead retained an autonomous character, to which, in some degree, the news agency itself was made to conform. The one-time manager of the New York Associated Press, Daniel H. Craig, indeed crowed before a committee of the United States Senate over the success of his agency's subservience to fact:

> Previous to this organization, in 1850, there was no regular or systematized arrangements for gathering the general domestic news of the country by telegraph, though there were numerous so-called news reporters, who were in the habit of telegraphing a few words, and then to draw

upon their imaginations for details, and with showy headings writing up and selling to the editors nearly as many paragraphs as there had been words telegraphed. A leading member of this news-reporting fraternity, on entering my employ, was greatly shocked when ordered to telegraph the details of all important news, and assured me that from an intimate acquaintance with the editors for more than two years, he was sure they didn't know real from imaginary news, and he thought it very foolish to waste money in telegraphing details of any event. (1885,2:1267)

Even before the AP commenced its operations, editors, as indicated above, are clearly seen as wishing to present only "real" news.

Craig's testimony has other implications relevant to the question of objectivity. According to Craig, who was in a position to know, the AP did not by any means uniformly cut telegraphed stories to the bare minimum required by economy and impartiality, but rather in some cases *added* details. Further, editors seem to have had some problem in differentiating between "real" and "imaginary" news. This suggests that stories could be written so as to make such a distinction difficult. A conventional mode of writing news, in other words, was implicitly relied upon by reporters to induce editors to accept their stories.

To claim that objectivity is a cultural form with its own set of conventions clearly challenges the more common assumption that objectivity equals the absence or reduction of political bias. The latter presumes that bias can be entirely avoided by newspapers, at least in principle. Within this view, however, there is disagreement over the correct dating and institutional source of the decline in what is now a reified entity, "bias." Phillips makes one relevant criticism of this position when she asserts that "the news media may indeed be biased, but in a direction which benefits the interests of political and economic elites, whether Democratic or Republican" (1977:64).

Also untenable is the assumption that, as Alden Williams puts it, bias may be properly thought of "as deviation from an unattainable but theoretically conceivable condition of unbias" (1975:191). A vast literature, embracing numerous research areas, now agrees that to conceive of the ideal of objectivity as the lack of bias is to misconceive it. In science and philosophy Polanyi (1962) and, from a different perspective, Habermas (1971) concur that such a definition of objectivity "deludes the sciences with the image of a self-subsistent world of facts structured in a lawlike manner; it thus conceals the a priori constitution of these facts" (Habermas 1971:69).[3] As Gouldner has put

---

3. Worth (1978) in the analysis of photography and Carey (1969:33), Chaney (1977), Gerbner

it, this kind of objectivism is a "pathology of cognition that entails silence about the speaker, about his interests and his desires, and how these are socially situated and structurally maintained" (1976:50). Of more immediate relevance is Gerbner's formulation: "there is no fundamentally non-ideological, apolitical, non-partisan, news gathering and reporting system": "all news is views" (1964:508, 495).

Moreover, the concept of bias is itself anachronistic. The immediate temptation is to believe that, if bias can be avoided in principle, it can also be identified by any who care to look for it—that, in short, bias is a universally recognizable quantity. One then merely assumes that what we today regard as biased was also seen to be biased by nineteenth-century readers. Shaw, for example, adopts this approach, defining bias as the "over-all impression . . . [of] positive or negative feeling . . . created upon today's reader" when given nineteenth-century journals to read (1967:5). Shaw clearly is aware that "today's reader" is different from his nineteenth-century counterpart; nevertheless, he is forced to assume an unchanging psychological type —an invariant human nature—in order to lend validity to his central concern with the telegraph's contribution to the decline of bias. Unfortunately, such an assumption is absolutely and inevitably invalid, because it does not test the development of news objectivity through previous time or the reduction of bias. The method at best details the reactions of twentieth-century experimental subjects to nineteenth-century newspapers.

We may, however, substitute a different basic assumption about the nature of news objectivity: lack of bias or news objectivity has been *attributed* to newspapers in American culture so often as to become, de facto, the accepted gauge of their performance. It is not the presence or absence of a reified bias that is vital, but rather the cultural configuration that permits readers to indulge their *belief* that bias indeed is present or absent. The critical analytical question may also be recast to agree with this assumption. We may ask, with respect to news objectivity, when and how and why the newspaper's special role as a purportedly transcendent purveyor of "the facts" was initiated, and how journalists animated this new role within newspaper content itself. How did the newspaper cultivate and attempt to confirm for its readers the idea that it merely reflected the world? How did reduction of political bias and partisanship become a feasible goal? When and

(1964), and Schiller (1973:11–13) in communications research also agree that such a definition excludes the activity of the scientist, the interpreter, or the news person, in producing a normative, conventionally structured work.

how did the newspaper first affirm that the ritual of objectivity might take precedence over all else within the compass of everyday operations?

With many of the other scholars discussed above, I assume that news objectivity did indeed arise in a predominantly commercial context. According to this view, objectivity is connected with the transformation of the newspaper into a commodity, which is now forced "to see in everyone the buyer in whose hand . . . it wants to nestle" (Benjamin 1973:54). It follows that the best period in which to study the development of objectivity in American journalism is not that of the rise of the wire services in the latter part of the nineteenth century, but the period beginning in the 1830s, when the newspaper first "was established as a capitalist institution" (Tebbel 1974: 180). We must turn, in other words, to the penny press.

This connection has been noticed before. Journalism historians have tied the emergence of objectivity to the decline in party journalism, beginning in the 1830s, when the commercial penny papers combined advanced print technology with a street-sale distribution system as a way of expanding and cultivating a new public. "The great change in that public occasioned by the advent of cheap dailies inevitably caused a shift in the news concept," states Frank Luther Mott (1962:243). Nothing less than "a revolution in news" was at hand. Local news, human interest news, and, above all, crime news became the commercial newspaper's staple fare while its foremost duty was "to give its readers the news, and not to support a party or a mercantile class" (ibid.:242–43). Despite this paradigmatic shift, objectivity itself is credited with having a distinctively evolutionary character, as it matured in tandem with the gradual passing of "the dark ages of partisan journalism" (ibid.:167). In the words of journalism historian Edwin Emery, by the 1830s the development of objectivity had "barely started" (1972:170). But why did it start at all? And in what sense can it be linked so precisely to the penny papers? Surely objectivity was not inherent in the Idea of the Newspaper, an ideal form awaiting a preordained birth and evolution?

Further, how does this early variant of objectivity accord with newspapers whose "sensationalism" has been so often remarked upon and whose use of crime news has been so closely identified with their transformation of news "into a readily saleable consumer commodity" (Davison, Boylan, and Yu 1976:11)? Because, as Chibnall asserts, crime news helps to "redefine the moral boundaries of communities," it may be that nowhere else more than here, in the penny press, will we see "the limits of newspaper values such as neutrality, objectivity, and balance revealed with such clarity" (1977:x). What limits were these?

Michael Schudson, in his pioneering study *Discovering the News* (1978), has devoted substantial space to the relation between objectivity and the penny press and has tried to clarify the unfortunately dim silhouette of journalism's foremost practice. His work deserves a close examination. Schudson begins by defining objectivity as "a faith in 'facts,' a distrust of 'values,' and a commitment to their segregation" (ibid.:6). Well and good. "If we are to understand the idea of objectivity in journalism," he continues, "the transformation of the press in the Jacksonian period must be examined" (ibid.:4). He suggests that massive economic and political changes in the 1830s were expressively integrated into the form and content of the penny press, which both drew upon and strengthened "the culture of a democratic market society" (ibid.:60). Nothing less than a virtual "middle-class revolution" against old aristocratic wealth and power underlies the emergence of the penny press. The revolution in journalism was closely connected, thus, to "the expansion of a market economy and political democracy or, put another way, the democratization of business and politics sponsored by an urban middle class which trumpeted 'equality' in social life." Schudson, in short, accepts that this was an "Age of Egalitarianism," an age when, increasingly, members of the growing middle class "acquired wealth and political power and brought with them a zeal for equal opportunity that led to the expansion of public education, the denial of government-granted monopolies to corporations and more flexible procedures for incorporating, the abolition of licensing regulations for doctors and lawyers, and other reforms we identify as 'Jacksonian' " (ibid.:43–44). The cheap commercial papers in their turn brazenly asserted their independence from party politics, their advocacy of laissez faire, their reliance on advertisements, their low price and high circulation, and their emphasis on news from any and all social spheres. In a nutshell, the rise of the penny press symbolized and strengthened "a new way of being in the world which we awkwardly summarize as 'middle class' " (ibid.:57).

Schudson's argument is especially interesting because of its concern with situating the penny press in the circumstances—economic, political, and cultural—of the new public. Schudson identifies the groups he labels as middle class; they include "the skilled craftsmen, the small and large merchants, the small and large tradesmen." In solidarity under the flag of equality, as "the entering wedge of a commercial middle class," they challenged and overcame the bastions of aristocratic conservatism, bringing "new institutions and a new consciousness that would radically affect every stratum of society" (ibid.:49). Prominent among such new institutions was the penny press. Boldly assaulting the social and intellectual deference that had guided the commonwealth, the press furnished "the groundwork on which a belief in facts and a distrust of the reality, or objectivity, of 'values' could thrive" (ibid.:60). This foundation built, objectivity would eventually arrive on the scene around World War I under the stewardship of professional journalists.

Schudson presents a unique and, in some ways, a forceful argument. In emphasizing the bond between the commercial cheap press and its new public, he has followed Carey's directive that journalism historians must search for "the intersection of journalistic style and vocabulary, created systems of meaning, and standards of reality shared by writer and audience" (1974:5). In certain concrete circumstances, the public as a collective entity may indeed help to determine the cultural form of an emergent media technology (acknowledging this, however, does not also imply that in all periods the media serve the public interest by giving the people what they want). Schudson's emphasis, on the other hand, permits us to circumvent the unsatisfactory "great man" theory of journalism, which holds that a few individuals—a James Gordon Bennett or a Joseph Pulitzer—may be singled out and asked to perform collective cultural chores, such as inventing the news concept. The emphasis on a collective public facilitates a more sensitive and compelling evaluation of the interaction between medium and public than is usually possible.

Nevertheless, there are serious problems with Schudson's work. His identification of the penny press with a rising middle class leads him to imply that, before this, newspaper advertising had borne little relation to the craftsman's business needs. Advertisements placed by tradesmen, however, were not lacking in the years before the penny press. Not less than 15,000 advertisers, including many artisans, bought space in the Philadelphia press between 1764 and 1794 (Steirer 1972); and Rock cites a collection of some 1,200 advertisements by artisans in New York City newspapers between 1800 and 1804 (1979:158). Had not the spirit of capitalism, after all, chosen a craftsman, Ben Franklin, as its exemplar, a full century before the eruption of the penny press?

Yet commercial interests and attitudes do not of themselves make one "middle class," and it is thus Schudson's characterization of the new public that is most troublesome. That craftsmen—the artisans and mechanics of the burgeoning Eastern cities, with a much smaller number of "large merchants" and "wealthy people" (ibid.:49, 51)—formed the primary public for the cheap press is, I think, indisputable. (I will continue discussion of this point in a later chapter.) But can these groups be considered, as Schudson strenuously insists, a middle-class public, with middle-class norms and values?

I think not. In keeping with his "culturalist" argument, Schudson attempts to match purportedly middle-class attributes of the penny press with demonstrable values of the social groups within the middle class. The supposed "democratization of business and politics" serves this cause by fusing press and public in a hypothesized "culture of the market." The middle class rolls in triumphantly as the Age of Egalitarianism smoothly displaces its predecessor. This phoenix, Jacksonian Democracy, should learn restraint; historians have been tolling its death knell for what seems an eternity.

There can be little doubt that, although *formal* equality in politics and commerce may have been achieved by the 1830s (and even then only for white men), *substantive* democracy proved typically more elusive. Also, his protestations to the contrary notwithstanding, there is now extensive evidence that sustained social conflicts were separating the two major groups in Schudson's middle class (merchants and artisans) into generally disparate and frequently hostile parties. By the 1830s one may indeed argue that an American working class—not a classic industrial proletariat, but a working class just the same —had traveled a good distance along the road to self-definition. But Schudson's argument does not hold up, because the middle class he envisions did not exist—not, at least, among the readers found by the penny papers.

The newspapers themselves, which for Schudson are the paeans of a new, middle-class "way of being in the world," must be reexamined to ascertain their particular historical shape, context, and character. In this book I attempt such a reappraisal and show that the success of the penny press stemmed largely from its remarkably fluent use of the idiom and ideology prevalent among its public of tradesmen. In the eyes of many readers the cheap papers turned to defend the rights of man, through crime news especially, at a time when those rights seemed to be threatened by changing social relations, and when other institutions only turned their backs on cardinal republican values. In particular, the belief of many republican tradesmen that knowledge, like property, should not be monopolized for exclusive use by private interests was expressed in the penny papers as a positive commitment to cheap, value-free information—to objective fact. Journalistic objectivity found further support from contemporary acceptance of positivist science and photographic realism, both of which claimed to reflect the world without reference to human subjectivity and selectivity. An intensive analysis of objectivity and the journalistic defense of natural rights in the early *National Police Gazette,* however, makes clear that these conventional cultural forms ultimately lent support to the state as well as to developing capitalist social relations.

1

A New Press for a New Public

In the mid-1830s the penny press launched the newspaper as an enduring and successful business enterprise. City-street sales supplanted subscriptions as the newspaper's dominant distribution mechanism.[1] Replacing party blocs, whose mercurial political fortunes meant both an unstable career for many journalists and a short life span for most newspapers, the public at large joined advertisers as a major newspaper patron.[2] Between 1828 and 1840 the number of daily journals published nationwide more than doubled, while total annual circulation of all newspapers expanded from perhaps 68 million to 148 million copies. Population increased by 40 percent, newspaper circulation by 117 percent (Pred 1973:21). In the 1840s, a few hundred dollars of capital could establish a major metropolitan journal; but by the end of that decade, with the incorporation of expensive new printing technology, the cost of entry into the New York City newspaper market had skyrocketed. In 1849 the New York *Sun* was sold for $250,000 (North 1884:100), a price that Horace Greeley, editor of the competing *Tribune,* called "very cheap" (House of Commons [*Report from the Select Committee on Newspaper*

---

1. Of this subscription-credit system Hudson observed that an *average* of 25 percent of subscriptions were never paid (1873:442). Doubtless this led proprietors to rely on strong patrons, with a corresponding increase in their vulnerability.
2. For examples of career instability in party journalism see Ames and Teeter (1971:50–63); Hammond (1842, 1:279); Hudson (1873:410–11); Pray (1855:136–50, 270–72); Wilmer (1859:32–33). Stewart notes that "fewer than half of the journals published before 1821 continued for two years, and only a fourth lasted four years or more" (1969:17–18). It should be observed, however, that the days of the party press were not over. Mott (1962) devotes no fewer than eight chapters in his *American Journalism* to the years from 1833 to 1860, under the main heading "The Party Press: Later Period." In his major interpretation of patronage and party journalism at the national level, Smith (1977) details the development of the party press up to its final eclipse, *in 1875.*

Stamps] 1851:395). By 1851 Henry Raymond could boast in the first issue of his paper of the "difficulties" of undertaking a newspaper like his *New York Times:* "We understand perfectly, that great capital, great industry, great patience are indispensable to its success" (18 September 1851).

Raymond understood that business growth was dependent not only on capital, to underwrite the technological capacity to engage in mass production of newspapers, but also on the existence of a large urban public eager to read papers. Both technology and the public were available in the 1830s. Harnessing steam, the same new source of power that sustained other emergent industries, printing technology granted the newspaper a physical capacity adequate—though only barely—to meet its needs. The Fourdrinier paper machine and the Napier steam press kicked off a period of innovation that, between 1820 and 1860, would drive printing productivity to increase by a factor of 100 (Pred 1973:286; Everett 1972: chap. 1, p. 8). The penny New York *Sun,* established in 1833, employed steam power in the first year that it became available (1835); reminiscing in 1851, the *Sun*'s first proprietor, the printer Benjamin Day, marveled that even this innovation "did not keep up with the increasing circulation of the Sun" (in Hudson 1873:418). Circulation had become an independent object of commercial desire and evolved quickly into a critical measure for setting advertising rates.[3]

Technology was itself outpaced by the growth of the public. Along with the spectacular growth of commerce in New York City, the center of the import and export trades, the city's population rose to 200,000 inhabitants in 1830 and accounted for nearly 20 percent of the total urban population of the United States.[4] Between 1830 and 1840 population in New York more than doubled, continuing to race on ahead of other cities in subsequent years. The city's swelling numbers formed an unprecedented, large, and compact local market, which could be exploited by expanding construction and consumer goods industries (Wilentz 1980). Newspapers were no exception: there was now a body of readers that might be reached through newsboys hawking their low-cost wares in the street.[5] Average daily circulation of sixpenny subscription journals of the era (by custom available at ten dollars a year) has been estimated at between 1,200 and 1,700 (Pred 1973:59; Hudson 1873:431). The New York *Herald,* at a penny, hoped, according to its prospectus, "to pick

3. Now termed "cost per thousand," this gauge apparently began to be used in the late 1840s and 1850s; see Hudson (1873:372, 469).
4. Ward defines urban areas as those numbering at least 2,500 inhabitants (1971:26).
5. Newsboys assumed critical importance at this juncture; cf. Whisnant (1972).

up at least twenty or thirty thousand" (6 May 1835), and, in fifteen months, the paper boasted a circulation of 40,000 (Tebbel 1974:183). This estimate is probably inflated; in 1851 Horace Greeley testified before the British House of Commons Committee on Newspaper Stamps that the five cheap dailies then published in New York commanded a total daily circulation of about 100,000. Within this group, he claimed, the *Sun* had 50,000 buyers, the *Tribune* just under 20,000, while the *Herald* and two other papers shared the remaining 30,000. Ten sixpenny papers, he said, found an additional group of 30,000 buyers (1851:389–95). A census report for 1860 noted matter-of-factly that newspapers now composed "a part of the reading matter of all" (Kennedy 1862:101), and a *Herald* correspondent commented a few years earlier that his journal had always aimed at "universal circulation" (Pray 1855:197). In a scant two decades the penny papers clearly had effected a fundamental change in the status and presence of the urban newspaper.[6]

So much, but little more, about the penny press is common knowledge. It is, however, a platitude of journalism history to say that, with the rise of the new public and its cheap press, the institutional foundations of public communication were radically altered. "The newly-recognized public was more interested in *news* than in *views*," asserts Edwin Emery. "The *Sun* and its galaxy of imitators proved that news was a valuable commodity" (1972: 169).

They did indeed. The commercial nature of the penny papers can not be doubted. Their boisterous arrival, nonetheless, has been but poorly understood. Scholars need to reexamine the very terms of perception through which they are accustomed to apprehending the emergence of the cheap press. For closer inspection reveals that the presumed dichotomy between news and views is historically facile. Emery himself notes that "papers like the *Herald* took up issues every day, and often fought for them as violently as in the old partisan-press days" (ibid.:170).[7] Again, one has only to glance at the penny papers themselves to grasp their often sportively polemical character. What, then, *was* truly unprecedented about newspapers that, as Emery concedes, were only "a little more impersonal" than their explicitly partisan rivals (ibid.)? How, over a mere two decades, did the newspaper

6. For purposes of comparison it is instructive to note that between 1922 and 1939 radio receivers were produced and purchased in sufficient numbers to average one set for every three persons by the latter date. One out of every three Americans had a television receiver (again, this is a statistical proportion rather than a social reality) seventeen years after TV sets were first produced for the market (1946). The achievement of the penny press is in line with the penetration levels attained by successive media. See Sterling and Haight (1978:325).

7. Again, note that the "old" days were not really gone.

transform itself from a thing of "luxury" into a "necessity" (Pray 1855:265)?

Posing this question in psychological terms, Helen Hughes suggests that the "invasion of the newspaper" by the "human interest story" explains the rowdy acclaim that the penny journals received (1940:2). The human interest story, she asserts, exhibits an "intrinsic" psychological appeal, allowing it to be "read for its own sake" (ibid.:xxi). Perhaps, with sociobiology now in the ascendant, her view will once again find acceptance. Does it not concede too much, though, to an undemonstrated and unchanging universal psyche? Is it not, as C. Wright Mills once protested, "a violation of the social and historical specificity that careful work in the human studies requires," that is, "an abstraction that social students have not earned the right to make" (1967:164)?

The transformation of the press doubtless had a psychological dimension, but it was fundamentally a *social* process. As a business, the newspaper's foremost task was to sell itself and, through its efforts, other products. It accomplished this, not through the utilization of human interest stories, but through the assumption of a new and major role within political society, a role that, in key respects, was urged upon it by the new public. The commercial cheap press staked a preemptive claim to the exercise of reason in the public sphere; it was the success of this claim that allowed it to boast of its function as the vox populi.

To comprehend this development we must focus not merely on newspaper content but also on the public at which the penny papers were aimed. This public has been considered up to now primarily as a quantitative entity: something that must have been expanded for a mass press to have been possible, an urban agglomeration of faceless purchasers. This is insufficient. We must ask who, socially and culturally, constituted the major public for the cheap journals; we must ascertain what sort of a public this was. Not individuals alone, but persons in a given social context formed the audience for these tabloids. What accounts for their eagerness to read them? We must search for the principles of social, cultural, and ideological organization that mark *these* people as a group for which *these* newspapers were appropriate. That is the task of this chapter. Because the penny press replaced subscription lists with street sales, we lack detailed information on the exact dimensions of this bygone public. This, however, does not by any means prevent informed judgment on the general composition of the penny public. According to the claims of the penny papers themselves, they appealed to the entire population. Ben Day's New York *Sun* proclaimed on its masthead, "It Shines for All." James Gordon Bennett insisted that his *Herald* was "equally intended for the great masses of the community—the merchant, mechanic, working people—the private family as well as the public hotel—the journeyman and his employer—the clerk and his principal" (6 May 1835). We shall find later that this assertion of universality was vital to the endeavor of the cheap journals; at the moment, however, we must confine ourselves to an estimate of the actual public that gathered to read them.

The penny tabloids doubtless penetrated many levels of the social scale through taverns, coffeehouses, workshops, and informal clubs of readers, which afforded numerous chances for the poorer classes to read or be read to. And merchants, businessmen, and white-collared clerks must soon have become readers of the new press as its commercial success became evident.[8] But most readers must have been drawn from the ranks of artisans and mechanics, who constituted approximately 40 to 50 percent of New York City's wage-earning population in this period.[9]

It has been noted repeatedly that these journals circulated largely among the less well-to-do (Pred 1973:293); Emery and Emery argue that they related specifically to the "common man," and point to the *Sun* as an example of a species of newspaper that "was not printed for the property class" (1978: 121). Frederic Hudson, who drew upon personal experience in journalism during this era, stated that the *Sun* was indeed circulated largely among mechanics (1873:420). Frank Luther Mott (1962:241) both accepts this estimate and generalizes from it about the penny papers per se. To turn once again to contemporary sources, the Philadelphia *Public Ledger,* a penny daily consciously modeled on its predecessors in New York, stated in its first issue that "the affluent are well supplied" with sixpenny papers. "But our large cities contain a numerous and daily increasing population," the *Ledger* con-

8. "In the cities of New York and Brooklyn," announced the Philadelphia *Public Ledger* in its first issue, "containing together a population of 300,000, the daily circulation of the penny papers is not less than SEVENTY THOUSAND. This is nearly sufficient to place a newspaper in the hands of every man in the two cities, and even every boy old enough to read. These papers are to be found in every street, lane and alley; in every hotel, tavern, counting house, shop and store" (25 March 1836). The sex-biased character of the penny papers deserves more study. Sex was not the only boundary of circulation and popularity, however, despite the *Ledger*'s claim. The *Ledger* itself went on to admit in the same issue that "the common good is its object; and in seeking this object, it will have especial regard to the moral and intellectual improvement of the laboring classes, the great sinew of all civilized communities."

9. Rock asserts that, between 1790 and 1820, the percentage of the city's population composed of artisans and mechanics remained at "between 50 and 60 percent," despite the swelling overall population (1979:12). One presumes he means fifty to sixty percent of the wage-earning population. Wilentz believes that Rock's "artisan" category is too broad, because it takes in occupations (carters, for example) that would not have been classed as trades; nonetheless, Wilentz stated in a private conversation that, even in 1855, forty to forty-five percent of the adult male population were craftsmen.

tinued, desirous of "rational amusement and useful instruction." Who constituted this group?—"our artizans and laborers." "Almost every porter and dray-man, while not engaged in his occupation," declared the *Ledger,* "may be seen with a paper in his hands" (25 March 1836). Porters and draymen, minimally skilled, worked near the bottom of the craft hierarchy; they may even have been considered laborers, working at an altogether lower level than artisans with a trade. Yet when wages of $1.00 to $2.00 a day were normal (cf. Wilentz 1980) even for various skilled craftsmen, the stratum of porters and draymen cannot have constituted the highest level of readership. Rather, in its crucial first years the major public for the penny papers must surely have been the artisans and mechanics of New York City.

In the 1830s the artisans' economic status, political presence, and ideological temperament (all of which were influenced and shaped to some degree by a particular trade and its specific place in an unstable society) were undergoing distinctive processes of transition and transformation, which led to changes that, in the end, were expressed through new institutions and new perceptions of the nature of society. In grappling with the concrete character of this public, it will be well to emphasize that the experience of its members was far from unitary because individuals lived discretely according to different trades. It would be equally incorrect, though, to move to the opposite pole by refusing to consider this public as an embodiment of shared social experience, because the bulk of the artisan public did participate in a common socioeconomic shift of epic proportions, as a still unformed and mutable working class. The remainder of the public, much smaller in number, belonged to an emerging class of capitalist industrialists and merchants. That the penny press found a way to speak to both groups at once was its most ingenious and fundamental contribution to American society and culture. In attempting to frame some of the more vital features of emerging class relationships below, we shall find, moreover, that the equality that has been trumpeted as the victory shout of the common man was instead the battle cry of hard-pressed journeymen and downwardly mobile artisans.

Production, Politics, and Artisans

An explosively expanding port, antebellum New York was also the principal node of the nation's information-circulation system and the hub of the country's finance (Pred 1973:142). Beyond, though not by any means apart from this, New York was a city of crafts. Metalworkers, builders, masons, carpenters, caulkers, shipwrights, coopers, glaziers, butchers, tailors, cabinet-makers, bakers, morocco dressers, shoemakers, coachmakers, printers—the list could descend endlessly down the page—built New York into the nation's preeminent center of commerce and manufacture. They plied their trades at home or, more frequently as the years went by, in relatively small manufactories. Even in 1869 the "typical" American firm employed an average of only 8.15 wage earners (Montgomery 1967:8). Factory production, when it did become socially important in the late 1830s and 1840s, began close to the rivers or coal fields, which alone could fuel it, and only later moved into the heart of the city, unevenly incorporating new technologies like the sewing machine (1846) to refashion industry. When factories did appear, they were superimposed on a well-articulated and elaborate system of handicraft production. Industrial production, in other words, built upon a previous transformation of the crafts.

While small shops persisted as the basic productive units across many trades, while many artisans continued to be self-employed, and while mechanics themselves owned most of the tools with which they worked, a reigning vision of gradual advancement toward the propertied independence of master status continued to fire the imagination and effort of the small producer. But in the decades leading to the Civil War, the transformation of the crafts and the widening division between the interests of masters and journeymen, which such a transformation entailed, made this an increasingly beleaguered and defensive vision.

Between 1790 and 1820 improvements in transportation and communication and a progressively greater demand for goods in thriving local markets like New York permitted a wide field of enterprise for eager entrepreneurs. Merchant capital underwrote an expansion of many crafts—frequently those responsible for consumer goods—by procuring the markets and, critically, the credit, without which expanded production would be unjustified. Artisans began to compete not merely within neighborhoods and cities but also within regional and, increasingly, national markets (Montgomery 1967:12). The larger markets put a premium on efficient, low-cost, high-volume production. Marketing techniques were developed to suit the potentialities inherent in expanded operations: branch stores, salesmen, out-of-town advertising, and the liberal extension of credit helped carve out profitable markets for different commodities (Wilentz 1980: chap. 3, pp. 22–23). On the other hand, the consequences of expanded production were distributed unevenly across different trades. Butchers, coopers, and shipwrights remained in key respects "traditional," while printers, shoemakers, and tailors radically changed their styles and standards of work. For the entire period between 1800 and 1860 craftsmen remained and a handicraft economy predominated, but, as Wilentz has shown so well, "the terms of their work were completely altered" (1980: chap. 3, p. 18). Even by the 1820s, Rock has argued, "no artisan could totally escape the consequences of the developing American marketplace" (1979: 243).

Merchant middlemen shattered the relative harmony of an earlier age by flooding many local markets with inexpensive goods, goods made more cheaply by less skilled workers. The apprenticeship system, through which youths were indentured to serve masters for a period as long as seven years, thereby acquiring the skills needed to strike out on their own, began to break down: apprentices formed a ready source for the recruitment of semiskilled, inexpensive labor (Rock 1979:242). Immigrants, hungry for work, added to the labor force, particularly after the mid-1840s; by about 1870, of the nation's six largest cities only Philadelphia had more native-born workers than immigrants in manufacturing (Montgomery 1967:37). In the complex of enterprises that produced wearing apparel, women began to dominate the labor force; as elsewhere, their appearance coincided with an extensive reliance on sweated labor, introduction of new technologies, and lower wages (Wilentz 1980: chap. 3, pp. 19–26). Master craftsmen survived, in a newly competitive world, by slashing wages to match falling prices, stepping up productivity by introducing piecework in crafts where it had been atypical, and often supervising workers more closely as well (Mayer 1978:9–13; Montgomery 1968:6–9; Wilentz 1980: chap. 3). Outwork became frequent, intensive specialization of duties grew in importance, and piece masters or foremen became independent agents in production (Wilentz 1980: chap. 3). Journeymen found themselves caught "in dependency to merchants whose capital enabled them to control the supply of raw materials and the marketing of the finished products" (Rogers 1978:22). Even by 1819 inequality between masters and journeymen in six "conflict trades" studied by Rock—shoemakers, masons, carpenters, tailors, cabinetmakers, and printers, who then constituted a full forty percent of the city's mechanic community—was strikingly pronounced (1979:268). Although in exceptional cases artisans from this group might still advance upward, journeyman status could no longer be considered a temporary position. Rather, there was a "good likelihood" that they would become permanent wage earners, "making a subsistence salary and struggling with their family under the constant threat of poverty" (ibid.). More generally, over the antebellum years, the changes characteristic of metropolitan industrialization in New York "challenged fundamental assumptions about craft work," notably, about the "independence" of master status, the nature of "virtue" in labor, and control of the work process (Wilentz 1980: chap. 3, pp. 54–55). We shall find below that this transformation of craft production was accompanied by what Wilentz calls "an ideological crisis" (1980: chap. 3, p. 57).

Statistics on property concentration in New York City may supplement our view of the dynamic growth of inequality within Gotham. In the Fourth Ward, the lowest 80 percent of the people possessed 13.4 percent of the area's personal property in 1815, as compared with 33.1 percent in 1789 (Rock 1979:254). Pessen estimates that by 1828 the wealthiest 4 percent of New York's entire population had amassed 63 percent of the corporate and personal property. He calculates that by 1845, however, this same top 4 percent owned over 80 percent of the city's wealth. The number of tax-paying families owning at least some property, on the other hand, markedly decreased. In Brooklyn, across the river from New York, it diminished from seven out of eight in 1810 to one out of five in 1841 (Pessen 1973:35–36, 38).

Business historian Alfred D. Chandler remarks, however, that the small shop and mill, craft work, and water power "remained a basic part of the industrial scene for the rest of the nineteenth century" (1972:178). Even as late as 1869 only about thirty percent of total power (steam and water) in New England was generated by steam. In the antebellum years at least, artisans and mechanics could cling to ideals engendered in a system of handicraft production while they were propelled into relations of unprecedented inequality with their fellow citizens.

Crucial to the increase in social inequality was business law, the edifice of rules vital to economic planning and resource allocation, which consolidated the position of the emerging business elite. As an instrument of individually or corporately guided economic activity, business law was thoroughly revised to support developmental economic policies. It is important to focus on the metamorphosis of American law because it reinforced market inequality with crucial support from the state sector.

Commercial transport by steamboat and canal permitted entrepreneurs with access to credit to revise the role of contract by undermining the importance of customary or "just" prices more appropriate to local markets.[10] Far into the eighteenth century such "just" prices of exchange were

10. "Transport improvements within a national political area defined by the United States Constitution, and confirmed by the Supreme Court, increased the size of the national economy by enlarging and interrelating its regional markets. The external economies and those of scale thereby made increasingly possible accrued both to agricultural and industrial producers, and augmented the profits out of which additional capital could be formed to speed the pace of

the basis of a law that awarded contract damages according to measures of fairness "independent of the terms agreed to by the contracting parties" (Horwitz 1977:173). The new law, on the other hand, accepted some injurious use of property as an inevitable consequence of competitive economic activity (ibid.:40).[11] Whereas, previously, contract law had assumed that economic relations were largely fixed and had actually impeded individual attempts to alter inherited economic status in keeping with the dominance of landed property, by the nineteenth century law assumed that "a fluctuating market-place was the central institution in the economy and left individuals free to manipulate its workings so that they rather than their neighbors would most benefit from it" (Nelson 1975:143).

The new view of contract was perhaps most forcefully enacted in the doctrine called "assumption of risk" in workmen's injury cases. Contrary to prior conceptions of substantive justice, the law now held that the paid worker "takes upon himself the natural and ordinary risks and perils incident to the performance" of his job, pronounced Massachusetts Chief Justice Shaw in 1842 (in Horwitz 1977:210). Skilled workers, who proudly preserved an ideological heritage "blended of Ben Franklin's maxims and Tom Paine's 'rights of man'," now found themselves increasingly subordinated by law to the dictates of an expanding market (Montgomery 1968:13). American law was being turned into "the most favorable to expanding business of any jurisprudence in the world" (Cochran 1977:31).

The corporation, considered as a legal entity, was transformed. Before the War for Independence, the corporate form had been utilized chiefly as a means of pooling resources in the pursuit of political, educational, and religious ends (Cochran 1977:15–18). By the 1830s the modern rule of limited liability had become the norm, however, and business corporations, at first mainly in transportation and banking, seeking private aggrandizement became typical. New York was the first state to pass a general incorporation law, which facilitated and made less public a previously difficult legal process. Whereas in all the colonies only about half a dozen charters had been granted to business corporations, in New York alone between 1811 (when the incorporation law was passed) and 1818, 129 corporate charters were given to manu-

---

further growth" (Bruchey 1968:160).

11. Mayer discusses New York Supreme Court Chief Justice John Savage, who testified in an important precedent to the importance of the enlarged market and its concomitant erosion of local demand for products made-to-order. Savage undermined tradesmen's ability to organize unions by holding them to be "conspiracies" in restraint of trade and commerce. "Coarse boots and shoes," ordained the Judge in 1835, "are made in many parts of our country; not for particular persons who are to wear them, but as an article of trade and commerce" (1978:11).

facturers (Miller 1970:109–10; cf. Seavoy 1972). By 1828 New York City's corporations, mainly banks and insurance companies, were assessed for $23,984,660, or 21 percent of the city's total assessed wealth excluding partnerships (Pessen 1973:34). Substantive legal encouragement was offered to this growing private sphere when business corporations were conceded citizen status in a Supreme Court ruling of 1844 (Green 1945:216–17).

The legal development of the corporation occurred through a long series of judicial decisions, significantly called private law. Lacking the visibility of statutory law, private law nonetheless served "to adjust constitutional law to the needs of the corporation" (Bruchey 1968:137). Horwitz, an outstanding authority on the transformation of American law, thus delineates a "basic ambiguity" between a public or statutory law "devoted to preventing redistribution" of wealth and a private law "undergoing massive doctrinal change and bringing economic redistribution about" (1977:256). Tocqueville's well-known comment is still pertinent for its insight into the contemporary significance of private law: "when a judge contests a law, applied to some particular case in an obscure proceeding, the importance of his attack is concealed from the public gaze" (1961, 1:105). "The political power which the Americans have intrusted to their courts of justice," declared Tocqueville, was "immense"; "the courts of justice are the most visible organs by which the legal profession is enabled to control the democracy" (ibid.:329). The judiciary achieved this level of power in part through a transfer, during the first decade of the nineteenth century, of the law-finding function from jury to judge. The shift permitted a greater measure of certainty in legally enforceable transactions; and this subjugation of juries was needed, thus, not only to control particular verdicts but also to develop "a uniform and predictable body of judge-made commercial rules" (Horwitz 1977:143). The law of evidence, which Langbein calls "the law of jury control" because it allows judicial supervision of the fact-finding process (1973:317), correspondingly became a more crucial aspect of litigation.

Protection of the fruits of private economic activity became the criminal law's paramount concern (Nelson 1975:136).[12] Centralizing political institutions no longer sought consensus on the morality of a ruling, but instead secured only as much support for a decision as was needed to make it "politically acceptable and militarily enforceable" (Nelson 1975:173). The

12. As the result of a gradual shift in the definition of the criminal, who was no longer condemned first and foremost as a sinner against God but rather as one who "preyed on the property of his fellow citizens" (Nelson 1975:117–18), prosecution for theft rose dramatically. See also Hindus (1977) and Flaherty (1971:248).

nature of moral offenses that were prosecuted shifted toward those acts that indirectly threatened property, such as drunkenness, vagrancy, and unlicensed sale of liquor (Hindus 1977:221–22). The maintenance of "public order" in the business districts of expanding cities became the prime police function (Schneider 1978; cf. Monkkonen 1979). Law was striving to become "the one undisputed and authoritative source of rules for regulating commercial life" (Horwitz 1977:155), and activities that interfered formally with its assumption of this role, no less than those that challenged the law's specific substance, were prosecuted increasingly as criminal assaults on social order.

The demand for law and order thus was transformed into "a constitutional imperative," and all infringement of legal process was in effect now criminal (Silver 1967:20). The rule of law simply invalidated recourse to extralegal sanctions by those with lesser access to the law itself.[13] In the colonial era riotous mobs had been unhappily tolerated (sometimes their behavior could be directed against England), but in the 1830s and 1840s they provoked a property-conscious and increasingly urban upper class to demand and, ultimately, to obtain reorganization of the antiquated "watch" system of policing. Urban police forces were revived as professional bureaucracies designed "to penetrate civil society" and thereby "to supervise daily life more closely and continuously than ever before" (Silver 1967:12, 15; cf. Weinbaum 1979).[14]

Legal ideology emasculated all prior conceptions of substantive justice, and an unspoken premise of equal bargaining power was established as the foundation of legal and economic analysis: "the law had come simply to ratify those forms of inequality that the market system produced" (Horwitz 1977: 210). Law had become an instrument of private economic activity, which enabled the market to expand into new areas, while access to law was markedly restricted by class privilege, and extralegal sanctions were rigorously constrained. To many of those whose socioeconomic status was progressively undermined by this series of changes, the state appeared to be indifferent, if not actively hostile, to the natural rights of men.

The wedding of law to private economic development occurred, paradoxically, as political power was being formally democratized and popular

13. Consonant with the certainty, predictability, and rationality that Hindus deems essential "for the prosperity of the new economic order" (1977:237), the availability of extralegal forms of dispute settlement to the commercial classes was also sharply curtailed at this time (Horwitz 1977:145).
14. On the emerging field of police history see also Miller (1977); Monkkonen (1979); Richardson (1970); Walker (1976). Weinbaum (1979) has some interesting materials on mobs in the 1830s, as does Grimsted (1972).

participation newly legitimated. The rise of popular politics, in which artisans participated (often, however, with no formal voting rights), dates to colonial times (Nash 1979:76–101; 154–57). Even in the eighteenth century, craftsmen and, to a varying degree, craftsmen's interests could not easily be ignored by any individual or faction seeking public office. As Nash relates, though, artisan participation "did not necessarily mean artisan power" (ibid.:364). New York's tradesmen were characteristically unable to unite as a single political interest or movement during the years preceding the War for Independence. Instead, artisans most often served as uneasy hostages to upper-class factions. Economic dependency on merchants, lawyers, and urban landholders, who controlled rents, job opportunities, and credit, translated into political loyalty. This was so, not because artisans owed some abstract fealty or deference to men higher up on the social scale, but because voice voting made it very difficult to conceal one's political preferences from one's patrons on election day (ibid.:365–66).

Craftsmen struggled to obtain greater political stature throughout the dawning years of the new republic. Mobs gave substance to public opinion in ways polling organizations today systematically overlook. But the informal presence of strongly voiced artisan interests, as well as the interests of those beneath them, is clearly attested by such urban crowds. In their capacity as voters, candidates, and officeholders, on the other hand, property-owning mechanics through the early national period might both assert their place in the body politic and punish "those who opposed them" (Rock 1979:8–9). But formal participation took place within a party framework, which neither centered on nor solved the specific problems of the trades. Journeymen in particular found "no political ally in their struggles in the marketplace" (ibid.:69). Elitism by party leaders and manipulation of artisans' interests were common; even the proper standing of artisans in the political order still ranked as an issue in its own right (ibid.:9, 125, 45).

It was an issue that, by the 1820s, began to be resolved. Universal white manhood suffrage was conceded in a New York State Constitutional Amendment of 1826. By the second quarter of the century the right of all citizens not only to vote but also to hold the highest municipal offices in New York signified, in the words of a leading student of the period, that formal democracy had been "substantially achieved" (Pessen 1978:21). Though important in reflecting a modern sensitivity to public opinion (Larson 1977:116), this newly popular politics also implied that, throughout its formative years, an emerging American working class could claim the Declaration of Independence and the Bill of Rights as "its own heritage" (Dawley 1976:237). Unlike their counterparts, the Parisian sans-culottes and the English Jacobins, American artisans could justify the state, because they had reason to believe "that the structure of authority, if not particular officials and policies, rested on popular sovereignty" (ibid.:71).

The extension of the suffrage to previously unenfranchised groups, however, did *not* lead to an Age of Egalitarianism, but, rather, to a less cohesive political state. Formal democratization of politics must not be confused with substantive popular democracy. Elite control remained the norm, in politics as in the economy. "The city was governed largely for, as well as by, its large propertied interests," states Pessen (1978:26). "The Whigs and Democrats set the terms of political debate: they posed the relevant issues," argues another authority, and "they also selected the opposing candidates" (Wallace 1973: chap. 12, p. 448). Despite its increasingly boisterous appeals to workingmen, the two-party system itself may have helped to prevent the emergence of serious third-party contenders, by virtue of its increasingly professional stranglehold over the extensive machinery of state patronage (ibid.).

It was in this context that, in the late 1820s, straitened journeymen founded economic, political, and cultural organizations of an unprecedented kind. It is imperative that we briefly scrutinize the ideological character of the crafts' struggle for equality, because this culturally patterned logic exerted a profound influence on the penny press. Again, only when we understand this new public as a dynamic, concrete entity will a correct understanding of the cheap press be possible.

Antimonopoly and Equal Rights: The Labor Press Objects

"For nearly half a century," wrote William Maclure in his analysis of American society published in 1831, the industrious working classes had "imprudently, indolently, and ignorantly permitted the consuming classes, who live on the produce of their labor, to legislate for the interest of their own class. . . . Exclusive charters, corporations, and monopolies, heaping and fixing wealth on the already rich at the expense of the industrious laborers," had been too easily procured. But, declared Maclure, the times were changing:

> It is only now that the accumulating consequence of so long and so patiently suffering injustice, has brought on the pinching of poverty and starvation that they begin to claim their long neglected rights and legal privileges of freedom and equality. (In Harris 1966:74)

Maclure articulated the complaints of the most radical segment of the artisan population. There can, however, be no question that the era in which he wrote witnessed a massive increase in agitation by laboring people as a whole. Although the artisans and mechanics did not consciously come to see themselves as members of a working class, as happened in England (Thompson 1968), their struggles contributed significantly to the same process.

Protesting tradesmen experimented with economic, political, and cultural action. In 1827 the first city-wide federation of workers was organized in Philadelphia. William Heighton, principal editor of the *Philadelphia Times, Mechanics' Free Press and Working Man's Register* (or simply, as it is often known, the *Mechanics' Free Press*), the organ of this group, testified to the emergence of a form of class consciousness among journeymen:

> We must . . . no longer speak contemptuously of our fellow-workmen, because they do not follow the same occupation as ourselves. . . . The different trades can never become united, so long as the members of one trade consider themselves better than those of another; and without a union of the different trades, we must ever remain the slaves of accumulators. (In Harris 1966:85)

It would be naive to assume that such unity as Heighton proposed was achieved, or even that it was considered desirable, by large numbers of craftsmen. It would be similarly wrong, however, to ignore the energizing force of this ideal of class unity—to underestimate its vital normative presence. An anonymous correspondent to the Utica *Mechanics' Press* thus expressed the more modest and probably more widespread sentiment: "I rejoice to see some indications that the mechanics of this state are awakening to the importance of uniting in support of their rights" (21 November 1829). Between 1833 and 1836 city-wide trade unions were formed in thirteen cities, including New York, where a General Trades Union was attempted in 1834 (Wilentz 1980: chap. 6). The latter numbered some 11,000 members, from a core of ten different trades. New York's artisans organized at least 43 different unions and called at least 18 strikes between 1833 and 1835 (Weinbaum 1979:83). Nationally, union membership grew from 26,000 to 300,000 in the years between 1833 and 1837 (Foner 1947:108)—this in an era when unions were often put down by law as "conspiracies" in restraint of trade. Independent political parties were initiated in 61 cities and towns in the period between 1828 and 1834, while mechanics' clubs advocated legislation and engaged in pressure politics across much of the land (ibid.:122).

The ideology of these journeyman agitators was artisan republicanism, a coherent system of political and social thought that recent historians have tried to analyze and understand.[15] In the ferment of old and new ideas that arose, wage-earning craftsmen grappled "with the concepts of 'class,' 'capital,' and 'republicanism' " (Wilentz 1980: chap. 6, p. 3). In its classical phrasing, which went back to Paine and the American War for Independence, artisan republicanism stressed the evils of "aristocracy" and "corruption," but made little attempt to explain how "aristocracy" arose or became socially entrenched. At the radical edge of artisan republicanism were those who moved to accept a labor theory of value—and who tried to link the elevation of an aristocracy to the deterioration of the trades (ibid.). Even the most radical thinkers of this movement, however, almost never directly challenged the need for private property and the state, although, in their present form, both were sometimes found wanting.

It cannot be overemphasized that, by and large, journeymen accepted individual private property as entirely legitimate, and general acceptance of this core value had profound implications for analysis and discussion of social relations and the state. Paine had earlier helped to define the right to property so that it came to include not only goods and instruments of production but craft skill as well: "The right of property consists in every man's being master in the disposal, at his will, of his goods, capital, income, and industry" (Paine 1967,3:130). When artisans protested their declining status in the market, it was the subordination of their capacity to exercise independent willful choice that was singled out and excoriated. "The labor of their hands and intelligence of their minds is their actual property," after all, "and they consider it their province to put a fair and just value on their own articles, and not leave the prices to the mercy of those who would grind them and give them just what they pleased," argued the journeymen curriers of Newark in 1835. "As labor is the only merchandise which the journeymen have in the market," asserted the New York Piano Forte Makers and Organ Builders, "they have a right to set a price on it" (in Foner 1947:119; cf. Rogers 1978:30). "It has been universally acknowledged, that the LABOUR of the mechanick is the same to him, as the *capital* of the merchant is to the rich man," generalized the New York *Evening Post* (13 June 1836). Mechanics who owned their

15. Foner's outstanding work on Paine (1976) delves deeply into the sources of artisan republicanism. Works on the emergent English working class, notably, Thompson (1968) and Prothero (1979), have great relevance to developments in the United States, although the striking differences between the two nations are nowhere more apparent than in the contrast between subjective class formation and consciousness in their respective working classes.

own tools, who invested years in acquiring highly specialized skills, and who hoped to become masters of households in which family life would center on production might well come to regard their labor as a form of property, particularly as true factory production was almost never to be seen. Thomas Skidmore, perhaps the most radical socialist of his day, nevertheless seems generally to have favored individual over collective ownership of property, although he did make exceptions in the form of state ownership of banks and public works such as roads, bridges, and canals (Harris 1966:108). An early leader of the New York Working Men's Party (formed in 1829), Skidmore, however, declared that in practice there could be no equal right to life, liberty, and the pursuit of happiness without an equal right to property. His scheme for securing this goal (by redistribution of property at each generation) proved visionary; at a general meeting of mechanics and other workingmen of New York City, Skidmore was not permitted to speak. "We have no desire or intention of disturbing the rights of property in individuals, or the public," the group resolved. Rather, it considered "the acquirement of property to soften the asperities of sickness, of age, and for the benefit of our posterity, as one of the great incentives to industry" (*The Mechanics' Press,* 23 January 1830). "Let it be explicitly understood," the participants continued,

> that the mechanics, working men, and those friendly to their interests, hold the rights of individuals, both as to property and religion, as sacred as the instrument that declared our Independence, or that which binds together these United States.[16]

The second resolution adopted by the meeting restated this concern, adding that individual rights to property and religion were "as sacred as life, not to be approached by ruthless despots, or visionary fanatics" (ibid.).

The abuse of state power by "ruthless despots" and the utopianism of

---

16. Perhaps not all artisans subscribed so completely to beliefs in the mainstream of liberal political philosophy; yet those who did not would have constituted a distinct minority. Montgomery claims that there is little evidence that prior to the 1830s the artisan "identified with 'the poor' or felt in any way alienated from the existing social order" (1968:13). Although subsequent research has qualified this, it cannot be doubted that the main goal of politicized craftsmen in the 1830s was equal rights to property, power, and knowledge. It is significant that at the same meeting discussed above, however, the people complained of "the unjust influence of property, which has been too sensibly felt in many instances and various ways" (*The Mechanics' Press,* 23 January 1830). The mechanics went so far as to argue that, in the case of "existing monopolies" held by auctioneers and importers, "extraordinary checks and restrictions must, for a time, be imposed. This is necessary to equalize business, and cause fair distribution of profits" (ibid.). This, clearly, was no systematic critique of class relations but a particular appeal to substantive standards of justice as a means to "equalize business." Miller observes, correspondingly, that in 1830 "laborers still did not think of themselves as a separate class, especially the skilled artisans who made up the majority of organized labor" (1967:41–42).

"visionary fanatics" were polar beacons, between which most artisans hoped to steer on the ship of their purportedly unitary common interest or, in the language of the time, of the "public good." The core of the problem was "monopoly," and the solution, the rigorous pursuit of equal justice. Monopolies, it was asserted by workingmen of New York's Fifteenth Ward in 1835, were "all exclusive privileges, or powers, or facilities, for the accumulation of wealth, or the exclusive use and enjoyment of the bounties of Providence secured to individuals or combinations of men by legislative enactments, the free and uninterrupted enjoyment of which are denied by laws to other members of the same community" (Hugins 1960:149). Monopolies arose in three interconnected spheres and thus were seen to obstruct alike "the free circulation of property, knowledge, or power" (Maclure in Harris 1966:59). In the economy, in the polity, and, for want of a better term, in the public sphere, monopoly rose in like proportion to the preponderance "of the interest of the few over the interest of the many" (ibid.).

Antimonopoly was founded on the belief in equal justice long-held by the industrious classes of craftsmen and those beneath them on the social scale (Hill 1975:60; Capp 1979:109). The Declaration of Independence had stated that "all men are created equal," and Paine, in 1793, had declared that "the law should be equal for all, whether it rewards or punishes, protects or represses" (Paine 1967,3:129). Equal rights, argues Wilentz astutely, "quickly assumed a cluster of meanings." The term might apply to the need for a just wage, to the journeymen's hope of abolishing privileged monopolies, or to the right of journeymen to organize on their own (1980: chap. 6, p. 40). "Equal justice" thus found a powerful advocate in William Sampson, who defended the New York cordwainers, on trial for conspiracy to raise their wages in 1809:

> Shall all others, except only the industrious mechanic, be allowed to meet and plot; merchants to determine their prices current, or settle the markets, politicians to electioneer, sportsmen for horse-racing and games, ladies and gentlemen for balls, parties and bouquets; and yet these poor men be indicted for combining against starvation? I ask again, is this repugnant to the rights of man? If it be, is it not repugnant to our constitution? If it be repugnant to our constitution, is it law? And if it is not law, shall we be put to answer for it? (In Commons et al. 1958: 3:279)

Aside from these meanings, equal rights held another and very important signification—the right of entrepreneurs "to have equal access to economic opportunity" (Wilentz 1980: chap. 6, p. 51). Yet this variant, entrepreneurial equal rights, was not explicitly posed as contradictory to the other uses of the term. All, rather, were encompassed by the single phrase. Equal rights customarily, therefore, attacked neither property nor the need for the state to supervise the public good. Instead, the state was charged with being subservient to special interests in its administration of its prime theoretical function. That these interests were related to certain social classes was not as vital as that they appeared to be private interests in contrast to a unitary "cause of right" in whose name the craftsmen lodged their protests. (Class, it must be admitted, was occasionally evident in a palpable way, as in the General Trades Union's refusal to admit masters into its ranks.) Class was seen not as a fundamental social reality, but as an increasingly intrusive *imposition* on reality by special interests. Class might be recognized and assailed, but only insofar as it evinced a capacity, especially a political capacity, to impede the journeyman's effort to secure independence and a just wage. Natural rights, in short, rather than social class, formed the basis of this critique, and it was the doctrine of natural rights that led to a hostility toward class: class was the expression of preferred economic standing in the political and public realms. Polity and economy were to be kept strictly separate so that a pristine state might justly supervise the republic. Insofar as polity and economy became intertwined, corruption entered the commonwealth.

The Mechanics' Press, a weekly published in Utica, promised in its first issue, therefore, only "to advance the cause of those whom we advocate—the cause of justice—the cause of right—and fearlessly to fling our gauntlet in the face of iniquity and wrong, under what roles soever they present themselves to our view" (14 November 1829). The "cause of justice" here was universalized, while "the bickerings of faction" and "the threatenings of power" were brought to task as sources of inequality. It is difficult for modern readers to appreciate that, precisely *because* private interest was the chief villain, the mechanics were able to voice their own cause as a universal "cause of right."

And because the interests of journeymen could thus be universalized, the notion of public good could also be revitalized. Its substantive connotations of civic virtue had long been tarnished by exposure to the pragmatic realities of factional politics (Nash 1979:156), but it had been resurrected in the War for Independence as "the exclusive end of government" (Wood 1969:53). Paine put the case with characteristic pungency: "The word *republic* means the *public good,* or the good of the whole" (ibid.:55). In turn the citizenry was conceived of as "a homogeneous body with a definable common interest" (Foner 1976:88). Party and faction and class, on the other hand, insofar as they interfered with the impartiality of the state in making decisions and enacting laws, could be broadly reviled for their "disorganizing" consequences, or vilified when they produced monopolies. Partiality in the exercise of state power, though frequently recognized as an almost inevitable or necessary evil—the two words being stressed differently by different groups and in various contexts—not only sapped the state of its integrity but vitiated the all-important public good as well.

Equal rights, antimonopoly, public good: these were not simply rhetoric. They represented, rather, ideological foundations, derived from the current and well-used idiom through which artisans sought to solve the unprecedented problems that confronted them. Both in its expression of a formal concern for a unitary public good grounded in individual natural rights and in its expression of substantive criticism of the state for being subservient to private interests, this language could be used to illuminate and cultivate crucial common ground between the labor movement and the penny press. Before turning to the latter, then, we must dig a little deeper into the use of this idiom by the contemporary artisans who would form the new public.

In 1830 *The Mechanics' Press* took up what would soon become an increasingly troublesome issue: what to do about new technologies that might effect alterations in the pace and character of many skilled crafts, while downgrading or even eliminating others. Reprinting an article from a kindred journal, the Utica organ took a clear stand in an article entitled "Labor Saving Machinery." Readers should not consider machinery's impact "upon a particular set of men, but upon the whole community." From this perspective, "every invention by which labor is saved, is a blessing to mankind precisely in the degree to which this result is produced." In Great Britain, the article continued, "all labor saving machinery has subserved as an instrument of oppression to the people"; yet this was "not a fair exhibition of the natural effects of the system," being attributable "to the state of society, and to the laws":

In a country where all are entitled to equal privileges, the effect is entirely different. Here the exertions of every individual conduce wholly to his own personal advancement, and the government instead of wrenching from him his earnings like a task master, protects him in the rights to which he is entitled. The sources of wealth and to the highest stations of the country are open to all, and where none enjoy exclusive privileges, it is clear that what tends to increase the aggregate of wealth or improvement is a common blessing. . . . It is admitted that the effect of an invention, even in this country is sometimes to injure individuals. But on the other hand, the effect of every useful invention is to benefit the public, and where all are equal, the interest of the whole should be consulted before that of individuals.[17] (27 February 1830)

In the American polity all white men were identically citizens, and they could use their *political* power to halt the slide toward monopoly and special privilege. Artisans, complained *The Mechanics' Press,* "have been too long neglected by our legislature, and we have too long, as a body, remained quiet, while almost every year brings into operation some law, or some plan of our state which bears down upon the different classes of mechanics" (21 November 1829). In a very important sense then, as Wilentz (1980) suggests, it was artisan republicanism itself that bridged the narrower interests of the trades, permitting a more encompassing critique of state and society. Still, it must be reiterated that journeymen throughout this period, despite their critical dissatisfaction with the status quo, shared what Montgomery aptly calls a devoted commitment "to the world's only political democracy." This staunch belief was fundamental to the positions adopted by workingmen into the Civil War (1967:92).

There were, however, serious problems besetting the republic. The question that needed asking, thought Skidmore, was: "Is there one sort of rights for one class of men, and another for another? May one do lawfully what the other will do criminally; have we two codes of law among us?" (in Harris 1966:119). Use of the first-person plural here may denote the defensiveness of this radical's vision. The prospect was frightening in its clarity: the necessary division between groups who exercised power in either the political or economic realms was threatened with collapse. Those who found places of political power, as Maclure put it, were "the rich and nonproductive," while the governed were "the laborers and producers" (ibid.:58). Inequality of this sort had, of course, been practiced throughout the history of human society but—and this must be an all-important qualification—never before had class control of the state been observable, over decades, in a *republic.* It was

17. It should be underscored that this perspective on new technology was offered in a prefatory era, when the extensive changes in production centered more on the prevalence of outwork, sweated labor, specialization of tasks, degradation of skills, use of cheaper materials, and the introduction of women and children into the wage-earning labor force.

frequently clear that laws were "as much as possible, in favour of the Governors and the class they belong to" (ibid.). Or, as Langdon Byllesby, another early radical, put it in 1826:

> An examination of the object of the multitude of laws with which all civilized states are encumbered, will show at least nine tenths of them to be directed to the service and defence of that superabundance, which the prevalence of the existing systems generates for *the few*, against the inroads which the oppression and distress of *the many*, flowing from the same source, induce them to make for the gratification of their wants, and thousands of lives have been sacrificed by their operation. (Ibid.:41)

It was not merely a few visionaries who thought in these hard-shell radical terms. On 13 June 1836 (a date we shall have reason to return to below), no fewer than 27,000 people rallied to a meeting in New York City to protest Judge Ogden Edwards's sentencing of twenty journeyman tailors to pay fines totaling $1,150 for their part in a "conspiracy" to raise wages (cf. Mayer 1978:7).[18] The protestors viewed the statutes that condemned the journeymen as unfair and partial because they prevented equal justice by barring workingmen from participating in the regulation of the price of labor, their only property. Or, as an anonymous "coffin" handbill circulated widely in advance of the rally proclaimed, "the Rich are the only judges of the wants of the Poor Man!"[19]

Equal justice was thought to be systematically impeded by a corrupt legal system. Subservience to private interest was incarnate in the person of the lawyer, "whose principal study is to acquire the knack of deceiving and perplexing a jury, and whose practice is to take a bribe, as often, and almost as readily, to defend a bad cause, as a fee to support a good one," claimed the *Man,* the organ of the workingmen of New York City, in its first issue (18 February 1834).[20] The lawyer was viewed as a key architect of the disturb-

---

18. *People* v. *Fisher,* decided by the New York Supreme Court in 1835, was the precedent-setting case (Mayer 1978). See below, pages 61–65.

19. The handbill is reprinted in Mayer (1978:6) and in the New York *Herald* (7 June 1836).

20. This response can be differentiated from the more typical, middle-class complaint that lawyers charged exorbitant fees. The former questioned the substantive justice of law and its susceptibility to institutionalized corruption; the latter pouted over the expense of a class privilege. Bloomfield cites a fifth grade text of the mid-nineteenth century: "To fit up a village with tackle for tillage / Jack Carter he took to the Saw. / To pluck and to pillage the same little village / Tim Gordon he took to the law" (1976:184). With its implied contrast of useful and unproductive labor, such a verse could perhaps be read in either way. The *Spirit of the Times* poeticized about "GOING TO LAW": "An upper and a lower mill, / Fell out about their water; / To war they went—that is, to law—/ Resolved to give no quarter. / A lawyer was by each engaged, / And hotly they contended; / When fees grew slack, the war they waged, / They

ing socioeconomic changes that both reflected and grew out of the transformation of the crafts. In one labor paper a correspondent charged in 1832 that

> the lawyers want office, power, patronage, sinecures, pensions. . . . To obtain distinction and emoluments of this sort, they very naturally unite with men of wealth, and give them banks, monopolies, etc., and with priests and other literary men, to endow colleges and universities for the benefit of a class of men separate and distinct from the working men. (In Hugins 1960:142)

Property, power, and knowledge alike were controlled by the private interests of the corrupt and iniquitous men who steered the state. Writing about "Laws and Lawyers," a correspondent taking the name "Public Good" exclaimed in the *Man:* "It is high time that the people sent other men than lawyers to our State and National Legislatures to make laws for them. Can they expect to have laws made by such men that will benefit the whole equally?" (24 February 1834).

The alliance between legal and business interests was contested, too, by the Locofocos, a radical offshoot of the Democratic party. At their 1836 convention the Locofocos emphasized the centrality of equal rights to knowledge and justice: "In a Republic but few laws are necessary, and those few plain, simple, and easy of comprehension" (in Hugins 1960:143). Law ought to be made by statute, with the judge's power to indulge in "judicial legislation" severely circumscribed. The Locofocos declared that "the practices of our courts of law are as aristocratic, arbitrary and oppressive as they were in the dark ages of feudalism," and they demanded the election of judges for a limited term and the reinvestment of the jury with substantive power "to determine according to the principles of natural right and justice" (ibid.:143, 142).[21]

This demand for a thorough reform of the political-legal sphere forced a new awareness of the very basis of political society. The *Man* announced the gravity of the crisis:

> The time has arrived when the people of the United States must decide whether they will be a Republic in fact, or only a Republic in name;

judged, were better ended. / The heavy costs remaining still, / Were settled without bother— / One Lawyer took the upper Mill, / The lower Mill the other" (21 January 1842).
21. More responsive to electoral politics, legislative bodies enacted statutory law between 1820 and 1850 that reflected the growing demands of the newly expanded polity for codification of criminal and civil law, reform of judicial procedure, and popular election of the judiciary. Provisions addressing all these demands were enacted in the New York State Constitution of 1846 (Miller 1977:149).

whether they will act upon, or only continue to assert, the principle, that
ALL MEN ARE BORN FREE AND EQUAL. (18 February 1834)

Political action was urgently needed. In this lead article of its first issue, the
Man launched its career by grounding the nation's problems in the political
system, where they could be solved by political redress: "It is *because* every
working man has *not* been a politician that bad legislation has taken place; that
laws have been made granting privileges to a few, which privileges have
enabled them to live without labor on the industry of the useful classes" (ibid.).

Insofar as the interests of journeymen conflicted with those of other
groups, equal justice could furnish the only equitable solution. A correspondent, one "K.L.," expressed this moderate but consistent position in clear-cut
terms:

> We should be careful not to encroach upon the rights of other classes
> of community. . . . The object of the great majority of mechanics, is not,
> I trust, to blot out all distinction between vice and virtue, or to exhibit
> themselves before the world as disorganizers, or as wishing to draw a
> dividing line between themselves and those who do not belong to their
> number. It is to press their claims upon that protection from our laws,
> which should be extended alike to all classes of community. (*The Me-
> chanics' Press,* 21 November 1829)

If the republic itself was the fundamental unit of social analysis, the journeymen's critique of unequal law merged easily with their resistance to the
emergent two-party system. William Heighton thought the problem arose
from the forms of practical politics: "the *first choice* which is that of *nominat-
ing,* is always assumed by the useless and accumulating classes . . . and after
that the *second choice* (election) is but a matter of form" (in Harris 1966:86).
And Skidmore insisted that workingmen should not allow themselves "to be
attached to the cause of a Clay or a Jackson, since neither of these will do
any thing to make your condition equal to their own" (ibid.:133). Although
it cannot but be admitted that journeymen were indeed drawn into the
two-party system, it must also be stated that their incorporation was accompanied by substantial political alienation—a fact that has been amply noted
by Michael Wallace (1973: chap. 12, pp. 461–65, 467–68).

Dissatisfaction with the party system spread easily to the newspapers of
the time, which by the 1820s had become a major conduit for patronage
monies and, indeed, a fulcrum for the mobilization of party allegiance (cf.
Smith 1977). Newspapers selected and paid by the United States secretary of

state to publish the laws passed by Congress, for example, varied more and more as the 1820s came to an end. For the 20th Congress of 1827–1829, 40 percent of the newspapers selected differed from the choices of the Monroe Administration; the comparable figure for the first Jackson Administration of 1829–1831 was 71 percent (Smith 1977:256–74). The number of journals enmeshed in party politics also increased. One newspaper estimated in 1827 that the current Adams Administration had 400 papers in its service (ibid.:290)—at a time when the number of journals in the United States numbered about 850. Hezekiah Niles, a prominent journalist, lamented in 1825 that "the press is now so conditioned in the United States, that nearly every publisher is compelled to take a side in personal electioneering" (in Mott 1962:168). A member of the Virginia Convention for Revising the State Constitution (1829) explored the ramifications of this:

> Look at the daily press. . . . Why is it, that upon all political questions —the presidential elections, or what not—the whole argument turns on the single point, which side will get the majority? because this is the most effectual argument to carry the majority; for the party that shall prevail, is to have the disposal of honors, and office, and emoluments, and partisans are to be excited to exertion or acquired only by the hope of reward. (*The Mechanics' Press,* 5 December 1829)

In this context there arose a labor critique of the party press that has been neglected by journalism historians but that in actuality explained the success achieved by the penny press. Maclure announced in 1831 that the majority of the country's presses, "supported by the subscriptions of the rich and influential, are forced to advocate the aristocratic party, and cease to be entitled to the appellation of free" (in Harris 1966:63). Hostility to the party press focused closely on its usurpation by private interests, in particular, by banks. One set of verses penned in 1834 castigated James Watson Webb, editor of the ten-dollar-a-year New York *Courier and Morning Enquirer,* for abandoning his previous Democratic principles and shifting to the Whigs:

> Who is't edits the blanket sheet,
> And garbles statements very neat,
> At No. 56 Wall street?
> James Double W.
>
> . . . .
>
> Who sold himself to one Nick Biddle,
> And said the Democrats he'd diddle,

Were he allowed to play first fiddle?
James Double W.

. . . .

Who said aristocratic rights
Should supercede the poorer wights,
And calls mechanics 'troglydytes'?
James Double W.

. . . .

Whose plighted faith and consequences,
His boasted knowledge—all pretence—
Was lately valued at *six pence?*
James Double W.

And who, to sum up all together,
Has changed with every change of weather,
A mocking bird, of Noah's feather?
James Double W.
(In Foner 1975:35–36)

These lines were published in the *Working Man's Advocate* (8 November 1834). The reference to (Major) Noah indicted another notorious sixpenny editor, and both drew fire from the artisans not only because they so clearly spoke to elite interests but also because their "boasted knowledge" was priced monopolistically above the heads of journeymen. Such knowledge was "all pretence"—aristocratic puffery. The *Working Man's Advocate,* perhaps the leading labor paper of the era, spoke often of "hireling presses" and linked the corruption of the press directly to their presentation and content: "Are our Democrats arousing, / No dangers still these drones descry; / The base born press in wealth carousing, / Soothes them with its lullaby!" (29 May 1834; in Foner 1975:31) The republic was sailing in rough and rocky waters, but the party press, instead of urging a speedy change of course, curried favor with dandies and nabobs.

An unusually precise and illuminating statement of resistance by artisans to the mainstream party press is given in an article entitled "Newspaper Reading" published by the *Mechanics' Free Press* of Philadelphia:

The vehicles of party political discussion, have set the nation by the ears. . . . The great mass of newspapers and periodicals, are thus mischievously involved in doing worse than nothing. . . .

Notwithstanding the diversity of character and object, discoverable in the aggregate of periodicals, with which this country is filled, they are all precisely alike, as regards the interests of the poorer classes, who are either entirely neglected by them, or noticed only with contempt.

They pay their court to the rich, under whose guidance and control they have contributed much to the creation of injurious monopolies in trade and manufactures; to the maintaining and defending the system of exhorbitant profits; and of late years to an illiberal and almost insufferable reduction in the price of labor. (3 May 1828)

Class, Politics, and the Press. Probably a poster issued for the Workingmen's Party in 1829, this anonymous engraving displays the contemporary language of class. While a corrupt aristocrat tries to buy out the upcoming election for monopoly, employing venal newspapers to prevent the poor from getting their rights, a mechanic casts his vote for "Liberty and the Rights of man." Note the liberty cap and the figure of Columbia. Courtesy of the Kilroe Collection, Rare Book and Manuscript Library, Columbia University.

Given the key position that mercantile newspapers then occupied in the circulation of shipping news, prices current, and other commercial information of immediate and outstanding value to the trader, banker, broker, and merchant (Pred 1973), this appraisal should not be thought extravagant. Newspapers seemed not only to abet monopoly and to contribute to the general corruption of the republic but also to be employed in doing "worse than nothing" by falsifying and obstructing the enlightenment of artisans and mechanics. This was, perhaps, their most heinous crime, for enlightened public opinion was seen—even by the most radical thinkers of the day—to be the only solid foundation for social reconstruction.

Knowledge, as politicized journeymen repeated again and again, would lead to that proper exercise of the vote, without which workingmen would never be able to win back their beleaguered rights and liberties (Foner 1947: 103, 141; Harris 1966:88). The evils complained of by artisans, "having been produced by legislation, will also have to be cured by legislation," pronounced the *Mechanics' Free Press* (5 June 1830). Just laws, however, could only be procured by a populace cognizant of its true situation and its real needs. Education was the only answer. "READ—READ," urged *The Mechanics' Press* (16 January 1830), in common with other artisan-backed journals. "Next to life and liberty, we consider education the greatest blessing bestowed upon mankind," averred the workingmen of New York City (ibid., 23 January 1830).

Many New York craftsmen of this era followed in the path of the London artisans who subscribed to "the universal radical belief that political change would come about through enlightenment, when the people would no longer tolerate the exclusive power of wealth and privilege" (Prothero 1979: 315). In England this sentiment flowed into the contemporary political struggle for an unstamped (untaxed) press, leading to reform. In New York, where the suffrage had already been won, the same sentiment underlay a demand for an "honest press":

> If for your wrongs you would obtain redress,
> With heart and hand support an *honest Press.*
> Mighty its influence, and supreme its pow'r,
> Falsehood and Av'rice must before it cow'r;
> Truth for its motto, Justice for its end,
> Revere the *Press, it is the Poor Man's Friend.*
> (*National Trades Union,* 1 January 1836; in Foner 1975:17)

THE DOWNFALL OF MOTHER BANK.

Class, Politics, and the Press. When President Jackson removed federal deposits from the United States Bank, thereby focusing on the issue of monopoly versus equal rights —the "Monster Bank" being the symbol and reputed agent of the former—the Bank's support of the elite press was publicly chastised. Here, the New York *Courier and Enquirer,* in debt to the bank for over $50,000, and other elite journals find their IOUs no longer safe within the Bank's walls—while editors and bank men flee and the Devil cries: "It is time for me to resign my presidency." Courtesy of the Library Company of Philadelphia.

Or again:

> No weapons we'll use, nor for aught do we care
> > But knowledge and union to bring on the field;
> For those are the keenest and those will we bear,
> > Whilst the *press* will inspire us and be our safe shield.
> (*Working Man's Advocate,* 15 March 1834; in Foner 1975:26)

The press was a mighty power for reason,[22] which, in its perversion by private interest, became a dangerous malignancy inflicting grievous damage on the

---

22. The association between reason and the press was manifested not only in the United States but also in France and England and other countries as well at about this time (see chapter 2).

American republic. Through its agency, to borrow the words of a journalist writing four decades before, reason "turns pimp to faction and enlists as a mercenary soldier" (in Stewart 1969:639).

Like all "place-hunters," the complaint ran, editors had become "marketable commodities; they put up their principles, their opinions, their votes at auction, to the highest bidder, setting the highest value to their services, but willing to take any price they can get" (*The Mechanics' Press,* 5 December 1829). James Gordon Bennett's erstwhile patron, Jesse Hoyt, informed him when he sought patrons for his newspaper (thus helping to precipitate Bennett's break with the party press), "the people are jealous of the public press":

> I am satisfied the press has lost some portion of its hold upon public confidence; recent developments have had a tendency to satisfy the people that its conductors, or many of them at least, are as negotiable as a promissory note. (16 August 1833; in Hudson 1873:413)

Hoyt's metaphor was quite apt. For many craftsmen the press appeared to have been wrested from its rightful place as it was incorporated by the monopolies, the banks, and the emerging party system. The arrogance of the elite press in deigning to notice developments of interest to the artisan population was angrily attacked by "Hamden":

> Among the whole host of the editorial fraternity of this city, I believe there is but one of them who has even had the courage to notice either the existence or the character of the 'Mechanics' Free Press.' . . . If this large body of the community can tamely brook such an insult, then indeed are they too despicable to be noticed either by the editors of our newspaper, or any other, who may lay claim to self-assumed superiority. What! shall the predictions of those useless animals be verified, who declare that the operative part of the community, particularly mechanics, are not capable of supporting or conducting a newspaper; that they are fit for nothing but manual and mechanical labour, having little more intellect than the brute creation and little else to distinguish them from the latter, than the circumstances of their possessing human form. (*Mechanics' Free Press,* 17 May 1828)

The partisanship against which the mechanics railed was conceived, not as an abstract entity that held reason to ransom, but rather as a form of social disorganization created by increasingly noticeable class objectives. "Each class that speaks or writes," announced Maclure, "assumes that the public good consists in their good" (in Harris 1966:65). Artisans distrusted the party

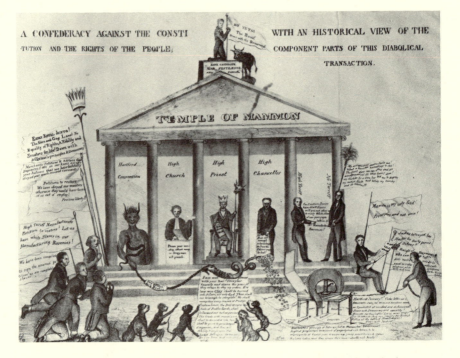

Class, Politics, and the Press. In this engraving of 1833 the plight of black slaves was explicitly compared to that of white workers "in our Manufacturing Baronies." While monkeys—ancient symbols of avarice—gather to read a statement proclaiming the advantage of monopoly and aristocracy, the "High Chancellor" of the Temple of Mammon pours money into the elite press. The words inscribed on the sack of coins he holds read: "It is not enough to have bought the Press the Editors must be fed!" Courtesy of the Library Company of Philadelphia.

press because they believed it to be dominated by "the monied and mercantile aristocracy." Such a press might only be called free in the sense that it was "free and open to every thing in favor of their supporters and shut against every species of reasoning, be it ever so true, that can militate against them" (ibid.:63). The monopoly held by this exclusive press over public information systemically obstructed the exercise of reason in the all-important process of the formation of public opinion. The elite press was, therefore, deeply implicated in the corruption of the republic. In this it had something in common with medicine, law, and religion, which, in the 1830s, were the objects of suspicion and animosity by working people (Hugins 1960:166–71; Larson

1977:118–20, 133–35). Like them, whose "whole stock in trade is a species of knowledge," journalism shared "a direct interest in preventing the article they deal in from becoming common and cheap" (Maclure in Harris 1966:67). Skidmore argued, in contrast, for leveling "the differences in the minds of men," so that "the most intelligent person" could not "extract property from the one who knows least." "With such an equality of both property and knowledge it will be impossible for anyone to accumulate a fortune substantially larger than that of any other person" (in Harris 1966:112). Again, wrote Skidmore in a remarkable passage:

> The discoveries, that yet remain to be made in every department of human knowledge, are inexhaustible, as will be the wealth which they will afford to the generations that shall make them, and to those that shall succeed them. But, in order that we may have a multitude, and the greatest multitude possible, of explorers of new truths; the *situation,* the *condition,* in one word, the *possessions* of all men, at their first mature entrance into life, together with their education, must be equal. Artificial and unequal wealth must not be nor remain built up, by the suicidal consent of society, to place those who possess it, in situations of ease, such as they need not, desire, and will not care to contribute *their* quantum of knowledge and discovery, to the common fund; nor must others be depressed into the gulf of poverty, discouragement and degradation, by withholding from them that which is their own, in right of their being; and without which, *they also,* will add little to the stock of science, and be unable even to preserve that which is now in existence. (Ibid.:131)

It is a formidable and modern vision. The radicals Maclure and Skidmore voiced it explicitly, but a wide stratum of artisans also found it necessary to insist that public education, being indispensable to human progress, should be supported by government (Hugins 1960:131–35). Access to knowledge, for such people as these, must ideally be unrestricted. "Perhaps the greatest improvement that can be effected in education," advised Maclure, "is to free the pupil as much as possible from the ipse dixit of the master, by teaching him to derive his knowledge directly from the things themselves, or accurate representations of them" (in Harris 1966:70). We shall see below what penny press made of this widespread concern for enlightenment and direct knowledge. First, however, we must recognize that the penny press was not unique in its recognition of these ideals.

Patronized either by independent subscription or trade unions and supported mainly by artisans and mechanics, aggressive labor papers had proliferated by the 1830s. This labor press, speaking to a portion of the same public

THE UPPER AND LOWER ORDER OF SOCIETY.

Class and Popular Culture. Comic almanacs—an amalgam of cheap woodcut engravings, puns, jokes, and obscure references—were a ubiquitous and popular genre throughout antebellum years. In this illustration from Elton's Comic *All-My-Nack* of 1845, the airs of the upper class are singled out for ridicule and class-based animosity. Courtesy of the Library Company of Philadelphia.

that would soon be taken over by the commercial penny papers, supplied a living model according to which the latter could formulate its appeal. Almost fifty labor papers were established between 1827 and 1832; more were added between 1833 and 1836 (Foner 1975:17). Enlightened reason, these journals proclaimed, had too long been restrained in the press by self-interested factions, bank men, and unprincipled, petty editors. But it could not be expected, one of the first of these labor journals proudly announced, "while light and knowledge is diffusing itself through every portion of the community, that the labouring classes should longer remain totally ignorant of the causes which have contributed to their degradation":

> nor is it a matter of astonishment, if perceiving the advantages obtained by the higher classes through the agency of newspapers, they should at length desire a journal of their own. The time has arrived that shall develope the energies of these classes, who are now beginning to discover the artifices by which they have been misled. (*Mechanics' Free Press*, 3 May 1828)

The Mechanics' Press, published "for the public good," explicitly renounced in its first issue "a rank among the leaders of party" (14 November 1829). "It is asserted," stated the editors in laying down their challenge, "and generally believed, that a periodical publication cannot long sustain itself and receive the patronage of the public, unless it sides with a political party. It may be so; we do not choose to dispute the truth of the assertion by words, but are content to prove its truth or falsity by experiment" (20 February 1830). The *New York Mechanic*, a penny daily, assured "the mechanics of the city of New York" that it was "attached to no party—belonging to no sect." Instead, "immemorably devoted to republican institutions," the journal purported to "attack or defend MEASURES *not* MEN . . . to effect the GREATEST POSSIBLE GOOD, for the GREATEST POSSIBLE NUMBER" (21 July 1834). Pursuing impartiality and independence, the cardinal virtues of the artisans (Wilentz 1980: chap. 6, p. 39), the editors of the *New York Mechanic* hoped to "view dispassionately the events passing around us, and in our capacity as public journalists submit calmly and unprejudiced our opinions upon their various results" (21 July 1834). The *Mechanics' Free Press*, "A Journal of Practical and Useful Knowledge," ran a prospectus for a new semimonthly to be called "The Liberal Press." The latter would be devoted to the interests of "the mechanic or labouring classes," so that "their minds should not continue to lay prostrate before that immolating Juggernaut, SUPERSTITION."

The objects of this journal here proposed to be published, are the development of the human intellect—the dissemination of truth—the promotion of happiness and virtue. It will utter the shibboleth of no party; for the creed of REASON is coextensive with illimitable nature —but it will be open to all parties, so long as their communications are conducted with candour, good temper and kindly feeling. (24 May 1828)

For enlightenment to be possible, independent pursuit of equal rights was indispensable. The New York Working Men in 1829 openly disclaimed "all connexion with any and every religious or irreligious sect, or political party, heretofore existing," and resolved to view any attempt to give their association such a partisan cast as "in no way friendly to the association" (*The Mechanics' Press*, 23 January 1830). This was not merely a strategic move to avoid dissension within the artisan community, for many craftsmen were indeed committed to extant party politics. It was also an attempt to lay the basis for rational understanding and enlightenment, which was conceived of in unitary and absolute terms. The *Awl*, journal of the shoemakers of Lynn, Massachusetts, in their battles against a more fully developed industrial capitalism, could state in 1844 that "the object of the paper is the benefit of *all* connected with the trade. We do not advocate the claim of the jour in opposition to those of the employer, nor seek to benefit one at the expense of the other" (in Dawley 1976:63). Equal rights, developed in defense of the foundering republic, demanded no less.

With the emergence of a vigorous labor press, the appeal to reason entered the arena of public discourse in a sustained and systematic way. The press, though, did not last beyond the Panic of 1837 and the ensuing deep depression, in which, Foner claims, 50,000 New Yorkers were thrown out of work, leaving fully one-third of the work force unemployed (1947:167). Again, this press cannot have spoken for all artisans and mechanics, let alone for all of the laboring classes. Yet what the labor papers initiated through their declaration of independence from monopolists and factions invited imitation from a different but even more explosive breed of journalism. Improved print technology was available; the need of business for the press was omnipresent; and now, disillusioned with newspapers serving political and mercantile elites, the artisan public was eager for a change. The penny press, which rode out the depression, which claimed to speak alike to the politicized and the less-politicized, the journeyman and the merchant, and which appropriated and softened the anger of the labor press into a blustery rhetoric of equal rights, enlightenment, and political independence, was eager to give them that change.

2

The Penny Press:
Private Defender of Public Good

In the 1850s the journalist George Foster remarked that the penny press, "commencing at the bottom," had now reached "the very topmost round of journalism, as understood in this country: while the old-fashioned 'respectable sixpennies' are getting farther and farther out of sight and mind" (1854:25–26). In less than two decades, sturdy new journalistic institutions had been planted; through them, the sociocultural role of the newspaper was ineradicably changed. These cheap papers succeeded by combining business acumen with explicit adherence to the chief artisan ideals in order to define and cultivate their new role. How they did this is the subject of this chapter.

The business orientation of the penny journals has often been noted. James Gordon Bennett linked the content of his New York *Herald* quite openly to his ultimate goal—business success. "The merchants generally are just beginning to find that the small daily press is becoming a much better vehicle for advertising than the large ten dollar papers," he boomed, nine months after his paper had commenced. Why? Because the public gave keen attention to the *Herald:* "People see, read, and remember." "This tells at once," he continued, in the best tradition of the media representative, "on buying and selling." "The independent, honourable, and liberal plan on which the Herald has been conducted" infused both editorial matter and advertising policy (1 January 1836). Bennett later claimed that his plan evinced a successful adaptation "to the public interests and public tastes" (2 March 1836).

Like other penny editors, Bennett espoused a variant of entrepreneurial equal rights. The cheap papers made much of the "impartiality" of their advertising columns and thereby linked their business needs directly to artisan republicanism. The *Public Ledger* in Philadelphia hoped to "admit any advertisement of any thing or any opinion, from any persons who will pay the price, excepting what is forbidden by the laws of the land, or what, in the opinion of all, is offensive to decency and morals" (in Atwan 1979:16). The Boston *Daily Times* similarly proclaimed that "one man has as good a right as another to have his wares, his goods, his panaceas, his profession, published to the world in a newspaper, provided he pays for it" (ibid.). The founder of the first full-time American advertising business, Volney B. Palmer, asserted that advertising released the press "from pecuniary dependence upon cliques and monopolies, insuring to it . . . the free expression of opinion which it only nominally enjoys while deriving its main support from an opinional constituency" (ibid.:18). As we shall see, entrepreneurial equal rights in commercial journalism produced what Bennett termed "a complete victory over interested opponents and private foes" (*Herald,* 1 January 1836).

The New York *Sun*'s logo—"It Shines for All"—profoundly captured the democratic promise of the penny press: extension of public access to information and metamorphosis of the character of public information itself. A newspaper costing only a penny could easily overwhelm a sixpenny paper with a limited subscription public, while the reputedly impartial reports that graced the former's pages resonated with the independence called for so heartily by the new artisan public. By giving all citizens an equal access to knowledge and direct personal knowledge of impartially presented news, the penny press could boast of its thorough revision of the language of the public sphere. Bennett pitched his *Herald* to "the great masses of the community," trumpeting that the paper's only guide would be "good, sound, practical common sense" (6 May 1835). Common sense spoke immediately to the political culture of journeymen in its emphasis not only on that which was plain or obvious but also on popular, accessible, unrestricted truth. And with Tom Paine's views (at least some of them) well established in political tradition, Bennett's appeal to common sense also maintained a resolutely political emphasis.

The penny journals appropriated vast reaches of republican rhetoric. The *Herald* openly disclaimed "all party—all politics," by which Bennett meant that it would "support no party—be the organ of no faction or coterie, and care nothing for any election or candidate from president down to a constable" (6 May 1835). This suddenly "independent" newspaper claimed incessantly that it impartially expressed "the public voice" (Pray 1855:252).

"Aloof from all cliques and parties"; standing above "money or private interests"; "more powerful than all the political alliances and bartering of factions" (ibid.); this commercial newspaper now claimed to act as an "upright censor" and an "impartial judge" (ibid.:311). A less boisterous journal than the *Herald,* the New York *Sun* also definitively aligned itself with "the whole people":

> Great statesmen and good magistrates administer laws for the benefit of *the* people. Knaves, demagogues, and narrow minded men, add an epithet. They incline to favor some particular class of the people, as the rich people, the working people, the religious people, the poor people, the temperate people. The politician, whose mind is not broad enough to take in *the* people, the whole people, is unworthy of confidence or regard. (17 April 1834)

The power of the journalistic equation of mass circulation and a unitary public was framed, too, in a contemporary account of Bennett's attempt to enter a brothel where a murder had been committed. As he pushed his way through the clamor of the crowd, someone called out to the police officer guarding the entrance, "Why do you let that man in?" The officer replied, "He is an editor—he is on public duty" (*Herald,* 12 April 1836).[1] "May journalists ever keep glowing in their minds," wrote *Herald* correspondent Isaac Pray, animating the new credo,

> those words in which they may find a manual of practice as efficient for the country and for the elevation of their own profession, as any conventional usages, or any codes of maxims and laws: IRREPROACHABLE TASTE—CHARITY—FRATERNITY—JUSTICE—THE PUBLIC GOOD. (1855:488)

This much-vaunted independence was not the benign voice of middle-class progress sweeping away vestiges of premodern mentalities but the angry protest of journeymen filtering through the self-interest of the cheap journals. The masthead of Philadelphia's *Public Ledger* bore the chief artisan ideals in proud view of its readership: "Virtue Liberty Independence" (25 March 1836). For many, the last translated at once into both political and economic terms. As the masthead of the Philadelphia *Spirit of the Times,* a consistently radical journal, boldly announced: "Democratic and Fearless; Devoted to No

---

1. This anecdote may also be found in Francke (1974: chap. 2, p. 44) and in a chapbook called *Sketch of the Life of Miss Ellen Jewett. By One Who Knew Her* (1836:21).

Clique, and Bound to No Master" (1 January 1842). And something of the urgency of the labor press was at stake when the commercial journals defended their forceful penetration of political life by recourse to the constituting rights of the polity itself. "If we are not allowed to give our readers an impartial history of the proceedings of our courts of justice," argued Ben Day of the *Sun,* characteristically, when threatened with a lawsuit for exercising "a right guaranteed by the constitution of the state," then "the boasted liberty of the American press is not worth a fig" (*Sun,* 17 April 1834). The penny press seemed to echo the journeymen's bark—but what about its bite?

As James Gordon Bennett would have it, his *Herald,* which made its appearance a full year and a half after the New York *Sun* hit the streets, brought business legitimacy to the small papers. "Before May last," he wrote, "the business and intelligent classes did not patronise the penny papers— now, probably two-thirds of these classes, if not more, take them" (2 March 1836). Bennett was never one given to understatement, but there can be no doubt that the distinction between the commercial journals and the labor papers upon which they drew was very often minimized in the first years of the penny press. *New-York as It Is, in 1834; and Citizens' Advertising Directory,* one of several business directories issued annually for the convenience of the commercial community, listed eleven daily morning and evening broadsheets, and then stated: "There are several small daily papers published in the city, which are sold by carriers, to citizens and strangers, at *one cent* each, such as The Sun, The Bee, The Transcript, The Man, The Morning Star" (Williams 1834:156). Here labor and commercial journals were indiscriminately mixed together. Both sorts of journals were small tabloids, in an age when "blanket sheets" opening to a full five feet were the dominant form for the mercantile elite.

The political qualities of the cheap dailies were noticed by this elite press, when the latter were mentioned at all, as consonant with the labor movement. The sixpenny *Journal of Commerce* complained, for example, of "the subserviency which, from the nature of their circulation," the penny journals "are compelled to exercise towards Trades Unions and such like humbug affairs" (29 June 1835; in Hudson 1873:425). In truth, as Bennett wrote, "we are, and have always been, in favor of the right of journeymen, or any body of men, combining peacably for the regulation of their wages" (*Herald,* 7 June 1836). No wonder then that, while some trade unions initiated their own journals, others supported existing journals friendly to their objectives (Foner 1947:112). The *Sun* and the *Transcript,* both started by printers, also supported the right of workers to organize unions and, sometimes, even to demand a "just increase in their wages" (*Sun,* 25 February 1836; *Transcript,* 24 February 1836; in Weinbaum 1979:83–84). On other issues, also, the penny papers often supported the artisans. Shortly before the food riot of February 1837, the cheap press printed angry editorials denouncing inflation. The increase in prices was said to issue from "an atrocious and wicked conspiracy by rich speculators . . . to grind to the earth the great mass of society" (*Herald,* 9 February 1837; in Weinbaum 1979:95). Bennett urged tenants who were unable to afford soaring rents to refuse to vacate their apartments when their leases ran out. After the February riot, the journal warned that further disturbances would be avoided only if rents were deflated. Otherwise, "the whole body of the people" would be driven "out of all sense and moderation" (*Herald,* 4, 9, 15 February 1837; in Weinbaum 1979:95). (It should be mentioned that the *Herald* did not condone riots, but instead consistently backed "legislative action" as the only sure redress [7 June 1836].) In at least one instance, labor's relation to the penny press proved unusually intimate and tenacious. Horace Greeley's *Tribune* (1841), well known for its sympathy to labor on different issues, elicited correspondence from Karl Marx in London over a ten-year period (1852–1862), and Greeley himself became labor's choice in the New York Congressional elections of 1866 (Montgomery 1967:111). In short, like some preachers of the English Revolution who were newly dependent upon their congregations for their living, the penny press proved sympathetic on various counts to the stands of the artisans who formed much of its public.

Nowhere was this more obvious than in the penny journals' studied attempt to lift restrictions that barred the public from information and to excoriate the monopoly held by an elite press over the news. In 1841, Bennett's reporter was rebuffed when attempting to gain entry to the United States Senate. The only newspapermen then permitted in the Senate were chosen from journals printed at Washington, which allowed greater congressional control over the final product of the newspapers patronized and, therefore, also over the national information system, which relied heavily upon their accounts. Bennett charged that this restriction was "caused by the selfish and malign influences of the Washington newspapers, in order to maintain a monopoly of Washington news, and to rob the public treasury, under the color of public printing, in order to gratify their extravagant habits of life" (in Pray 1855:289). The *Herald* exposed Treasury payments of a reputed $420,000 to three Washington papers in 1838, and, triumphantly employing egalitarian logic, stated: "*We* propose, and will give, a daily report and circulation of these debates, better and more comprehensive, without asking a cent of the public treasury" (ibid.:290).

And what of the notorious attack by the cheap press on the mercantile and party newspapers? Did it not also center on the obstructions that denied citizens participation in public enlightenment? "Who would expect," queried Bennett about the financial news offered by his rivals, "that the Courier & Enquirer would tell all the truth if it touched the United States Bank? or that the Journal of Commerce would not throw a mantle over the nakedness of the Manhattan Bank? or that the Times would not hide the small linen of the Commercial Bank?" (*Herald,* 4 September 1835). From the very fact that these papers, whose price alone assured their inaccessibility to much of the population, were "entirely dependent on this or that institution," Bennett went on, "they dare not for their soul's salvation, or the throwing out of their notes, give a free, candid, full, and truly scientific account of the recent panic, or the present state of the money market, or its future prospects. They only support a party in stocks, or a party in politics, or a party in religion." The party press, according to Bennett, had participated in the prostitution of reason itself: "These journals have obscured not enlightened the public. Devoted to party or politics, either on this or that side—owned body and soul by some banking institution or another," they would only discourse on those matters "to deceive on one side or entrap on the other" (ibid.). Running extravagantly expensive news expresses to beat the sixpennies, Bennett declared that "speculators should not have the advantage of earlier news than the public at large" (in Pray 1855:373). An additional advantage, of course, would follow if businessmen and merchants would look to the *Herald* for timely commercial news.

For its part, the *Sun* denounced the elite *Journal of Commerce* as "a company of rich, aristocratical men" and charged that the paper would take sides with any party "to gain a subscriber or a yearly advertiser." Moreover, the *Sun* revealed,

> its mechanical department is managed by what honorable printers term *rats* and *botches*—and edited, and conducted, by tyrants and hypocrites. We understand that an agreement has been entered into by Hale and Hallock, of the Journal, and Townsend & Dwight, of the Daily Advertiser, to keep the wages of their men two dollars a week below the Standard price. Shame! (16 April 1834)

"Rats" was printers' slang for those who accepted wages below standard; "botches" were shoddy craftsmen. What more forceful evidence of corruption could be offered up to a public of artisans? The *Sun* exposed a mutual corruption, linking "aristocratical" usurpers of public good with those who, in acquiescing to work for lower wages, also participated in the prostitution of public good by private interest.[2] Bennett's *Herald,* again, castigated the sixpennies for being "in the hands of stockjobbers," who would "pervert every public event from its proper hue and coloring, to raise one stock and depress another" (1 September 1835; in Pray 1855:204). It is entirely correct to call the antipathy between the sixpennies and the cheap commercial papers a form of "class conflict" (Schudson 1978:57), but it was not a battle between old aristocrats and a new middle class; rather, it was a battle between contemporary privilege and monopoly, typified perhaps best of all by the banks (Wilentz 1980), and artisan-backed equal rights.

The penny papers, in contrast to the sixpennies, occupied "altogether a different position" (*Herald,* 4 September 1835). Free of the insidious obligations borne by the elite press, because dependent not on parties but on the public as a whole, indebted to no bank and therefore without preordained "sympathy or antipathy towards them,"

> we shall—and can therefore—deal justly, honestly and fearlessly with every institution in Wall street—every broker—every bank—every capitalist. (Ibid.)

Released from the forcible restraints of monopoly by the dynamic combination of advertiser support and an ideology that made it possible to boast about business success without undermining his commitment to the public good, Bennett could brag about his commitment to democratic public information. "I have entered on a course of private enterprise," he allowed, "but also of public usefulness" (2 March 1836). In a more jubilant mood, he crowed that "the miserable tirades" of the elite press "will not disgrace the columns of the Herald" (4 September 1835). Again in keeping with the principles of the cheap press more generally, Bennett offered his *Herald* as a means by which enlightened public opinion might at last be placed on the unshakable foundation of reason. This effort received decisive support from the practice of journalistic exposure.

Exposure—of dark corners hidden throughout the city, of public vices

2. Pocock holds that republican virtue "consisted in a relation between equals" and, therefore, that "its loss was not private but mutual. It might be thought of as coming either when some became so strong that they could use others as their instruments, or when some became so weak that they could be so used" (1973:87).

and private lives—was used to reveal violations of the overarching standard of equal justice. By ferreting out such information, the penny press displayed, indeed, flaunted, its commitment to public enlightenment. Through exposure, also, the cheap papers claimed to play a powerful remedial role in redressing the corruption that connived at permanent class divisions. Thus, at one stroke, they emphasized their proximity to the culture of the new public.

Exposure focused most closely on the abuse of state power and on criminal infringement of natural rights. Both of these areas, as we shall see in a more detailed analysis of the *National Police Gazette* below, were inextricably bound up with conceptions of class; but, in every case, exposure subjected concrete instances of a violated public good to "the ordeal of public opinion" ("The Press" 1811:526).[3] Thus, the public good was reaffirmed as the guiding light of the republic, and the commercial press cultivated a new social role. Unnamed, the *Herald* took first place among what Bennett in 1842 called "the resources within ourselves that enable us to correct every family error, rectify the balance of the world, and whip it into decency whenever it deserves it" (Pray 1855:309–10).

Before turning to exposure in more detail, it is worth noting that the tactic drew compelling force from its context: the time was not yet gone when a mob might give dramatic and forcible expression to the complaints of the dissatisfied. "A wicked and corrupt administration," cried John Wilkes (a pioneer agitator for popular liberties in Georgian England who knew quite well the uses of the crowd), "must naturally dread this appeal to the world" (*North Briton,* 5 June 1762). By the 1830s, in the closely packed streets of the city of New York, the "appeal to the world" had been cogently connected to the demand for equal justice. Skidmore thundered that it was up to the poor

> to vindicate your rights—by holding him up to public scorn and indignation, who, however remotely, however insidiously, however advantageously in appearance . . . attempts to place you, or to induce you to place yourselves below the level of the proudest nabob of the land. (In Harris 1966:126)

3. Francke decisively rejects the view that exposure dates only as far back as the Muckrake Era, around the turn of the twentieth century (1974: chap. 1, p. 17). He quotes the journalist Will Irwin in support: "The muckraking articles in the magazines were only improved examples of a device used by American editors ever since our press began to find itself in the 1830s—attacking some public evil or abuse, with a view to reforming it, by printing the news about it" (ibid., conclusion, p. 358). It is significant that such a view depends on a conception of enlightenment through public discourse, leading to decision-making by active, autonomous political participants.

Dozens of crowds shot through the streets of the city in the 1830s, bearing eloquent witness to the potency of Skidmore's demand (Grimsted 1972; Weinbaum 1979).

The manner of exposure also merits a brief word. When journeymen of the new republic declared their outrage against unjust masters, they directed their anger at particular offenders and not against "an economy that was becoming inherently exploitative" (Rock 1979:282). Precisely because a system of craft production predominated, individuals who undercut or threatened the social relationships upon which that system was founded remained just that—deviant individuals. Exposure, whether by newspaper or mob, or some combination of the two, arose as a means of achieving a localized, limited redress. Therefore, although exposure led to a new institutional role for the press, it posed no ultimately radical threat to the American state. On the contrary, while chastising particular abuses, the commercial newspaper consistently supported the state itself. By virtue of its inherent tendencies toward corruption by private design, government, in this view, was a necessary evil. Without in the least abridging the necessity of government—which, indeed, it insisted upon—the commercial press attempted to expose and publicly cauterize the specific evils that bedeviled it.

In the earliest months of the penny press, we find regular, patterned instances of exposure centering on the changing legal system and its evident abuses. Not only did the cheap press ritualistically oversee the operations of justice, in police and crime reports and commentary, to ensure that justice was acceptably attained, but also, more defensively, perhaps, commercial journals kept an eye on what was being *done* to justice by virtue of the transformation of the legal system. In this respect they again borrowed from contemporary labor papers. The *Man*, for example, published crime accounts frequently and, in recognition that these reports were directed at abuses of and by law, occasionally headlined its police news "LAW INTELLIGENCE" (18 February 1835). Crime news, embracing police reports from the magistrate's court, discussion and news of police activities, criminal biographies, and extensive trial coverage of noteworthy cases, dramatized a larger intention: to punish specific infractions of public good.

This infusion of crime news into the young commercial papers did not, therefore, merely reflect the hunger for "sensationalized" news that analysts so often attribute to the "mass" public. Crime news was absorbed by the penny journals only after a period of experimentation with the form and with its dramatic potential. In particular, the emergence of crime news was tied intimately to continuing trans-Atlantic struggles for individual rights. The crucial political basis of the form—that the trial of one man's rights not figuratively but *literally* brought the entire political nation to the bar of justice—was elaborated in eighteenth-century England, notably by John Wilkes. Wilkes had been arrested and imprisoned for seditious libel in April of 1763. When in May he appeared before the judges at Westminster, he prefaced his defense with words carefully calculated to evoke a response "among the varied throng of gentlemen, shopkeepers and craftsmen that crowded the galleries and approaches to the courtroom." "My Lords," rang out Wilkes, "the liberty of all peers and gentlemen, and, what touches me more sensibly, that of all the middling and inferior set of people, who stand most in need of protection, is in my case this day to be finally decided upon a question of such importance as to determine at once whether English liberty shall be a reality or a shadow" (Rude 1962:27). Wilkes's whole argument, claims his most successful chronicler, lay in his constantly repeated refrain "that the Englishman's liberties were, in his person, being invaded and violated by a tyrannical executive and, equally in his person, required to be defended" (ibid.:193). Paine, that remarkable citizen of the world, also helped to transform the trial of his person into a simple empirical test of civil rights. "My necessary absence from your country," Paine wrote on 11 November 1792 from Paris to the attorney general of England concerning the prosecution being waged against his *Rights of Man Part Two*,

> affords the opportunity of knowing whether the prosecution was intended against Thomas Paine, or against the Right of the People of England to investigate systems and principles of government; for as I cannot now be the object of the prosecution, the going on with the prosecution will show that something else was the object, and that something else can be no other than the People of England, for it is against *their Rights*, and not against me, that a verdict or sentence can operate.[4] (In Paine 1967,3:111)

The penny press consistently broached a formally identical appeal (we shall have occasion to examine this in detail through the analysis of the *National Police Gazette*, below). Isaac Pray's account of the *Herald*'s trial coverage of John C. Colt, for the killing of one Samuel Adams in 1842, gives a glimpse

---

4. One could also mention the "Queen Caroline" affair in the England of 1820–1821 in this connection. The new King George IV attempted to divorce and depose his estranged queen without a proper trial. The queen's rights were used by radical artisans and by the radical press as a test of the people's and as a chance to "recover the country's constitutional liberties" (Prothero 1979:132–55, especially 144).

of this appeal when he observes that the powerful and wealthy friends of the defendant "spare[d] neither money nor exertion to clear him." "The Time had come," Pray wrote, "when the power of money and the power of the majesty of law were to be tried, as well as the accused" (1855:296). Here, however, the content of crime news had clearly shifted. Modified and adapted, crime news in the penny press focused not only on the integrity of the state but also on the unequal effect of social class on the political nation and, specifically, in the law. The cheap papers had only to station reporters at the police courts to pick through a constant flow of cases that might be used to reveal and dramatize the status of the citizenry's rights. This they lost no time in doing; the *Public Ledger* told the public in its very first issue that it had "secured the services of a police reporter and a collector of news, and it is hoped that their exertions will impart to its columns additional interest" (25 March 1836).

The Somers case, again involving well-placed principals (this time the prominent person was deceased, the victim during a mutiny of a superior Naval Officer's bullet), again dramatized the adversary relation between newspaper and legal system. Bennett's trial reports were notable, claimed Pray, because he "assailed the mercenary lawyers for their peculiar conduct at the time, while he endeavored to uphold the laws." Pray thought that this "was a bold course"; but, he countered, "it had its uses":

> Law was becoming a mockery in the eyes of the people. The poor man was condemned, and executed—the rich man was found guilty, and ingenuity could invent means in quibbles to avert his legal doom. Monroe Edwards, the forger, was only deserted when it was ascertained that he had no money, and the popular maxim was "with money enough, you can clear the vilest malefactor." (1855:301)

In the notorious Richard Robinson–Helen Jewett murder case of 1836 the use of crime news to report the standing of individual rights in the face of emergent class divisions reached its zenith. The case was something of a cause célèbre; it gave rise to no fewer than eleven chapbook accounts, published not only in New York City but also in New Haven, Boston, and Philadelphia, the last being a sixty-four-page edition published in 1878. George Wilkes, editor of the *Police Gazette,* catered to the apparent longstanding fascination that the case occasioned by producing a long chapbook chronicle of the debacle in 1849. Journalism historians have also proved to be susceptible to its enticements; the Emerys, for example, cannot resist a disapproving sniff over this "murder of a prostitute by a notorious man-about-town." This was, in their eyes, merely a "sordid" affair, which Bennett sensationalized to gain readers in a period before his *Herald* gained respectability and "gave way to an increasing interest in more significant news" (Emery and Emery 1978:123).

It would probably have been difficult to convince contemporaries of the merit of this judgment. Bennett, the Emerys assert, "stirred up so much interest in the case that the court could not continue hearing testimony when the defendant was up for trial" (ibid.). Bennett alone, however, evidently did not stimulate great interest in the case. Rather, the Robinson-Jewett affair appears to furnish a rare instance where the contemporary transformation of business law intersected with the proceedings of a criminal trial, to resounding effect among the city's population. The Philadelphia *Public Ledger* claimed that "the excitement in New York is tremendous; and certainly no criminal trial ever took place in that city, productive of such absorbing interest" (4 June 1836). To gain a glimpse into why this was so, we must turn to the case itself.

Helen (or Ellen, as some journals called her) Jewett was the victim of a brutal hatchet-murder on a Saturday night in a prominent and fashionable brothel. The crime sparked immediate interest. The *Herald* reported that the morning after the murder excitement in the city was "extraordinary" (12 April 1836); and Philip Hone, self-made man and one-time mayor of the city, recorded in his diary on 11 April 1836 that the perpetrator "was no doubt her paramour, a young man named Richard P. Robinson." From the very first there appears to have been something suspicious about the way the case was handled by the police. Robinson, a clerk, was to be examined "privately" in the Police Office, the *Herald* reported: "The Justices have agreed to exclude all reporters—and all the public. It is to be made a Holy Inquisition affair." The closed nature of the inquiry prompted Bennett to add: "There is some mysterious juggle going on. Look to it—look to it" (12 April 1836).

The *Sun* published incriminating correspondence, purportedly written by Robinson himself, which further excited speculation. In retrospect, the *Evening Post* would claim, as Robinson's trial closed, "the savageness of the assassination, the mysterious nature of some of the circumstances, together with the extravagant stories which had been put in circulation concerning it, had created in the publick a strong desire to know the truth of the case and a universal demand for the report of the testimony given on the trial" (8 June 1836). It was not, then, merely "sensationalism" abstractly conceived that made the case a burning topic of the day. Instead, as we shall see, it was the context in which sensationalism *made sense*—the specific cultural *form* of the sensation that lent the case such a tumultuous presence.

Helen Jewett herself contributed to this. A reader of Byron, an exotic personality, and "one of the most beautiful of her degraded caste," Jewett was said to have seduced "more young men than any known in the Police Records" (*Herald*, 12 April 1836). She worked at Rosina Townsend's City Hotel, a posh bordello; and Bennett declared that "a large number of fashionable young men, clerks and others were caught in the various apartments by the Police." The accent of class was at once clear in reports of the murder,[5] which resonated, perhaps, with what Bennett described as "a morbid excitement" pervading the city. "The house," he confided, "is in danger from the mob" (ibid.); a day later the *Herald* confirmed that "all yesterday morning dense groups of people, men and women, were . . . expecting to get a sight of Robinson on his way from Bridewell to the Police Office to be examined. The prison was nearly surrounded" (13 April 1836).

By this time Bennett was ready to sermonize. "The question now before the public," he began, "involves more than the guilt of one person":

it involves the guilt of a system of society—the wickedness of a state of morals—the atrocity of permitting establishments of such infamy to be erected in every public and fashionable place in our city. (Ibid.)

The murder became a text for a classic lesson: *"We are all guilty alike,"* Bennett underscored. Supposing even that Robinson was found guilty and executed, "will that take away from the awful guilt of the present age—of this city—of our leaders in society—of our whole frame of morals and manners in permitting such a state of things to exist in a respectable, moral, and Christian city?" (ibid.). Bennett's jeremiad was strikingly similar to those proffered by eighteenth-century preachers intent on giving their flocks lessons in damnation and original sin (Bosco 1978). But by 15 April, Bennett was prepared to be radically modern.

The pretext for this abrupt shift was evidently an article published in the penny *Transcript,* which accused Robinson "alone" of being "the guilty individual" (in *Herald* 15 April 1836). Bennett responded to this assertion by arguing that the *Transcript* article had as its chief object

---

5. The Robinson-Jewett newspaper coverage exudes a sense of mystery—of things left purposely unsaid. In view of later developments in the case, it seems likely that suspicion of particular individuals besides Robinson was present soon after the discovery of the murder. This may be the best opportunity to mention that the Jewett murder and subsequent trial of Robinson can also be approached from the point of view of sex relations and sex roles, for which it would also yield much illuminating material.

to protect from suspicion the inmates of the house in Thomas street. It might endanger the business of certain men, the confidential clerks, and so forth, to break up and shut up, and blow it up, a system of society which has led to crime of the deepest die. . . . Ellen Jewett was the goddess of a large race of merchants, dealers, clerks, and their instruments. (Ibid.)

In keeping with Bennett's earlier insistence that a "juggle" was taking place, the case was now redefined as a cover-up by men of wealth, seeking to keep themselves above the glare of public exposure of their nighttime misdeeds. This redefinition proved to be persistent and sweeping in its application. By 25 April, three days after a grand jury had handed up a bill of indictment against Robinson, Bennett could deftly insert the story into a climate of antibank sentiment. It was Maine-bred Ellen Jewett's misfortune, he said, "under the promise to marry, to have fallen an early victim to the arts of a cashier, belonging to one of the contemptible set of $200,000 banks in Maine, whose promises to pay in specie are about equal to the promises of their cashiers to marry. Here may be found another illustration of paper money, and paper currency, which we trust the public meeting to-night will take into consideration" (*Herald,* 25 April 1836).

By the day the trial opened on 2 June 1836, its class-embedded character had noticeably deepened. The wealthy Philip Hone, who gained entrance to the courtroom, recorded his experiences there in his diary on 4 June 1836: "the crowd is very great and I found my position so uncomfortable that I staid only a short time. . . . Yesterday," he went on,

> the mob was so great and their conduct so disorderly that the Court was compelled to retire into another room until order was in some degree restored. every avenue was filled, and on the opening of the doors a general rush was made, in which the Railings of the Court Room were broken down. Would to God, these are the only barriers between the sanctity of the Laws and the violence of an unrestrained populace which we are destined to see broken down and trampled under foot.

Hone himself, moreover, hinted that justice might be bought out:

> I perceived in Court a strong predilection in favour of the Prisoner. He is young, good looking, and supported by influential friends. . . . I observed a murmur of satisfaction, and of hardly suppressed applause, whenever any part of the testimony seemed to be in his favour, or when points were successfully raised by his Counsel. (Ibid.)

The trial received front-page coverage in the press, even in Philadelphia. A report of the proceedings on 4 June bears out Hone's testimony on the unruliness and disorder:

> For some time before the precise hour of meeting, a large concourse of people of all classes, rushed in, filled the court room outside the bar, and created a tremendous noise and clamor, which continued with deafening violence until the arrival of the Court. As soon as the Judges entered, they were saluted with loud shouts and outcries, and their presence insulted by a jargon of confused cries of the multitude, who, assuming the character of a numerously embodied mob, rushed upon the officers, resisted all their efforts to control their violence, and set all order, law, and decency at defiance. The police and sheriff's officers present, in vain attempted to control them. (*Public Ledger,* 6 June 1836)

Was such obvious tension the product merely of sensational reportage, as the Emerys would have us believe?

Assuredly not. The man who tried the Robinson case, Judge Edwards, was at the very same time also in the process of convicting and sentencing twenty journeymen tailors for their part in a "conspiracy" to resist wage reductions. Indeed, the 4 June scene in the packed court occurred because it was thought that on this day Judge Edwards would deliver a sentence on the tailors' case (*Evening Post,* 8 June 1836). Edwards, however, did not issue a sentence on that Saturday, but waited instead until the following one. The delay thus coincided precisely with the unfolding of the Robinson trial, and, in this tense period, it should not be surprising that the later case became linked to the earlier one.

Within the tailors' trade, as within the trades more generally, relations had deteriorated through spring 1836, as rapid production for a blossoming "ready-made" market led to lower pay and eroded the work practices of journeymen (cf. Wilentz 1980: chap. 3, pp. 19–29). In 1836 labor throughout the nation struck 96 times—the largest number of strikes in any year between 1827 and 1837 (Mayer 1978:8). On 29 March 1836 the *Herald* covered an "IMPORTANT TRIAL" to be heard before the next court of General Sessions "relative to strikes and combinations for the protection of the rights of journeymen mechanics." This was the result of an indictment against journeymen tailors for conspiracy—in restraint of trade and commerce—to combine to resist wage reductions. "For many weeks past," stated the *Herald,* "the city has been in a state of great excitement on the subject of strikes and Trades Unions":

All the feeling—all the sensibility afloat on that point will now be concentrated on the approaching trial. The Indictment we look upon as a most extraordinary event—the trial will be even more so. An involuntary combination is no doubt illegal—any force made use of by individuals to prevent the free action of others in the same trade is contrary to law. But the question now to be decided is whether voluntary associations among journeymen to protect themselves can be made punishable by law. If so why is not the Board of Brokers indicted? That body have no legal authority to meet—to make a President—enact bye-laws—and regulate the prices of stocks. (29 March 1836)

On 1 April 1836 the *Herald* headlined a front page story entitled "Renewal of the Strikes." Bennett reported on a parade by several hundred journeymen tailors "dressed in new suits" and looking "extremely neat and handsome." They carried flags expressing a "fixed determination to stand out for the old wages." Bennett placed responsibility for the events leading to this state of affairs squarely on the masters: "All the agitations of this city this spring have been produced by a strike of the master tailors, to reduce the old wages of the journeymen—a reduction too, in the very face of an advance of rents and provisions, which gives the whole movement the appearance of a gross insult." The journeymen, in response, "rally as one man, and traverse the streets in thousands." Suppose, asked Bennett, "they should take it into their heads to rally next week as politicians—nominate a corporation ticket—carry it in over every other party, (and they can do it,) where would be the officers of the Corporation in May?" "Are we not," he summarized, "on the eve of such another revolution as we witnessed among the mechanics in 1829?" (when the Working Man's Party had been founded). "Everything looks that way." Bennett's estimate of journeymen solidarity was inaccurate, but it is a useful indicator of the tension in the city as spring ripened.

On Sunday, 5 June, the day after Edwards unexpectedly did not move to sentence the tailors, an inflammatory handbill was posted "on the corner of every street in the city," and Bennett obligingly reprinted it:

THE RICH AGAINST THE POOR!—Judge Edwards, the tool of the Aristocracy, against the People! Mechanics and Working men! a deadly blow has been struck at your Liberty! . . .

On Monday the Liberty of the Working men will be interred!—Judge Edwards is to chant the requiem! Go, go, go, every Freeman! every Workingman, and hear the hollow and the melancholy sound of the earth on the Coffin of equality! Let the Court Room, the City Hall, yea! the whole Park be filled with Mourners! (*Herald*, 7 June 1836)

It is perhaps not entirely fanciful to entertain the idea that the Liberty invoked by these journeymen may have been personified by Helen Jewett, the beautiful prostitute, the "goddess," whose foul murder was being investigated under the stewardship of the reviled Edwards.[6] "In consequence of the posting and distributing of the coffin handbills on Sunday," Bennett claimed, "an immense crowd was assembled" awaiting Judge Edwards at court (7 June 1836). The explanation for the abusive nature of the throng lies, not in some abstract "sensationalism," but in the journeymen's rage against unequal justice, which barred their union as a conspiracy but allowed their masters to combine to lower wages. The *Herald*'s report on the incident suggests that discussion among the crowd spilled over naturally from the tailors to the Robinson trial:

> The several groups were discussing various questions. Some were engaged in a debate on the tailors—others on Robinson's fate—others on Bob Furlong's testimony[7]—and others gazing and gaping after wonders of any kind. At one corner, a man with large whiskers was talking of the hours of labor. "If," said he, "a man were to work only six hours, won't he spend the rest playing dominoes in a porter house?" "Well," said his opponent, "don't the rich man buy his keg of brandy, take it home, and play cards in his own house?" "Ha! ha! ha!" said a few voices. —"Pretty piece of business," said another, "that we should submit to the rich!" "But won't you submit to the laws?" "Oh! that's a different thing." (Ibid.)

The tenor of reportage itself can not be understood without keeping in mind that the Robinson case overlapped contextually with a hated conspiracy trial. When the young clerk was found not guilty by the jury, the *Herald* proclaimed that "a wicked and atrocious conspiracy" had consistently attempted "to take away the life of an innocent youth" (9 June 1836): the word "conspiracy" cannot have failed to implicate Judge Edwards. We can be quite explicit here. A letter from "Critick" to the *Evening Post* substantiated what must have been general fears by arguing that in court "there seemed to be a tacit understanding not to scrutinize too closely the defendant's *alibi,* or the privacies of the brothel; while the court, with grave impartiality, respected the secrets of both parties. What a farce! What mockery of the forms of

---

6. The image of Liberty as a woman of godlike stature is well known. Describing the scene as the people swept through the Tuileries in 1848, Flaubert wrote: "In the vestibule, on a pile of clothes, stood a prostitute, posed as a statue of Liberty, motionless, with staring eyes—a figure of terror" (1962:271).
7. Furlong gave crucial—and suspicious—testimony during the trial in support of Robinson.

justice! to amuse the publick by a show of investigation, for five long days, while the decisive points of the cause were mutually avoided! . . . How could it be imagined," Critick inquired darkly, "that an intelligent and discreet jury would convict . . . while there were six men in the house at the time, not one of whose names were permitted to be mentioned, though some of them at least, were known; and no inquiry was made after them, nor any cause assigned why they were not identified and produced?" Under these circumstances of officially sanctioned public ignorance, it is not surprising that "there are some who perceive that the mystery of the trial, is not less than the mystery of the murder" (10 June 1836).

At loggerheads among themselves over who was guilty, the penny papers nevertheless amplified and shaped Critick's concern into an identical defense of violated rights. The *Sun,* having published incriminating correspondence ostensibly written by Robinson, used the verdict of the jury to charge that "any good-looking young man possessing or being able to raise among his friends the sum of fifteen hundred dollars to retain Messrs. Maxwell, Price, and Hoffman for his counsel, might murder any person he chose with perfect impunity" (in O'Brien 1928:69). The *Herald* impugned the *Sun* and the *Transcript,* for "these miserable organs . . . have received their orders and their cash to set aside the verdict of the jury" (10 June 1836). The real murderer, thought Bennett, got away. But "this bloody and unnatural conspiracy—must not pass away till it be thoroughly unriddled—till it be thoroughly revealed" (9 June 1836). Over and over again Bennett hammered home the point that another and more impartial search for the murderer "might unfrock some of the most respectable men in New York," who had been at the brothel "on that very night" (10 June 1836). Part of the police establishment, "which is rotten to the heart," together with the "licentious inmates" of a brothel and the *Sun*'s editor, the *Herald* inveighed, had formed "a most wicked and atrocious conspiracy, in violation of law—in violation of truth" (9 June 1836). On "the very bench of the Police Office" Robinson's private papers had been filched, only to be published in the *Sun* "for the purpose of prejudging public opinion, and finding in advance the innocent guilty." This attempt "to forestall the verdict of a Jury" was coupled with an audacious declaration "that the *Police Department believed him* to be the real murderer, from evidence in their possession" (ibid.).

Nor did the conspiracy end here. "Even during the pending of the trial, and while the jury was in a state of seclusion," Bennett protested, "one of the *attaches* of the Police, had the daring insolence to come to our office, and state on Sunday last, that the jury had determined to convict the young man, and *that he knew the fact from the best authority.*" Thus stood revealed the final, foulest sins of all:

> Forgetting their oaths—forgetting their duty, these creatures of a wicked and foul conspiracy, endeavored during the pending of this trial, by every species of falsehood, to give a new direction to public opinion, and to make this paper—this independent Herald as polluted, as corrupt, as unprincipled as they themselves were. (Ibid.)

Gathering together the colorful threads of the case, Bennett knit a vividly clear, ideological design, eschewing retributive justice, spurning "to ungown the miserable hangers on of corruption": duty prompted that "we strike at higher game." The "atrocious conspiracy" must be dragged to light. Conspirators "must be placed before this community . . . whoever they be, justices, officers, auctioneers, Pearl street merchants, Broadway fashionable storekeepers" (ibid.). Bennett was relentless in his assault on class-structured justice and unbending in defense of all men's natural rights:

> The trial is a juggle—the arrest was a juggle—the whole affair is a juggle. It is a juggle to criminate Robinson, in order to save others, some of them worth $150,000, who were in that house, from public exposure. (10 June 1836)

Did Bennett too have specific, unnamed men in mind? "On this trial," he said, summarizing two months of proceedings, "the clerks are dragged before the community, and the employers escape." This was the kind of logic that the outraged artisan public found irresistible, even if Bennett's particular conclusions lacked definitive evidence.

Although we may never know the truth of the Jewett murder, we must not doubt that the penny papers spun available facts into a pattern expressive of basic class tensions and antagonisms. In so doing, they relied upon the artisan-republican ideology of equal rights for all citizens. Reliance on this ideology persisted. In George Wilkes's recounting of the story a dozen years later, there echoes the claim "that evidence of the murder had been sequestered, and an indifference shown to the rights of The People that was peculiarly significant in the case of a person, who like the prisoner, could command so much influence and means" (1849:131; cf. Saxton 1979).

It would be a grave error to stop here and thereby neglect to mention a limit on this apparently radical rhetoric. On 14 June 1836, after the tailors had been convicted at law, Bennett turned his *Herald* against the union men:

"We seriously and solemnly believe that all the evils and disasters of which mechanics of all classes have to complain of during the last two years, have arisen entirely from the precipitate measures of their own—listening to agitators—running into strikes—neglecting their work—and trying by coercion—sometimes legal, sometimes illegal—to obtain an advance in wages, which might easily have been obtained by milder measures, and more considerate conduct." In the face of the legal decision, Bennett could no longer view the journeymen's conduct as a defensive or, for that matter, a defensible, act: "It is an idle and preposterous attempt for any combination or any association, either of masters or journeymen, to seek to regulate by force the wages of labor," he asserted. Laissez faire, the natural action of the market, could be the only arbiter of wages: "When trade is brisk, wages will rise—when slack, they will fall" (ibid.). We must remember here that the ideological heritage of the bulk of the public blended Tom Paine's rights of man with Ben Franklin's maxims (Montgomery 1968:13). Bennett and, presumably, many of his readers found it possible to make the jump with little difficulty:

> Let the mechanics do as we do rise early—be always at work—take what wages you can get—don't quarrel—visit no porter-houses—stick to your own wives, you that are married—you that are single, seduce not your sweethearts, or if you do, go to Alderman Brady, and make the weeping girls (poor things!) honest at once—meddle not with other men's wives, they're pitch—avoid politics and politicians—support Gen. Houston for the Presidency—don't bother yourself about Robinson's case—kick the Trades Union to the devil, and Eli Moore & A. Ming after it—go to no public meetings or riots, much better to kiss your wives at home, or your sweethearts behind the door—they will slap your cheek and say 'Fie, Tom!'—go to bed at half past nine o'clock, and get up early, and read the Herald. (14 June 1836)

In the face of adverse circumstances, stoicism and personal fortitude, with a heavy emphasis on upstanding, hard work, would have to serve. The obvious tension between this stance and the emphasis on Paineian equal rights was, in passages such as this, left glaringly unresolved.

It may be objected that most of the unadorned accounts of crime published in the penny journals made little of the rights and liberties of men, nor did the editors assail the public on the need for diligent, hard work. Short, dry paragraphs listed nothing but the who, the what, and sometimes the where. Even these sketchy reports, though, might serve to underscore the key institutional role claimed by the commercial papers in their purported defense of public good. Thus, Bennett noted, "instead of relating the recent awful tragedy of Ellen Jewett as a dull police report, we made it the starting point to open a full view upon the morals of society" (*Herald,* 30 April 1836).

In a story headlined "Dangers of Bad Company," the *Sun* reflected on its own role in routinely publicizing even the most insignificant misdemeanors. A young man walks to the Five Points (an area of the city notorious for its criminal vice) and soon is among "the most abandoned of the female sex." The youth's watch is taken from him by a "colored girl" he takes up with, and, desperate, he carries her to the policeman nearby. All three return to the police office, where the magistrate delivers a lecture on the dangers of such behavior to the young man before returning his watch. To this peculiar story the *Sun* appends a revealing comment:

> Little do young men imagine, that by going into such company, however innocent at heart they may be, they are in danger of public exposure. And, many a young man, of respectable connexions, goes out at night, becomes a little intoxicated, gets involved in some disgraceful scrape— taken to the watch house,—and, though he may be comparatively innocent, what are the consequences? The next day he figures in a "police report" before ten thousand readers, as the hero of some disgraceful night occurrence. His reputation is stabbed—the feelings of virtuous parents and sisters wounded. Young men should take warning.[8] (18 April 1834)

Whether or not young men did take warning is not as relevant here as the evident belief that exposure by the newspaper could produce a public shame supportive of the common good. "Young men do not now, as formerly, treat being captured by the watch . . . as a mere joke," exclaimed the *New York Mechanic:* "they find serious injury is sustained both in character and pocket by midnight brawls, and very prudently refrain" (21 July 1834). This labor journal acknowledged that "the publicity now given to our police proceedings" was a major factor in the change. The social role undertaken above all by the commercial papers deserved praise:

> The public are certainly somewhat indebted to the morning reporters, and the great patronage it bestows on those papers who go to the expense of furnishing police reports, is good evidence that gratitude is by no means wanting.[9] (Ibid.)

8. For the growing importance of "reputation" and "character" as credentials when seeking employment, see Horlick (1975:162–63).
9. William H. Bell, police detective, noted in his *Diary* on 21 March 1851:

The attention editors gave to local crime news led to another important development—the growth of a cheap urban literature. Lavish description and detail were often used to flesh out cursory accounts from the police courts. To these as well as to the trials of natural rights, the commercial papers might frequently add elements of popular culture and occupational lore, exploring the narrative possibilities of news reports (Francke 1974: chap. 2, pp. 27–28) and incorporating dialect, impolite language, colloquialisms, slang, puns, and folklore. In this socioliterary experimentation, the cheap press was also distinguished unmistakably from the elite papers, which held proud ties to an exclusive literature as well as to a more restricted polity (cf. Dudek 1961). The *Evening Post,* whose late editor William Leggett, a "radical libertarian" and Locofoco (Meyers 1960:185–86), had shared various platforms with protesting artisans, by 1841 found the melodramatic style of crime accounts in the cheap press clearly objectionable: "The robber is at least one-half hero off the stage, and a perfect one on it; the murderer is an unfortunate man; the swindler is visited and comforted by sympathetic ladies, while the newspapers describe him to his very whiskers, as if he had performed some great action, which renders him an object of public admiration and gratitude" (5 November 1841). Detailed physiognomic description had previously been reserved for the upper classes (Schudson 1978: 26–27), but in the penny press fastidiousness of this kind was expunged by an unprecedented flow that recorded common, daily events, urban low-life, crime, corruption—New York "in Sunshine and in Shadow."[10] A single instance of this from the *Herald* issued on 1 September 1835 will suffice to illustrate its remarkable and fetching qualities.

POLICE, Monday, Aug. 31

> If you had drunk as I have drunk,
> You never could forget.

This afternoon an old Gentleman residing at Oyster Bay Long Island Called on me and stated that his son had left his House on the 19th inst. and came to this city—carrying with him or rather stealing his Silver Watch he wanted me to get his watch for him but was unwilling to have him arrested upon the charge on account of it getting in the papers and especially the Police Gazette which paper he said his son thought the world of.

10. This is how Smith (1868) describes it. This important genre, bounded on one side by the roman feuilleton (common to France, England, and the United States) as practiced by Dumas, Sue, Lippard, and many others and, on the other, by documentary works on the shape and coloration of the new, large cities written by Foster (1850a; 1850b), Martin (1868), Morrow (1860), and Smith (1868), deserves more serious scrutiny.

As we entered the office this morning, the first object, or rather subject, that presented itself to our view, was John Gooney, a sailor. His face was red as the refiner's furnace, and his hands, (O what hands) they looked like two door knockers. He had on a check shirt, which had evidently been dropped on the ground, for it was broken and cracked in divers places.

He stretched his broad, brawny, sun scorched arms over the desk, like two handspikes. His mouth looked like an open sepulchre; and O could the secrets of his throat be made known! they would unfold a tale as long as the cat o' nine tails, whose effects were visible on his back.

Mag. "You are charged with being drunk in Catherine Market."

The prisoner now stood bolt upright, rolled a quid of tobacco from one side of his mouth to the other, tipping his nor-wester, and striving to look gracious, with a phiz marvelously resembling a gnarled and split oak stump, struck by lightning. "I want not drunk," exclaims he indignantly, but I allow that sleep overtook me when I was woke up by this fellow of a watchman.

Watch. "He was rolling about like a tar barrel, Sir."

Gooney now looked more indignant than ever. He hitched up his breeches, drew his oaken fist across his eyes, pulled out his tobacco box and took a fresh quid: then casting a glance of ineffable contempt on the watchman, with a broad grin of infinite meaning, he said, "It was all a lie."

Watch. "You know you were drunk, as well as I do?"

"Do I," said the prisoner, in a deep sepulchral tone, sufficient to have petrified the stoutest watchman that ever handled a club. He then stated that he was waiting for the arrival of the steamboat, but that he had not tested a drop of liquor.

The Magistrate observed, that as it was the first offence, he should overlook it for that time, but that he would not get off so cheaply if he was brought there again. Jack, after rapping his knuckles on the desk by way of applause to the magistrate, hoisted the top gallant sail, let go the anchor, and made sail in a dashing style out of the office, firing salutes of indignation from his gleaming black eye, on the watchmen and officers in attendance.

Here was crime news that, while borrowing from a rich stock of lore ("Jack" was not only John Gooney but Jack Tar), was no longer bound by the preachy style of many of the chapbooks and broadsides, which had recounted stories of rogues for earlier generations. This style made the laboring classes a socioliterary force in the public arena. Crime news intertwined with the lived experience of the new public and thus testified to the essential propriety of reporting the varied forms of urban social life. Kicking off a series of accounts of this latter kind, the *Sun* began: "Reader, did you ever, just after nightfall, enter a pawnbroker's shop, and take note of the scenes that pass there? If you never did, step aside for a few minutes with us, and seat yourself here, in this obscure corner, behind the door, whence you can see what goes on without being yourself observed" (14 April 1834). The boundaries between news and literature were indeed thin.

Under the pseudonym of "Toney Blink," the novelist George Lippard, who soon became the nation's best-selling author, wrote city news for the Philadelphia *Spirit of the Times*. He recounted the story of one Jabez Coyle, "a gaunt country wight from the Eastern shore of Maryland," who was arrested for drunkenness. Lippard spun a story round this commonplace incident by elaborating on Coyle's defense of his actions. He had met a man, so he said, who told him that in Philadelphia one could go to a pub and order oysters and drink without charge. The two men proceeded to do exactly that, or at least so Coyle had thought. His companion, having eaten and drunk, left, saying he would be back shortly. Coyle waited two hours and then himself wanted to leave the pub:

> So I went and told the feller behind the counter, when my friend come in to tell him to wait for me. "Jest please to square off before you go," says the feller with a kind o' half laugh, "the bill's one dollar and three fips." "Why, my friend that went out told me there would be nothing to pay," says I, "he axed me to walk in and allowed he'd show me how they did things in Philadelphia." "Well, I s'pect he's kept his word," says the feller, "What more do you want?" "No; he hasn't shown me yet," says I. "Yes, but he has," says he;—"you're diddled; and that's a thing that's done here pretty extensively."

Resigned, Coyle drinks some more. Finally,

> I paid the bill and put out, but how I got in the watchhouse, heaven only knows, for I'm sure I don't. But I s'pose I shall be diddled again, before I get off. And so he was, to the tune of $1.50. (7 January 1842)

More work is needed to determine the proximity of the penny press to the shared social experience of the new public, but it is irrefutable that this relationship was qualitatively more intimate than that involving any previous newspaper press.

In the 1830s newspapers began to report on the actions of persons from every sphere, including the working classes, as citizens with natural rights and private lives—rights sometimes under siege, lives often teeming with reportable incident. In speaking to the living experience of the public, the penny papers presumed to represent the voice of the people as they discharged their obligation to the public good. They succeeded in this new role because the public—from large merchants down to journeymen and even laborers—generally accepted the rights of man to property. Even with its selective attacks on monopoly and on the unwholesome extension of class inequality by the state, the penny press could simultaneously align itself with both hard-pressed journeymen and successful capitalists. During the spring of 1836, for example, the *Herald* supported the right of journeymen tailors to organize while it ran a concurrent advertisement for Hobby, Husted & Company, which sought the services of no fewer than 300 tailors and 500 tailoresses "accustomed to Southern work" (*Herald,* 7 May–9 June 1836). The latter term denoted "rapid rather than artful" production for the ready-made markets (Wilentz 1980: chap. 3, p. 24), a chief grievance among journeymen as we have seen.

General acceptance of individual property right, the genius of the penny press in generating accounts attuned to the experience of much of the new public in its concrete social context, and, finally, the advertisers' patronage of the cheap papers all defined the triumphant emergence of the new public sphere. The commercial press claimed and held ground that the labor papers found unattainable. And, as the *Mechanics' Free Press* lamented, "very few" members of the laboring classes "possess any definite ideas, or correct notions of the character which a journal to be adapted to their purposes, ought to possess" (3 May 1828). In an era when these purposes were far from antagonistic to the state, the penny journals were sufficiently boisterous, intrusive, and popular in their support of equal rights to win wide acceptance.

The penny papers therefore were ultimately different from the labor press. If the latter, from which the cheap commercial dailies obviously borrowed, advocated impartial pursuit of public good, they did so as a necessary part of the struggle to achieve wide-ranging social reform. However laudable Bennett's or Day's intentions, in contrast, their journals held up the banner of equal rights first and foremost to dramatize and substantiate their own commitment to this ideal. What mechanics thought to accomplish as a political public in the name of reason and a universal justice based on natural rights, newspaper proprietors pursued as a means to ever-enlarging circulation and profits. The penny journals embodied entrepreneurial equal rights:

they spoke for themselves and only afterward for a distinct social stratum. Despite the initial coalescence of these roles, it did not take long for them to diverge.

The depression of 1837, which initiated a period of economic troubles lasting into the 1840s, knocked the labor press out of competition, as journeymen temporarily abandoned trade union activity and independent political organization, or moved to the fringes by advocating a form of utopian socialism, or declared support for nativism. Artisan republicanism lived on in the rhetoric of the penny journals, which assumed the institutional legitimacy of the republic and hence focused on individual deviations from this ideal. "Moral wars" led by sixpenny editors and clergymen prodded the *Herald* to "tone down" its coverage, while the comparative weakness of organized labor during the depression permitted the commercial press to cultivate a more "respectable" parlor presence (Emery and Emery 1978:125). New technology, in particular, the Hoe press, eliminated the job printer from mainstream, metropolitan journalism by the late 1840s (Cochran 1975). With him went the possibility of an easy return to more radical journalism in the central arena of the public sphere—costs were too great, in most cases, for any but the well-connected to establish lines of credit. Only a little more than a decade after its birth, the cheap newspaper edged toward a recognizably modern propriety (cf. Emery and Emery 1978:119; Pray 1855:265). When Raymond launched the *New York Times,* he declared in the first issue that some of his rivals were "objectionable upon grounds of morality" and promised that the *Times* would seek "to be temperate and measured in all our language. We do not mean to write as if we were in a passion" (18 September 1851).

Even from the beginning, however, these papers had sought the same legitimacy that they took to be inherent in the form of the republic. Bennett boasted that "the first men of the country subscribe to the Herald. Not longer than Saturday, we had an order to send our paper by mail to Washington, to the Minister of one of the leading powers of Europe—Shoals of members of Congress, diplomatists, &c., have ordered the Herald, and we learn that it is a constant companion of the breakfast table of the President and Vice President at Washington" (1 January 1836). A decade later he wrote:

> We ought to guard the reputation of our great men—to whatever party they belong—better than to make them the sport of other nations, by revealing every little thing, by a forced construction, to their discredit. . . . [Daniel Webster's] reputation ought to be cherished, encouraged, and taken care of. (In Pray 1855:380)

It is only in light of its commitment, from the first, to individual property and the American state, that the new content of the cheap press can be judged.

The success of the penny journals was occasionally contested. An unusually biting appraisal was made by Lambert Wilmer, who found the fact that public opinion was "evidently *manufactured* by the public journals" deplorable (1859:62). Wilmer argued that, owing to its hold over public opinion, the commercial newspaper "audaciously encroaches on the *political* rights of the American people." For, he continued, "the Newspaper Press controls the state and the church; it directs the family, the legislator, the magistrate and the minister. None rise above its influence, none sink below its authority. The newspaper press is the GREATEST POWER IN THE STATE; and, from its very nature, it places every other power, to a greater or less extent, in subjection to its laws" (ibid.:64). A similar anxiety had been expressed somewhat less abstractly by Richard P. Robinson after his acquittal of the murder of Helen Jewett, when the *Sun* and the *Transcript* nonetheless persisted in their condemnations of him. Robinson wrote of the "persecution" he had suffered at the hands of the "petty editors," and his friend Thomas Armstrong added:

> If Jurymen are not permitted to abide by their oath's [*sic*], for fear of the anathemas of the press, I fear trial by Jury must cease, curts [*sic*] of judicature be abolished, and the *Penny editors* become the arbitrators of our lives, liberty, character, and property. (1837:13, 16)

More often, however, the institutional presence of the commercial press was roundly applauded.

The Boy's Manual, one of many guides to respectable conduct available through this era, echoed the cheap journals' own claim in stating that newspapers

> awe the proudest into the conviction of keeping some terms with morality and public opinion. They deter the flagitious from crime, lest they should be held up to the public detestation: and, in fine, they watch over individual and public liberty, which never can be violated with impunity, while the press remains pure and free. (1842:169)

In the estimate of the German observer Francis Grund, public opinion had become "a mighty police-agent of morality." Why? Because "the whole people of the United States are empannelled as a permanent jury to pronounce their verdict of 'guilty' or 'not guilty' on the conduct and actions of men, from the President down to the laborer; and there is no appeal from their decision" (1837:166). Isaac Pray agreed that the *Herald*'s power "consists in holding rods which have been placed in its hands by those with whom love of country is an abiding thought . . . These are the fasces of its authority; and while they surround the axe, the blows which are given are dictated by justice itself. Traitors alone will tremble!" (1855:317). The commercial newspaper's conceit was to transform its own capacity to expose deviations from the public good into the foremost criterion of the people's security. By attempting to substantiate that vox populi is vox dei, the penny press cultivated its predominance over both. "It ought never to be forgotten," wrote E. L. Godkin in the *Nation,* "that a republic without a press is an impossibility, almost a contradiction in terms. The modern newspaper is the equivalent of the Greek agora, the only means possessed by the citizens of interchanging thought and concerting action" (1865:165).

In contrast to the unstamped press of England, which was a major device for the application of "pressure from without" on the institutions of the state, the commercial press of the United States was an equally vital lever for the application of pressure "from within." An emerging American working class—white and male—confronted newspapers that accepted and amplified belief in individual property, the market, and the state, and that simultaneously drew heavily on its own experience. We can hardly appreciate in our time the effects on individuals of such a press, but it is obvious that, by virtue of its politicocultural proximity to the artisan public, the penny press in turn contributed to the legitimation of the state.

A comparison with the press of Europe is instructive. In contrast to Germany, France, or even England, where government controls over the press—overt censorship, police harassment, taxes, state subsidies, press bureaus (O'Boyle 1968; Ruud 1979)—long persisted, in the United States the commercial newspaper was left relatively free to develop alongside the working class itself. Even in England, liberalization was a calculated policy to permit the development of a popular press in the face of formidable class antagonisms. Indeed, while the English working class found the newspapers a vital contributor to an unfolding class consciousness over two crucial decades (1815–1836; cf. Thompson 1968:788–806), the American working class had barely begun to employ the press as an agency of class identity when the commercial penny papers began to enlist the interest and identification of laboring men.[11] This was no sleight of hand. It was, rather, an authentic expression of dominant values among the emerging white, male working-class public. And it was the authenticity itself that marked the American experience as unique; only in the United States was mass communication left free to develop as a private business *before* class relations hardened the terms of perception that it employed.

The American newspaper was therefore capable of capturing the polity's moral core in a way that made it the envy of others round the world. The impartiality and independence claimed by the penny press successfully ushered in its stewardship of the pursuit of enlightened reason in the public sphere. Although different penny journals had distinct identities, which were subject to change in various contexts, they shared what Bennett termed "the great focus of intelligence, news, wit, business, independence, and true knowledge" (*Herald,* 31 March 1836). The preemptive claim staked by the cheap journals to the defense of natural rights and public good was, as we are now in a position to see, the enduring foundation upon which the structure of news objectivity was built.

---

11. As the radical Bronterre O'Brien put it, the English press was "the portal" through which the lower classes would enter into political society (in Hollis 1970:23). A woodcut by Charles Jameson Grant, a caricaturist whose work "was most closely associated with working-class radicalism in London," applauded: "three cheers for Cheap Knowledge and defiance to our oppressors" (Fox 1978:235, 244–45), a sentiment that American artisans of the same era (c. 1835) would not have shared. In the United States, rather, the lower classes (of white men) were already in the polity and used newspapers to expand their role there. The critical difference, once again, was that English workers utilized newspapers to advance the interests of a clearly felt and well-recognized class, whereas American workers employed newspapers to defend their natural rights as citizens against the incursions of the emerging class society. In both countries, however, the extension of the political press and the expansion of the polity were closely intertwined. In England the most farsighted spokesmen for the ruling order saw clearly that this dual movement might be controlled, but it could not be prevented. In a speech centering on the need to reduce the stamp tax, thereby affording greater circulation of newspapers at lower prices (reprinted in the House of Commons *Report from the Select Committee on Newspaper Stamps*), Lord Henry Brougham stated (in the 1830s): "it is no longer a question whether [the people] shall be politicians, and take part in the discussions of their own interests or not; that is decided long and long ago. The only question to answer, and the only problem to solve is, how they shall be instructed politically, and have political habits formed the most safe for the constitution of the country and the best for their own interests" (1851:407). The answer was purposeful liberalization, a strategy to which the United States contributed, for example, in the form of Horace Greeley's testimony to the Select Committee on the utility of a cheap press.

3

A World of Fact

Freeing itself from the trammels of monopoly and party patronage, the young commercial press suggested and cultivated a new social role through its declaration of protection of the public good. Independence, virtue, impartial defense of life, liberty, and property: support of these core values facilitated the transformation of the infamous self-interest of the elite press into an interest that seemed to embrace the whole people. The penny papers' defense of this ostensibly unitary and universal interest in turn enabled them to wrap themselves in the mantle of public rationality. Released from the corrupt embrace of monopoly, the cheap press, it was thought, would be free to spearhead the advance of enlightened reason, progress, benevolent reform. Exposure of abuses in state and society carried the commercial journals into an implicit third zone, omniscient over both. A "cheap engine of instruction," as the *Public Ledger* called it in its first issue, the press would be a "source of rational amusement and useful instruction, . . . carrying light where darkness had long reigned" (25 March 1836). Although the ideal of objectivity was unproblematic for contemporaries, it cannot be so for us. We must ask, Why was this superordinate position so easily accessible? Why was widespread acceptance of the ideal of absolute truth, untinged by relativism, uninflected by values, so easily assumed? What, in brief, were the sources for this mechanical variant of journalistic objectivity that arose in tandem with the commercial newspaper's enveloping, transcendent perspective?

The series entitled "Discoveries in the Moon," a legendary journalistic hoax perpetrated in a series of articles in the New York *Sun* in late August 1835, permits an illuminating glimpse into the early development of journalistic objectivity. The Moon Hoax grew out of the tension between the penny papers and their more respectable sixpenny rivals. The latter apparently made a habit of lifting news items from the former without giving due credit. At least, so the *Sun* charged: "Will the Journal of Commerce give us the proper credit, when it publishes editorial articles from our paper" (11 April 1834). Aside from being good fun and an early example of press boosterism, the Moon Hoax was a clever attempt to outwit the elite papers of New York City.

Probably inspired by Richard Adams Locke, a police reporter, the moon stories began as an inconspicuous paragraph buried in the edition of the *Sun* issued on 21 August 1835:

> CELESTIAL DISCOVERIES—The Edinburgh *Courant* says—"We have just learnt from an eminent publisher in this city that Sir John Herschel, at the Cape of Good Hope, has made some astronomical discoveries of the most wonderful description, by means of an immense telescope of an entirely new description.

This innocuous statement permitted the editors to claim that the astounding revelations they began to publish on 25 August had been handed on to them (in the form of a spurious "supplement" to the fictitious *Edinburgh Journal of Science*) "by a medical gentleman immediately from Scotland, in consequence of a paragraph which appeared on Friday last from the Edinburgh *Courant*" (*Sun,* 25 August 1835).

And on 25 August the big story began to break. The *Sun* claimed to be reprinting from the *Edinburgh Journal of Science,* and gave three front-page columns to an impeccable scientific discussion of the invention and construction of Sir John's fabulous telescope. This telescope, which was to play a crucial role in the pacing of the "discoveries" throughout, utilized a 14,826 pound lens; with it, the *Sun* reported, Herschel was confident of "his ultimate ability to study even the entomology of the moon, in case she contained insects upon her surface" (the full story was reprinted in the *Daily Albany Argus,* 1 September 1835). The next day the *Sun*'s exquisitely plotted and paced narrative had Herschel finding tall mountains, lush forests, and, finally, "specimens of conscious existence"—herds of "brown quadrupeds," similar to but "more diminutive than any species of the bos genus" (bison) known to man on earth (in *Daily Albany Argus,* ibid.). The *Sun* continued to detail the geology, geography, and natural history of the moon—and to build circulation—on 27 August. Now "bluish lead" goatlike animals were discovered, now water birds; in the Endymion region alone, Dr. Herschel "classified nine species of mammalia, and five of oviparia." Finally, on 28 August, the *Sun* produced humanoids: "man-bats" with huge, semitransparent, membranous wings, "expanded in curvilineal divisions by means of straight radii, united at the back by the dorsal integuments." Averaging four feet in height, they were covered "except on the face" with "short and glossy copper-colored hair" (ibid.).

Responses to the story varied, but until 31 August they were either noncommittal or highly laudatory and receptive. The New York *Daily Advertiser* noted that "Sir John has added a stock of knowledge to the present age that will immortalize his name, and place it high on the page of science" (in Levermore 1901:457). The *Mercantile Advertiser* began reprinting the story in full, with the remark "that the document appeared to have intrinsic evidence of authenticity" (O'Brien 1928:47). A delegation of scientists from Yale College was sent to New York to investigate the report (MacDougall 1958:229–31; O'Brien 1928:53–54); many scientists, Pray claimed, were "completely deceived" (1855:190). Philip Hone noted soberly in his diary on 28 August 1835: "if this account is true, it is most enormously wonderful. And if it is a fable, the manner of its relation, with all its scientific details, names of persons employed, and the beauty of its glowing description, will give this ingenious history a place with Gulliver's Travels and Robinson Crusoe." The judicious Hezekiah Niles agreed in the *Niles' Weekly Register* that the moon stories were "very ably prepared" (5 September 1835).

The stories were a careful weave of fact and fiction strengthened by continual reference to various forms of professional authority. Pointing to a fictitious scientific journal is one example of this technique; another is repeated reference to the British Royal Society, to whom Herschel had reputedly sent a copy of his full report. The *Sun* also hastened to explain, through the *Journal of Science* article it "quoted," that the report had been prepared by Herschel's longtime colleague, Dr. Andrew Grant, the "superintendant" of the telescope. The text referred to densely scientific footnotes—which were not included; a description of the manipulations of the telescope was supported by reference to "an optical phenomenon which you will find demonstrated in Note 5" (in *Daily Albany Argus,* 1 September 1835). Frequent allusions to illustrations, also not included, again were doubtless effective in creating the illusion of "facticity." The astronomers reported that their telescope obtained an image "as faithful and luminous as that of . . . a camera obscura" (ibid.). The telescope, indeed, mediated the introduction of important information throughout the report. Sighting the man-bats, Herschel, who had already increased the power of his lens three times in the preceding paragraph, commanded: "exchange for my number D":

> Having observed them at this distance for some minutes we introduced lens H.z. which brought them to the apparent proximity of eighty yards; the highest clear magnitude we possessed until the latter end of March, when we effected an improvement in the gas-burners. (Ibid.)

The Moon Hoax took the form, thus, of a long series of telescopic swivelings in conjunction with gradually increasing magnification.

The rebuttal of the moon story, which was made by the *Herald,* was difficult because people found the reports so convincing: Bennett hesitantly doubted "whether his optical principles correspond with fact" (*Herald,* 31 August 1835). And on 3 September of the same year the *Herald* complained that the *Sun* had gone too far: "But now, when that paper in order to get money out of a credulous public, seriously persists in averting its truth, it becomes highly improper, wicked, and in fact a species of impudent swindling." The "swindle," of course, occurred when the *Sun* placed its self-interest ahead of truth. A disgruntled reader of the *Herald* proclaimed, displaying this normative regard for truth in journalism, "I am determined never again to patronize a paper that has thus egregiously deceived the public —and instead subscribe to the 'Herald,' or some other paper, whose veracity can be relied upon" (3 September 1835).

Yet the fabricated objectivity of the moon stories permitted the penny press once again to expose what Pray called "the character and jealousies of the Sixpenny Press"—and in "a most glaring light":

> There was a general chagrin experienced by the old journals that a penny paper should outstrip, in its enterprise or knowledge, the "respectable dailies." Great ingenuity was displayed by the author in his description of the telescope of Herschel, and much external consistency marked his portraiture of the inhabitants of the Moon. The people and the editors, generally, received the statement as a narrative of truth—and nearly all the editors copied and commented on the news from a "cotemporary," "small morning paper," "recently established cheap paper," or anything else that would keep the *Sun* out of view. . . . The Albany *Daily Advertiser* said: "We have read with unspeakable emotions of pleasure and astonishment, an article *from* the last Edinburgh Scientific Journal, containing an account of the recent discoveries of Sir John Herschel." . . . It then seemed to the Penny Press that it had put its foot, for the first time, on the neck of its unnatural Elder Brother, who was passing

himself off for more than he was worth, and denying his relationship!
(1855:190–91)

The full impact of the hoax depended on its exposure as a fraud: its chief
purpose was to bring the elite journals back down to earth, where they were
shown to be unnatural and corrupt. Their veracity and their self-interest alike
were impeached.

The hoax was successful for so long because of its scientific garb, which
represented for readers its transcendent, value-free character. Indeed, scientific journalism alone promised a true public enlightenment.

Public Enlightenment through Scientific Journalism

Around 1840 James Gordon Bennett gave voice to a fundamental tenet of the
new commercial journalism: "I feel myself, in this land, to be engaged in a
great cause—the cause of truth, public faith, and science, against falsehood,
fraud, and ignorance" (in Pray 1855:267). The practice of impartial exposure,
which Bennett pioneered and which animated the new institutional role of
the commercial penny press, expressed and enlarged on a seminal theme of
the Enlightenment: scientific knowledge, once adopted by a public of earnest
truth-seekers, would lead to an enduring, beneficent social reconstruction.
"The more men are enlightened," wrote Condorcet in 1791, and "the more
(truth) spreads . . . the less societies need to be governed" (in Baker 1975:79).
As William Leiss puts it, "the cause of human happiness was claimed to be
identical with that of science" by all propagandists for enlightenment (1974:
78). "Truth is the enemy of power," wrote Condorcet (in Baker 1975:79), and
science served public good just as the commercial newspaper wished to do.
Bennett's "great cause," thus, would be implicitly but ultimately dependent
on the belief that the commercial newspaper could be a major social agency
for the organization of public enlightenment through a scientistic presentation of "the facts" of natural and social life. It *could* be, that is, if, akin to
most formal science and philosophy of the mid-nineteenth century, the newspaper also came to accept the notion of an objective universe lying at the very
core of its endeavor.

The rise of objectivism in modern science and philosophy is considered
the hallmark of their modernity. Copernicus dislodged humankind from the
center of the universe; as Matson says, "it remained for the Galilean-
Newtonian revolution to remove him from the universe altogether" (1966:4).
Only a "universal mechanics" based on the primary qualities of number,

figure, magnitude, position, and motion could illuminate the true nature of reality. This new universe was causal, determinate, and objective, in Oppenheimer's words, because "no human act or intervention qualified its behavior" (in ibid.:3).

Perhaps paradoxically, this objective universe afforded a unique opportunity for human experimentation and control. The great machine that was the substance of Descartes' famous dream in 1619 inflamed a radical doubt as the prime methodological feature of the scientific pursuit of knowledge. "Cogito ergo sum" became the measure of the man as man became the measurer of the universe. Traditional explanations of natural events were swept aside by the triumphant advances of an increasingly rigorous experimental science.

It yet remained for the other major segment of the universe to be claimed as part of the preserve of objectivist science—that segment defined and populated by people. Here, crucial preparatory work was performed by Hobbes, in whose hands politics first became an object for scientific scrutiny, based strictly upon the primary Galilean entities of matter and motion.[1] Adam Smith and others developed an objective economic regulator in the "hidden hand" of the market. But it was the French Enlightenment that went furthest toward the integration of all human activity and thought into the realm of objective measurement and explanation. William Leiss provides a general assessment of the Enlightenment's fundamental contribution:

> Men like Condillac, d'Alembert, and Condorcet brought to completion the idea that a single method could be applied in all the sciences, a method that was as valid for the study of society as it was for the investigation of nature. A "social mathematics" or "geometry of politics," utilizing the mathematics of probability, was envisaged as a way of rationally reconstructing the system of social relations, since by these means human actions could be analyzed, laws of behavior formulated, and institutional arrangements leading to more humane conduct established. (1974:78)

By the close of the eighteenth century, Matson writes, Newtonian mechanism "had become standard procedure throughout the respective sciences of nature, of life and of man" (1966:15). Despite their differences, Saint-Simon and his student Comte shared with Bentham and the Utilitarians an underlying confidence that a single science might encompass not merely the natural

1. On Hobbes, see Habermas (1974:41–81); Macpherson (1962); and Matson (1966:6–7).

world but also the affairs of politics, morals, and social life.[2] Science alone, with its powerful "copy theory of truth" (Habermas 1971:69) positing an isomorphic relation between statements of fact and the world they described, stood aloof from the relativization that progressively influenced other modes of thought.[3] Educated men, by the mid-nineteenth century, "were not merely proud of their sciences, but prepared to subordinate all other forms of intellectual activity to them" (Hobsbawm 1975:251). Scientism—acceptance of the epistemological primacy of scientific knowledge of an objective universe— was everywhere triumphant.

The role of the press in organizing popular enlightenment was widely thought to be especially vital. The French Revolution, claims Leith, taught that print, because it "ensured the ultimate conversion of mankind to enlightened philosophy," was a turning point in history (1968:11). Extravagant claims were made for the potential of the press, as when, for instance, the English radical Richard Carlile confidently stated that "the Printing-press may be strictly denominated a Multiplication Table as applicable to the mind of man" (in Thompson 1968:805). More modest was the claim of William Ellery Channing, who addressed himself in 1841 to the democratization of science: "Through the press, discoveries and theories, once the monopoly of philosophers, have become the property of multitudes. . . . Science, once the greatest of distinctions, is becoming popular." The definitive feature of the age, Channing thought, was "not the improvement of science, rapid as this is, so much as its extension to all men" (in Zochert 1976:7).

The prominence of science in the popular press has been frequently noted (cf. Mott 1967:1:446). Charles Rosenberg finds that "medical articles

2. For Utilitarianism see Halevy, who is illuminating in his remarks on the general context in which Utilitarianism, or Philosophic Radicalism, arose: "On the one hand the development of the physical sciences, the discovery of Newton's principle which made it possible to found on a single law a complete science of nature, and the conception of the hope of discovering an analogous principle capable of serving for the establishment of a synthetic science of the phenomena of moral and social life; on the other hand a profound crisis in society, a crisis which was itself due in part to the development of science and to the progress of its practical applications, a crisis which called for transformations of the judicial, economic, and political regimes and gave rise to schemes for reform and to reformers without number, a crisis, finally, which demanded a single principle capable of uniting into a single theoretic whole so many scattered notions:—these are the general causes of the formation of Philosophical Radicalism" (1955:3).
3. This relativization has occurred on a larger scale since the latter decades of the nineteenth century. The general point is taken from Feyerabend, who argues that science alone has largely retained its purported independence from "culture, ideology, prejudice" (1975:302). Hobsbawm states that " 'Positive' science, operating on objective and ascertained facts, connected by rigid links of cause and effect, and producing uniform, invariant general 'laws' beyond query or wilful modification, was the master-key to the universe, and the nineteenth century possessed it" (1975:269).

. . . of an impressively technical sort, were often printed in newspapers" (1962:238). Zochert examines the treatment of various sciences in the popular press, among them astronomy, botany, and geology, and concludes that newspapers contributed to nothing less than a "celebration of science" (1976: 27). The New York *Sun* found it easy to print a story entitled "The Minuteness of Atoms" (29 April 1834), and the paper's editor became the proprietor of *Scientific American* (cf. Mott 1962:227). That weekly, launched in 1845, described itself as

> especially entitled to the patronage of MECHANICS and MANUFAC-
> TURERS, being devoted to the interests of those classes. (*Scientific
> American,* 26 September 1846, p. 8)

Zochert confirms the democratic character of popular science when he remarks that "local observers, with unstated credentials, felt no reluctance in communicating their views on scientific subjects to the newspapers, and the newspapers felt no reluctance in publishing them" (1976:31). The design behind a regulated universe "was to be wrung from nature by a prodigious empiricism, the accumulated, perhaps endless, effort of observation and measurement" (ibid.:30), and to this process many might contribute. It is thus no surprise to find Bennett boasting from the popularity of one of his articles that "I have struck out the true Baconian path in commercial science" (*Herald,* 28 October 1836; in Schudson 1978:54). Baconian observation and deduction were the American variant of positivism. To comprehend Bennett's boasted allegiance to "truth, public faith, and science," therefore, we must examine American positivism.

Positivism in Natural and Social Studies

In the mid-nineteenth century, positivism nurtured widespread acceptance of a uniform, objective world. Scientific description and assessment of this world would lead, so it was thought, to valid knowledge of the natural and social laws to which things and persons alike must necessarily conform. The empirical method was explicitly endorsed in this cause. A Milwaukee editor commended an article by saying that its author "very properly confines himself almost entirely to an examination of the facts observed, and not being influenced by any preconceived theory . . . his observations may be relied upon with perfect confidence" (in Zochert 1976:30). Another writer of the same period (the 1840s) commented on an apparent scientific anomaly: "These facts, though we have not yet got at the reason of them, are still extremely interesting" (ibid.:15). "Let us gather all the facts before we begin to deduce our theories and form conjectures," was a common sentiment (ibid.:30).

George Daniels' study (1968) of American science at this juncture shows New York State at the very forefront of scientific advance, sponsoring more scientific societies and journals between 1815 and 1850 than any other state. Never before was such an enthusiastic confidence in science so widely shared (1968:61–62). Across the spectrum of scientific endeavor, Baconianism dictated the basic philosophical and methodological assumptions and presuppositions of practicing scientists. Baconianism, according to Daniels, was "universally acknowledged" and implied "a kind of naive rationalistic empiricism —a belief that the method of pure empiricism consistently pursued would lead to a rational understanding of the universe." Of fundamental importance to American Baconianism was the assumption, derived from the Scottish philosophers of "common sense," notably, Reid, Ferguson, and Stewart, "that the intuitions of the mind were direct, immediate perceptions of a real objective order." The absolute validity of the testimony of the senses could not even be doubted without, as one spokeman said in 1848, "questioning the truthfulness of our constitution, nay, the veracity of God himself" (ibid.:66–67). The only true foundations for knowledge were to be observation and experiment; and the spectacular success of Baconian science occurred in its continuing amassment of undigested facts.

Paradoxically, although scientists only rarely eschewed the theoretical foundations of Baconianism, their very success at accumulating data displaced older systems of data management and classification as unworkable or misleading and created an inescapable need for less cumbersome and confusing systems (ibid.:102). Baconianism, in brief, did not appear "to lead automatically into the higher classifications that were its aim" (ibid.:192). Although in botany and zoology, for example, scientists were agreed that a "natural system" of data classification, that is, an arrangement "indicated by nature itself," was needed, the choice of meaningful indicators was inevitably selective. Therefore, "the seemingly reasonable effort to classify things in terms of their real natures opened up the gateway for a whole philosophy of nature to enter a classification system" (ibid.:115). By the 1820s and 1830s, wild speculation on one side and a fierce disregard for theory in favor of palpable facts by the majority of scientists on the other became defining features of American science. Although Baconianism was never explicitly questioned, the role of theorizing and of the subjectivity of the scientist had become problematic issues.[4] Objectivism was generally espoused, but it was also tacitly abused.

At the very least, American science encouraged a deep reverence for "the facts." In this it was joined by the expanding and newly exalted category of history. In the first half of the nineteenth century, history was becoming a profoundly important means of validating the present, by dramatizing its organic and necessary connection to past events and past greatness.[5] A North Carolina promoter and developer, Archibald D. Murphey, chose an apt simile when, in 1821, he wrote: "To visit a people who have no history, is like going into a wilderness where there are no roads to direct a traveller."[6] Of 248 best-selling books published between 1800 and 1860, ninety or 36 percent dealt with history; the comparable figure both before 1800 and after 1860 was close to 15 percent. Of at least 111 historical societies organized before 1860, 85 were formed between 1830 and 1860.[7]

Since the Renaissance, history had been more and more carefully segregated from fiction. History was truth and thus was limited to "unadorned reporting of things that had happened, free of distortion, addition, or omission, as though it were possible to record human actions in words as faithfully as a musical performance might be recorded by an infallible phonograph," states Nelson (1973:40). Now history incurred an increasing obligation to recount verifiable fact—singly, honestly, accurately, and thoroughly. One critic in the middle third of the nineteenth century particularly sought accuracy, as "the *sine qua non* of history." Another argued: "Accuracy, that prime virtue of an historian, distinguishes the narrative and gives us, throughout, the impression of reality."[8] The discipline of history veered away from the previous Romantic conception, which had stressed the artistic and poetic nature of the past, and began to evince a growing concern—in Douglas's terms an "obsession" (1977:174)—for "the facts." Indeed, history was thought to be entering the ranks of the positive sciences, and, wrote one observer in 1851, it was only a matter of time

---

4. The fusion of rationalism and empiricism in Comtean positivism disclosed a similar tension. In Comte's words: "For if, on the one hand, every positive theory must necessarily be founded upon observations, it is, on the other hand, no less true that, in order to observe, our mind has need of some theory or other" (1970:4–5). Yet the "fundamental maxims of the positive method," which in Comte's vision supplanted, first, theology and, second, metaphysics, could not really be known and demonstrated apart from their applications in concrete scientific research (ibid.:18, 23). The role of scientific subjectivity thus was accommodated without being either acknowledged or understood.

5. On the rise of history in this context see Lukacs (1962:15–29). Ann Douglas argues, in her illuminating study, that "people began to believe that the most profound and meaningful way of viewing life was as a series of events unfolding uniquely in historical time. . . . Characters, places, scenes [were] subjected to a kind of transformational grammar of events" (1977:170, 179).

6. This quotation and other helpful comments are from Van Tassel (1960:104).

7. These statistics are from Callcott (1970:31, 35).

8. These critics wrote in 1836 and 1856, respectively, and are quoted in Callcott (1970:123).

before history would "reveal all the laws . . . and enable us . . . to predict the future."[9]

The obverse of reverence for fact was a deep and abiding distrust of fiction. "Fiction which has no relation to what has been, or what is to be, must be both vapid and valueless," cautioned a writer in *The United States Magazine and Democratic Review.* "Our daughters will decide between right and wrong with all the more distinctness, from never having had their natural perceptions warped by the perusal of fictions in which those boundaries are artfully or stupidly confused" ("Periodical Reading" 1845:61). From the characteristic perspective of a threatened clergy, the Reverend John Austin advised youthful readers to study any historical novel only "in connexion with that portion of history to which it refers, and with that portion of geography which describes its location, and carefully note what is fictitious and what is real" (1838:53).[10]

Concern for a definitive historical reality appeared in the journalistic sphere as well. Suppose, conjectured William Alcott in his popular *Young Man's Guide,* that in a newspaper you read about the death of a person who was "at *Yorktown,* in Virginia, during the whole *siege,* in the American *revolution*" (1839:212). Alcott then directed the reader to "find out, *when* the siege in question *happened,* by *whom,* and by *how many thousand troops* it was carried on; and *who,* and *how many* the besieged were. . . . He who follows out this plan," argued Alcott,

> will soon find his mind reaching beyond the mere events alluded to in the newspaper, both forward and backward. . . . If newspapers are not thus read, they dissipate the mind, and probably do about as much harm as good. (Ibid.:212–13)

The passion for historical fact here defined a way of reading newspapers that bore a remarkable resemblance to the newspaper's eventual incorporation of a "Who? What? When? Where? How?" format.

The Civil War marked the entrance of journalists on a large scale into the field of national historical writing, where they challenged and then upset the dominance of the minister and the lawyer. Because of their access to events (the war correspondent was a product of this era) and their acknowledged ability to separate fact from fiction, journalists produced histories of

9. This optimist is quoted in Callcott (1970:225).
10. In the opinion of such advisers historical novels alone were permissible. Austin insisted that "you must be cautious in your selections. None should be read but those of a purely moral tendency, and such as are illustrative of historical truths" (1838:52).

the Civil War that rang true. More important, perhaps, in both style and content such histories were similar to the previous versions of events circulated in newspapers.[11] Conservators of the nation's past at this time began to view newspapers as "valuable documentary history" and undertook to acquire and preserve extensive newspaper files at the Library of Congress and elsewhere.[12]

Positivism in science and history encouraged a general cultural acceptance of a reportable, objective world. News shared the same commitment. In the prospectus for his *Herald* Bennett wrote: "We shall endeavor to record facts on every public and proper subject, stripped of verbiage and coloring" (6 May 1835). Journalistic objectivity presumed a world prior to all imposed values, and the periodic construction of accurate and universally recognizable copies of events in this world became the newspaper's fundamental business. Objectivity, once again, was an *ideal*—and it was acceptance of the newspaper's right and capacity to pursue this ideal that was essential. Such acceptance allowed the press to cultivate and to accumulate a modern mass public by appearing to present simply *"facts,* in such a form and temper as to lead men of all parties to rely upon its statements," as the *New York Times* (22 March 1860) put it. The weekly journal the *Subterranean* published a poem on 24 May 1845 by one James Montgomery entitled "The Press" that conveyed this sentiment.[13] The third stanza of this tribute reads:

> What is the Press? 'Tis what the tongue
> Was to the world when Time was young,
> When, by tradition, sire to son
> Conveyed what'er was known or done;
> But fact and fiction so were mix'd,
> That boundaries never could be fixed.

The newspaper ostensibly permitted a definitive separation of fact from fiction; indeed, the press itself testified to their disengagement. Although generally falling within the compass of what was fit to print, news seemed not to result from editorial selectivity.[14] Rephrasing Geertz, we may therefore

11. On the entrance of journalists into history writing, see Van Tassel (1960:149).
12. On the accumulation of newspapers by libraries, see Ames (1874:133, 137).
13. The poem was probably taken from *The New World* (25 February 1843), edited by Park Benjamin.
14. There developed an apparent separation between literature, which retained the right to symbolic manipulation and selectivity, until literary realism challenged it, and journalism. An article entitled "The Decline of the Novel" in the *Nation* directly contrasted "periodical[s]

say that, each day, the commercial newspaper generated and regenerated the very objectivity that it pretended only to display (1973:451). This is also evident in a ubiquitous contemporary metaphor, which called the newspaper "the historical photographer of national acts" (Hudson 1873:xxvii).

Photography and Photographic Realism

Objectivity in American news reporting found a powerful ally in the new technology of daguerreotypy and its decisive animation of an entrenched style—realism. Before the Civil War era the newspaper periodically presented frozen moments of a historically unfolding present; news and history were fused in these glimpses of an objective reality. An article published in 1848 compared Bennett of the *Herald* with John Walter, proprietor of the London *Times:*

> The *New York Herald* is now the representative of American manners, of American thought. It is the daily daguerreotype of the heart and soul of the model republic. It delineates with faithfulness the American character in all its rapid changes and ever varying hues. The dominant character of European journals is Walterism—that of American journals is Bennettism. (In Pray 1855:412)

A compendium to the Seventh Census entitled a *Statistical View of the United States* claimed that newspaper readers saw "as in a telescope, and often as in a mirror, every thing that is transacted in the most distant regions" (1854:154). News objectivity was compared metaphorically to instruments whose capacity for photographic accuracy was widely known and uncontested. "The most important purpose of the newspaper press," stated a lead editorial in the *Minnesota Pioneer* in 1851, "is to mirror back to the world, the events, the peculiarities and the whole features of the new world by which it is surrounded. . . . We would rather, now, present a daguerreotype of Saint Paul . . . than write a political homily as long as the Mississippi river, and twice as turbid" (in Hage 1967:5). The widespread typification of the newspaper as a daguerreotype was sustained also by the guiding credo of the new professional journalist. Isaac Pray, for example, wrote:

---

devoted to literary and social subjects" with newspapers, which, "more and more exclusively devote[d] . . . to news," had become an "immensely powerful unliterary" next of kin (1868: 389–90).

A reporter should be as a mere machine to repeat, in spite of editorial suggestion or dictation. He should know no master but his duty, and that is to give the exact truth. His profession is a superior one, and no love of place or popularity should swerve him from giving the truth in its integrity. If he depart from this course, he inflicts an injury on himself, on his profession, and on the journal which employs him.[15] (1855:472)

What was implied by this machinelike role and by the evident tie to daguerreotypy more generally?

Daguerreotypy helped to bring about a new sort of realism in mid-nineteenth-century America. Photographic realism was defined by and in turn sustained a sweeping series of changes in the conventional design, execution, and significance of painting and literature. The key assumption of photographic realism—that precise, accurate, and universally recognizable copies of reality could be produced from symbolic materials—was accepted generally, both within and outside the conventional domains of art.

The style of realism long antedates photography.[16] Auerbach (1953), for example, has discussed the representation of reality, or "mimesis," widely thought to be basic to the style, in Western literature from Homer up to the twentieth century. Ian Watt (1957) has persuasively demonstrated the hold of realism over the novel in eighteenth-century England. Properly speaking, photography itself emerged partly out of artists' attempts to create a more realistic art.[17] It would be anachronistic, however, to separate the innovation of early photographic technologies from the scientific domain.[18] Lindquist-Cock, in her illuminating discussion of the impact of photography on painting, insists that the invention of photography

15. For a later example of a reporter claiming to copy an event, see Martin (1868:132). I have explored some of the links between objectivity and professionalism elsewhere (1979). Tuchman (1978a, 1978b, 1980) has contributed much to the discussion of the "web of facticity" as an institutional presence that underlies the development of a public opinion "from above."

16. I take it as axiomatic that languages, codes, conventions, and styles, which formally embody an active communicative competence, vary historically (Williams 1976:505). Codes may be thought of as formally organized but historically open-ended subsets of "the total range of elements, operations, and ordering principles that are possible in a given mode. In the simplest sense, then, any single language is a code existing within the verbal mode" (Gross 1973:192). For more discussion, see Schiller (1977).

17. Gernsheim states that by the eighteenth century the camera obscura, a precursor of photography lacking the latter's ability to fix images, "had become a craze. . . . As an aid in painting its use was widespread, and such phrases as 'Everything is represented with such exquisite exactness as far surpasses the utmost skill of any painter to express'. . . constantly recur as if to challenge artists" (1969:27).

18. For a more general argument that, historically, artists have had more to do with the development of new technologies than is customarily thought, see Ferguson (1977).

"demonstrated an absolute identification of artistic and scientific strivings" (1977:6).

The creation of photographic technology in the mid-nineteenth century, in any case, was motivated by expanding academic and commercial art markets. Daguerre, one of the inventors of photography, hoped to fix images in order to reproduce scenes upon canvas without the labor of painting them. In this way his dioramas (large sets of painted scenes passed before observers) could be made to assume an even more lifelike and illusionistic quality. The other major inventor of photography, Joseph Niepce, was trying to reproduce designs on lithographic stone without actually copying them by hand.[19] Photography was impelled by a commercial impulse to save labor and to obtain completely accurate imitations of Nature and of works of art that were also reproducible.

The cultural impact of daguerreotypy, the first major photographic technology, was immediate and wide ranging, and the French Government's benevolent gesture of freeing daguerreotypy from most international patent restrictions was certainly instrumental. Before the end of 1839, the year marking the culmination of the technical achievement, Daguerre's pamphlet describing his process had been through thirty editions and published in nearly as many languages. Daguerreotypy's acceptance, however, was nowhere else as quick and as complete as in the United States. Beaumont Newhall, an authority on early photography, asserts that, by 1845, "daguerreotypes were so popular in America that the word was assimilated . . . into everyday language" (1976:33). A best-selling periodical, *Godey's Lady's Book,* stated in 1849 that "it is hard to find the man who has not gone through the 'operator's' hands from once to half-a-dozen times, or who has not the shadowy faces of his wife and children done up in purple morocco and velvet, together or singly, among his household treasures."[20] Photographic historian Richard Rudisill claims that by 1850 Americans spent between eight and twelve million dollars a year on photographs (1971:198); at the time, states Taft, some three million daguerreotypes were taken annually (1938:76).[21] By

19. The labor-saving impetus behind the daguerreotype is described by Taft (1938:5).
20. The quotation is from Rudisill (1971:70). In 1853 a New York *Tribune* article claimed that "the enormous practice which our operators now enjoy combines to render the daguerreotype a necessary contributor to the comforts of life. . . . The readiness with which a likeness may be obtained, the truthfulness of the image, and the smallness of the cost, render it the current pledge of friendship; and the immense number of operators who are supported by the art, in this country, shows how widely the love of sun-pictures is diffused" (in Greeley 1853:171–72). Daguerreotypists commonly were termed "operators," as if to denote the mechanical certainty of the process and its result.
21. A single firm, the Edward & H. T. Anthony Photographic Company, listed sales of $600,000

the early 1850s technological innovation had made multiple prints possible, and in the late 1850s stereoscopic views were developed.[22]

American photographic realism at once attributed to these ubiquitous pictures an unappealable, exclusive, and universally recognizable accuracy.[23] As Poe put it in 1840:

> In truth the daguerreotype plate is infinitely more accurate than any painting by human hands. If we examine a work of ordinary art, by means of a powerful microscope, all traces of resemblance to nature will disappear—but the closest scrutiny of the photographic drawing discloses only a more absolute truth, more perfect identity of aspect with the thing represented. (In Rudisill 1971:54)

Daguerreotypes appeared to embody nothing less than natural truth. Speaking to the National Academy of Design in 1840, Samuel Morse—the artist, scientist, and inventor who was mainly responsible for bringing daguerreotypy to the United States immediately after it was developed in France—asserted that daguerreotypes were

> painted by Nature's self with a minuteness of detail, which the pencil of light in her hands alone can trace, and with a rapidity, too, which will enable [the artist] to enrich his collection with a superabundance of *materials* and not *copies;—they cannot be called copies of nature, but portions of nature herself.* (In Rudisill 1971:57)

Seemingly both of and about nature, both imitator and imitated, daguerreotypy drew compelling force from its apparently effortless transcendence of human fallibility. "What a wonderful reputation for veracity photography has acquired," stated the *Philadelphia Photograher* in 1876: "From its earliest days it has been looked upon as strictly truthful by all classes of people, with perhaps an occasional exception, as in the case of dissatisfied sitters" (in Peters and Mergen 1977:292).[24]

---

in 1864 (Jenkins 1975:50). In 1872, in a massive collection of essays entitled *The Great Industries of the United States,* edited by Horace Greeley, one writer calculated, on the basis of figures gathered on the importation of special albumenized photographic paper, that 50,400,000 photographs were made every year (1872:880).

22. For technological innovation, see Jenkins (1975:39); on stereo views, see Darrah (1964).

23. Respect for the accuracy of daguerreotypy coincided with large-scale rationalization of production, with the simultaneous and intertwined needs for precise machine tools, for a labor force capable and willing to relinquish old procedures and tools for these emergent new technologies, and for sales records and accounting procedures able to itemize, record, and justify incomes and expenditures of members of corporations, which were now becoming legal entities.

24. Jussim observes that at this juncture the photograph "was not viewed as a message about

The uncanny ability of photography to re-present reality—to depict, apparently without human intervention, an entire world of referents—bolstered the apparently universal recognition of it as a supreme standard of accuracy and truth. An article published in 1840 in a Cincinnati newspaper expressed this in lasting and significant terms:

> Its perfection is unapproachable by human hand, and its truth raises it high above all language, painting, or poetry. It is the first universal language, addressing itself to all who possess vision, and in characters alike understood in the courts of civilization and the hut of the savage. The pictorial language of Mexico, the hieroglyphics of Egypt, are now superseded by reality. (In Rudisill 1971:54)

In the universality accorded to the language of photography there was an exclusive standard of visual truth.[25]

As early as 1842 the 27th United States Congress had accepted daguerreotypes as "undeniably accurate evidence," claims Rudisill, in settling the Maine-Canada boundary (1971:240). In 1851 a panoramic series of daguerreotype views of San Francisco elicited the following comment from a local paper:

> It is a picture, too, which cannot be disputed—it carries with it evidence which God himself gives through the unerring light of the world's greatest luminary. . . . [the view] will tell its own story, and the sun . . . testify to its truth. (In Newhall 1976:86)

Photographic realism posited a universally recognizable symmetry to the correspondence between picture and reality. So empowered, photography would hold its creators to account by helping to redefine the ways in which people saw. Photography paradigmatically revised the nature of visual "accuracy"; for, rather than merely manipulating symbols, photography appeared, and claimed, to reveal Nature. Photographic realism insisted and seemed to

---

reality, but as reality itself, somehow magically compressed and flattened onto the printed page, but, nevertheless, equivalent to, rather than symbolic of, three-dimensional reality" (1974:289).
25. Worth has rightly attacked this notion of a universal language of art: "the knowledge that there are many codes and languages of speaking—does not seem to extend to our understanding of visual signs. . . . Somehow the notion persists that . . . pictures in general, [have] no individual cultures that 'speak' . . . in differing languages, or articulate in differing codes" (1978:1–2). A visual "universal language of nature" had been sought much earlier. In 1709, for example, George Berkeley produced *An Essay towards a New Theory of Vision* (Turbayne 1970). It seems more important, though, to inquire: How is verisimilitude to be recognized across time and culture? How is a particular "realism" achieved within a specific culture?

confirm that the only form of true knowledge was nonsymbolic "reflection" of an objective world.

Triumphantly consonant with Baconian science, photography similarly began to redefine the nature of American painting.[26] Thus, the painter Thomas Cole wrote, in the mid-nineteenth century, that photography was destined to produce "a great revolution in the pictorial arts":

> and one thing appears to me evident, that it will have the effect of annihilating the false lying artists who of late have deluged the world with their production—those things called views—purporting to be sketched on the spot. . . . Nature herself will now confront the liars in paint and black and white and their monstrosities will be revealed to the eyes of the much abused public—their exaggerated mountains, their pitchy skies, their suns setting in the south, their full moons setting in companionship with the sun and all those violations of truth . . . will be exposed, and I trust better taste will be the result. (In Lindquist-Cock 1977:27)

Photography was expected, claims Lindquist-Cock, to set "the permissible levels of verisimilitude by which both portrait and landscape painter were to judge their success" (ibid.:39). She speaks of a "vast difference" in the painted portrait after the mid-1840s, when the influence of the daguerreotype was at its height; some of the changes she notes are: static poses, a subdued range of hues, harsh lighting, a lack of plastic quality, and, "most of all, an objectivity approaching the objectivity of the camera's lens" (ibid.:45). To remain true to the new *form* of visual truth, the content of art and the practice of artists had to change.[27]

26. Photography, states Ivins, though not a perfect report, "can and does in practice tell a great many more things than any of the old graphic processes was able to" (1953:139). The point is not that photography indeed can copy natural events but, rather, that belief in its objectivity both encouraged and allowed unprecedented human control of the natural and social world. Within science, photography found an important place in astronomy (Taft 1938:198–200); in geographic exploration (Newhall 1976:84–91); and cartography (Woodward 1975:137–55). Generally, as Rudisill claims, "a common ground of trust was soon established which equated a picture made by the camera with the truth of a direct perception. Once this sort of reliability was attributed to the medium and it was placed into wide use, it was inevitable that national imagery should henceforth have to base itself on the evidence of the machine. Political candidates must 'daguerreotype' themselves on the public imagination; popular portraiture of statesmen, entertainers, or criminals in the press had to credit origin in the daguerreotype when laying claim to accuracy" (1971:231).

27. On photography and painting, see Scharf (1974). There were of course dissenters to the standard imposed by photographic realism, and their sometimes acid comments lace many contemporary debates on aesthetics. With Hobsbawm, it is vital to note that realists themselves might resist "the simple identification of art with exact and naturalistic reproduction. . . . Photography was useful, because it could help the painter to rise above a mere mechanical copy of objects" (1975:292).

The belief that photographs are, in Ivins's words, "exactly repeatable visual images made without any of the syntactical elements implicit in all hand made pictures" (1953:122) has endured to the present day.[28] It must be made clear, however, that, despite its central importance as a cultural construct, the notion that photographs are equivalent to reality itself is both mistaken and fundamentally misleading. In Worth's terms, "it is impossible —physiologically and culturally—by the nature of our nervous system and the symbolic modes or codes we employ, to make unstructured *copies* of natural events" (1976:15). The purported lack of syntax in photography, its seemingly transparent form, has been demolished analytically by Jussim, for "what it records can be manipulated by an individual or restricted either by the technological limitations of lens or emulsion or by 'artistic', i.e., subjective, manipulations in the making of photographic positives on paper" (1974: 298). In one vital sense, though, Jussim's refutation is unimportant, because the illusion of photographic objectivity has without question been real enough in American *culture* to convince even some of the most astute critics, Poe and Ivins, for example, of its existence.[29]

Photographic realism underlined and extended belief in a direct and completely accurate symmetry between art and reality. As we have seen, this congruence was also sought outside the domain of art—in writing as well as in painting and sculpture. A review in the *Atlantic Monthly* in 1858, for example, stated that "to copy Nature faithfully and heartily is certainly not less needful when stories are presented in words than when they are told on canvas or in marble" (in McMahon 1973:11). The impact of photographic realism on American literature reached its zenith in the decades following the Civil War.[30] Just as surely as the camera appeared to destroy the need for pictorial syntax, writers were called upon to eliminate any blatant traces of their own subjective presence within their work. Once the author's figure was no longer seen to intervene in, interrupt, or redirect the narrative, the reader

28. On the current status of photographic objectivity, see Leighten (1977–78:135–36).
29. Some of the consequences of photographic realism for symbolic production and appreciation in codes customarily located outside the realm of art have been extensively studied by Gerbner and Gross: "the premise of realism is a Trojan horse which carries within it a highly selective, synthetic, and purposeful image of the facts of life" (1976:178). See also Fiske and Hartley (1978).
30. Literary realism antedates this period, and Edel believes that, correspondingly, "novelists have sought almost from the first to become a camera" (1974:177). Wilsher confirms the subordination of photographic technology to cultural form, which preceded it: "The readers of Fanny Burney's romance *Cecilia* (1782) were delighted with the realism of her descriptions of London life; a friend, Mrs. Thrale, remarked that the novel was just like a 'camera obscura in a window of Piccadilly' " (1977:84). See also Gernsheim (1969:27–28). A useful study of American literary realism is Kolb (1969a).

might apprehend the story as an unmediated progression of visual images, a series of verbal stereoscopic views.[31]

Fiske and Hartley assert that "realism requires that it be accepted not as *one* way of seeing but as *the* way of seeing" (1978:165). In this, I believe, it shared extensive common ground with journalistic objectivity. Students of American literary realism might do well to study the formal practices of American journalism, with an eye toward their influence on realist literature, because, as Hofstadter remarks, "with few exceptions the makers of American realism . . . were men who had training in journalistic observation" (1955:198). And journalistic observation before the Civil War meant conventional adherence to the rigorous separation of fact from value and to an exclusive and universal language of empirical fact.

Science and popular photography were culturally patterned constructs whose veracity was not disputed. By explicitly invoking them, journalists grounded their defense of natural rights in the authority of the natural world itself. Following Barthes, we may characterize journalistic objectivity as a myth of primary import for an evolving American society, for, like myth, objectivity "transforms history into nature" (1975:129). Arising in homologous relation to the paths taken by science and by art, the myth of journalistic objectivity allowed the penny papers to oversee the public good—to supervise public enlightenment—without betraying any self-interest.

At a macrocultural level, science and photography made it possible for the commercial newspaper to incorporate the standard of objectivity. Yet, at a microcultural level, that is, *within* the content and form of journalism, how was this claim routinely animated and publicly certified? How was objectivity *specifically* generated within newspapers? In the following chapter I analyze the cultivation of news objectivity within one prominent newspaper, the *National Police Gazette,* between 1845 and 1850. In chapters 5 and 6 I extend the analysis to the transcendent pursuit of public good, which, in accordance with its cultivation of objectivity, the *Police Gazette* was able to indulge in.

31. The explicitly visual frame created by literary realism was often remarked upon. In an 1862 review of Harriet B. Stowe's *The Pearl of Orr's Island,* E. P. Whipple noted the author's ability "to impress us with a sense of the substantial reality of what she makes us mentally see"; and he approved the "foundation of the story in palpable realities which every Yankee recognizes as true the moment they are presented to his eye" (in McMahon 1973:12).

4

Anchoring the Facts:
The Pattern of Objectivity
in the *National Police Gazette* 1845–1850

In mid-eighteenth-century London, the novelist Henry Fielding was determined to start a police force to suppress the thieves and robbers who too often
enjoyed the freedom of the city. After his death, his half-brother John Fielding expanded on his effort. In 1761 John submitted to the Prime Minister a
plan for curtailing "the frequent robberies in and near London" (in Pringle
1955:160–61). One of his suggestions was that there be published an official
police gazette: regular lists with descriptions of wanted criminals, printed in
sufficient number to send copies to magistrates throughout Britain (ibid.:190).
In the fall of 1772, Fielding's police gazette got under way. Called the "Quarterly Pursuit" (and supplemented by a more frequent edition, the "Weekly
or Extraordinary Pursuit"), the first issue contained descriptions of thirty-six
"offenders at large":

> Elizabeth Austin, alias Williams, alias Robinson, a tall girl, flaxen
> hair, fair complexion, cast in her eyes, broadshouldered, has a scar under
> her chin, charged with felony in Middlesex. . . .
> William Thompson, by trade a butcher, about five feet five inches
> high, pale complexion, effeminate voice, light curled hair, flat nose, the
> end of which turns up, charged with felony in Westminster. (Ibid.:193)

A lineal descendant of Fielding's police gazette provided an explicit model
for the journalist George Wilkes and his associate Enoch Camp (a lawyer),
when they joined forces in the late summer of 1845 to launch the *National*

Police Gazette in New York City. George Wilkes, the driving force behind the enterprise, was a spirit more nearly akin to the rogues whose careers he so carefully traced in his *Police Gazette* than he would perhaps have been prepared to admit. Probably the son of an artisan, he worked at different times as a law clerk, a journalist, a speech writer for David Broderick (senator for California in the 1850s), a political boss, a commentator on Shakespeare, horse racing, boxing, the prospect of a national railroad, the Paris Commune, and the Civil War, and a land speculator in Baja (Saxton 1979).[1] He had an instinct for the anomalous, the ironic, and the unjust; but he never failed to keep a keen eye out for the main chance. Wilkes was a freebooter, a sometime firebrand, and, in his bones, a muckrake journalist. His writing could be spicy and sharp. He specialized in crime news of all sorts and honed to a fine edge the razor that the cheap press used to shave the presumptuous airs of nabobs and corrupt officials. Indeed, the *Police Gazette* was a nationally known and thoroughly commercial undertaking from the very first. In the approach of the journalists and their systematic use of crime news, the *Police Gazette* is representative of the broader tendencies in journalism at that time.

In this chapter I will show that news objectivity was a recurrent, even a continual, and conventionally generated strategy in the *Police Gazette,* perhaps not so much in spite of that paper's strongly investigative proclivities as because of them. Objectivity, however, was contradictory: the ideal of a universally recognizable, democratically accessible "web of facticity" was concretely verified and bulwarked by a specific social hierarchy. Belief that access to knowledge should be equal for all citizens was belied by the particular *form* through which knowledge was expressed. For, in the *Police Gazette,* a specific social hierarchy authorized and defined a particular threshold of proof.

The sources on which the *National Police Gazette* drew were two. One was the London *Police Gazette,* which Wilkes saluted in his first issue. The London *Gazette* was a government-sponsored sheet that boasted that it was "Published by Authority" (*POLICE GAZETTE; or, Hue And Cry* No. 1, London, 18 January 1826). It was an agent of law enforcement, "Containing the Substance of all Information received in Cases of Felonies, and Misdemeanors of an aggravated nature, and against Receivers of Stolen Goods, reputed Thieves and Offenders escaped from Custody, with the time, the place, and every particular circumstance marking the Offence" (ibid.). On the

1. Saxton's (1979) penetrating study is the only thoroughly researched and analytic biography of Wilkes.

other side was the very different *Cleave's Weekly Police Gazette,* perhaps the most famous of the radical, working-class newspapers oriented to crime news that marked the eruption of the "unstamped" press into English life in the early 1830s. Dipping into *Cleave's,* more or less at random, we find political sentiments stressing the "impudence which the majority of newspaper proprietors . . . display in the advocacy of their own private interests in the name of public morals" (5 March 1836). The journal was founded, so it declared, "FOR A FREE PRESS AND EQUAL LAWS," and, it announced, "KNOWLEDGE IS POWER" (26 December 1835). More specifically, *Cleave's* stated:

> The working men of Great Britain are conscious that they live in the freest country on earth, with but one exception; yet they themselves are hardly above the condition of slaves. Unrepresented by the law-making power, their wants and their interests are wholly at the mercy of their rulers. Shut out of the courts of law as jurymen, and by the enormous expense of what is called justice, they are seldom seen in them, except when dragged there to be convicted for breaking statutes whose existence they were not permitted previously to know.
>
> The working men of Great Britain live in a country remarkable for the extensive and rapid circulation of intelligence and information; yet they, themselves, are positively, and almost in express terms, denied any participation whatever in the readiest, the commonest, the chief vehicle of knowledge—the newspaper. (23 April 1836)

In its lineage and in its own composition, then—as we shall see—the New York *National Police Gazette* combined the authority of the state with a focused concern for the impartial defense of equal rights and public enlightenment.

From 1845 until the early 1850s the *National Police Gazette* evidently prospered, but then the journal began to languish until, in 1857, it was sold to ex–Chief of Police of New York City George Washington Matsell.[2] Matsell experimented with different formats, but never managed to restore the *Police Gazette*'s previous good fortune. In 1876 an English émigré, Richard Kyle Fox, bought the *Police Gazette,* and within five years, it had become the most notorious, nationally circulated purveyor of sporting news and theatrical and crime coverage. In its heyday the *National Police Gazette* claimed a circulation of 500,000 (Bessie 1938:64); and its pink pages gave the "barbershop

2. What little history of the *National Police Gazette* is available is largely the work of Mott (1967) and Van Every (1930, 1931).

bible," as it was called, a flamboyant and eye-catching style. Beginning around World War I, however, "the tabloids beat the *Police Gazette* at its own game" (ibid.:65), by copying its format and appearing daily. Under a series of new publishers the journal has survived, living on the nostalgia that its masthead continues to evoke.

Owing to a paucity of information about its growth and commercial character, it is unlikely that an institutional or business history of the *National Police Gazette* will ever be written. Evidence from the *Police Gazette* itself suggests that between 1845 and 1850 the journal became the preeminent, nationally circulated newspaper for specialized crime news. Above all else, in these successful early years, the *Police Gazette* was a commercial journal, concerned primarily with circulation, readership, and advertising rates.

In one of its first issues the *Police Gazette* claimed a circulation of 15,000 —at two dollars a year, payable in advance. "Its extent of readers and circulation are already superior to any weekly periodical issued in this city" (New York), the editors boasted. A modern and commercial logic underlay their claim that this large and increasing circulation "renders it the most desirable medium for advertising in the United States" (8 November 1845). The proprietors employed the publishing house of Burgess, Stringer & Company as "General Subscription Agents." Other agents were maintained in other major Eastern cities, in smaller inland cities in New York, and in a surprising number of Southern and booming Western cities: Buffalo, Cleveland, Detroit, Chicago, Pittsburgh, Louisville, and Cincinnati, as well as Richmond, Norfolk, Charleston, Mobile, New Orleans, and Saint Louis. Advertising terms for one twenty-line "square" were one dollar for the first insertion and half price for each subsequent one. For ten lines or less the journal charged fifty cents, twenty-five cents for each additional insertion. All monies were payable in advance. Advertising policy thus clearly favored the stability of long-term advertisers, and the unit of commercial space was not yet entirely rationalized—ten lines cost the same as one.

The *National Police Gazette* appears to have done well. Midway through its first year three of its eight tabloid pages were given over to advertising. Patent medicines, tea, gold pens, daguerreotypes, tools, lost and found notices, and announcements of stolen property were prominently featured. A weekly list of United States Army deserters was published for the War Department "more for its preventive effects, than for rescue after escape" (25 April 1846). In return, "by order of the government," recruiting stations around the country were supplied with subscriptions to the *Police Gazette*. Circulation advanced, reaching a reported 23,000 in the first year (9 May

NATIONAL POLICE GAZETTE.

VOL. 1.   NEW-YORK, THURSDAY, OCTOBER 16, 1845.

Entered according to Act of Congress in the year 1845, by Enoch E. Camp and George Wilkes, in the Clerk's Office of the District Court of the United States for the Southern District of New York.

LIVES OF THE FELONS.

No. 1.

ROBERT SUTTON,

ALIAS "BOB THE WHEELER."

The criminal records of no country perhaps present in the compass of an individual career so much of painful and amazing interest as attach to the first era of this notorious felon's life; and were his exploits and their results not substantiated by irrefragable proofs still fresh in the minds of many of our citizens, they would be discarded by even the most susceptible imaginations and condemned as the merest vagaries of fiction.

That our readers may the sooner be able to judge of this fact for themselves, we will without further preface commence with the actual events of his career.

Robert Sutton was born, as near as we can learn, in a village near the city of London, early enough in the last century to make him at present from fifty-five to sixty years of age. He was at the proper time of life apprenticed out to a wheelwright, but possessing a remarkably muscular frame and an extraordinary degree of physical strength and prowess, he allowed himself at an early age to be persuaded to abandon his handicraft, and cast his stalwart fortune in the circle of the prize ring.

It is not for us to describe the history of his pugilistic career. Suffice it that he justified the presage of his renown, and in a number of severe pitched fights, they chronicled in "Boxiana," came off a creditable combatant and a conqueror. As a member of the fancy, Bob the Wheeler, (so nicknamed from his trade,) soon became acquainted with a number of the admiring swell mob, and from a boon companion of these genii, was easily moulded into a susceptible disciple. How far he progressed in their science or mingled in their practices on the other side of the water, there is no reliable account to say, but it is a fact, that in his twenty-fifth year he found London too hot to hold him, and deemed it more than advisable to seek an asylum in some foreign country. Having been brought to the state of mind, it is not strange to find that, like so many others of his class, he gave this land of the largest liberty his decided preference.

He arrived here somewhere in the immediate neighborhood of 1820, and after working at his trade a short time, set up an English beer-shop in Roosevelt street. This establishment he called the "Darby & Joan," and had its title properly certified by an illustration of that domestic couple on a sign before the door. It was situated nearly opposite a large livery stable, on the left hand side of the first block from Chatham street. The building, a small blue frame house, is still standing, and is known as number 24. This concern soon became the resort of all the most notorious English thieves and burglars in the city, and the pugilistic fame of Bob the Wheeler also drew together admiring crowds of the bellicose youngsters of the town.

Sparring exhibitions were given there; it was the place where all sporting matters from rat-catching to cock-fighting were discussed; and the respective qualities and merits of "shoulder hitters" and "artful dodgers" weighed and waged with the precision of philosophy. By encouraging this spirit, the landlord was reaping a very cheering harvest, and wherever the fever flagged, he revived it by throwing himself into the field for a match, for the purpose of keeping up the profitable excitement. This went on very prosperously for four or five years, during which time, not satisfied with the large profits of a legitimate business, he occasionally amused himself with picking a pocket; but was obliged to abandon this line, in consequence of having been arrested in 1824 for a very clumsy attempt of the kind. Immediately after this, he formed a secret connection with three other rogues, who, for desperation, cunning, and capacity, have never been exceeded. The first of these was James Holdgate, an English pewterer or maker of fancy leaden toys, who, at the above date, had but recently arrived in this country. This man was employed by the Gas Company to repair the fixtures and meters in rapid succession. At this period, a gentleman named "Moccasin" Jackson, deceived in the character of Holdgate, furnished him with $1000, to start him in the pewterer's business; and in accordance with the offer, the gas-man established a shop at No. 3 Murray street, in the small two-story brick house which stood so many years in the rear of Tenney's (then Brewster's) jewelry store, on the corner of that street and Broadway.

The next member of the coalition was an Englishman of remarkable abilities and liberal education, named James Stevens, and a New Yorker named John Reed, who was also a man of superior acuteness and address, was the fourth. This party fully appreciated each other's abilities and felt a substantial confidence that their connection was bound to eventuate in the most striking results.

This organization was effected, so far as the three first were concerned, as early as the fall of 1824, but though they doubtless safely effected many depredations in the two years immediately succeeding their nefarious companionship, we cannot fix the strong presumption of any particular offence upon them until 1826, when a daring attempt was made to enter Brewster's jewelry store by undermining it through the cellar. The robbers however, not being able to accomplish their purpose in a single night, had the progress of their operations discovered on the following day, and their designs of course defeated; but Holdgate, the honest and thriving pewterer next door, was never once suspected. He however shortly after moved away, and took up his residence in James street, near his old friend and pitcher, Bob the Wheeler.

About this time, Reed, who was a man of superior genius, began to exercise a controlling influence in the band, and proposed to change their system of downright burglaries, (the predominant policy of Bob the Wheeler,) to a more powerful and insinuating system of acquisition. This was forgery. He possessed acids which were capable of extracting from paper any name or figure, and his skill as a penman enabled him to counterfeit any name or sign with the most remarkable exactness.

His counsel prevailed, and the knavish cunning of the quartette set itself to work to invent modes of obtaining the desired signatures. Holdgate was entitled to the credit of suggesting the successful plan to effect this object; and Sutton, following his peculiar bent of mind, which was force, proposed that when address should fail, they should extend their operations by burglariously entering the stores of those merchants whose signatures they desired to obtain, and gather them from the papers or checks that they found therein,—Holdgate's design was to make inconsiderable purchases of goods from those whom they intended as their prey, and by offering them a note of large amount induce them to give a check in change. This was

to be used at pleasure or imitation. By this means $40 on the North [River Bank] was cash-ed from Duncan P[hyfe] Shouler, who, being m[anager] of a job, was, upon appl[ication] crates above named, all[owed] luck upon that gentleman. [So] far successful, Holdgate took [one] forged one from it for $19.00 [offer]ing to have it allowed to [Hold]gate's prudence [found the] sum. This was presented by the [other] party two hours after the good one had been paid, and it was cashed without demur. From this time we hear no more of Shouler, and his name vanishes from the records altogether. The probability is, that he was some poor journeyman knack, who was tossed this job by way of keeping him from starvation.

A forgery on Abraham Le Foy, for $700 on the North River Bank, another on James Grant, a tin worker, and several others, followed, which we will omit to enumerate, for the purpose of coming at the grand exploit of all.

It had long been the desire of the party to obtain the signature of the heavy firm of Howland & Aspinwall in Front street but all their attempts had failed. At length Bob Sutton's policy prevailed, and they determined to effect their primary object by a burglary. They therefore went together to that store on the evening of the 28th September, 1827, and at a little before nine o'clock, while all the clerks were busy in the counting room above, and while wayfarers were passing up and down the street, Reed, with unparalleled audacity, advanced from the pier where the other three lay secretly in wait, and with a bunch of keys commenced the process of fitting one to the lock. After trying several, he at length succeeded in getting one that turned the bolt, but this was only effected at the expense of severely straining the lock. He then returned to his associates, and Sutton and Holdgate went away with him, leaving Stevens to watch the effect which the discovery of the injury would have upon the inmates of the store. About ten o'clock the last clerk attempted to fasten up, but finding after several attempts some unexpected obstruction in the lock, he left off in despair, and walked up go down the next morning, and to ascertain what effect the circumstance had produced.

Sutton attended to the business an early hour on the following day, and lounging about the pier, discovered the colored porter of the store at work sweeping it out. He sauntered carelessly up to him, and falling into conversation, learned that the circumstance had occasioned no surprise, as the lock had been but recently repaired. While thus engaged, he noticed some bits of paper among the rubbish, which the porter's broom was scattering before it, in the street, and on observing them closely, was overjoyed to find that them they watched his opportunity to pick them up unperceived, and nothing some floating in the slip, he obtained them, by letting himself down in a boat and picking them out of the water. All of

SUTTON'S "DARBY & JOAN," 24 ROOSEVELT STREET, NEW-YORK.

The *National Police Gazette,* 16 October 1845. Engravings, published virtually every week, invariably appeared on the journal's front page. The address given here for the "Darby and Joan," the pub kept by the felon Robert Sutton, placed it in the Fourth Ward, a few blocks from the Bowery, near the notorious Five Points district, and five or six blocks from the wharves on the East River. The *Police Gazette* was edited and published in the same quarters.

The *National Police Gazette,* 16 October 1845. An early page of advertisements features the journal's prospectus, with Justice and her scale and sword. Advertisements for patent medicine for treatment of venereal disease fostered a disreputable image of the journal in "respectable" middle-class quarters.

1846), and purportedly numbering at least 3,700 in Boston and 5,000 in Philadelphia (14 March 1846). This "perfectly unparalleled" increase pulled the *Police Gazette* into regions "where scarcely any other papers from the Atlantic border ever reach" (10 January 1846). The newspaper felt compelled to notice three vital features of its circulation above mere quantity of copies sold. First, the quality of its readership, which was said to include, among others, Martin Van Buren and John C. Calhoun (25 April 1846). "There is scarcely an hotel or place of public resort in the country," claimed the *Police Gazette*'s proprietors, "where it cannot be found" (24 January 1846). Second, the extent of secondary readership as opposed to circulation was noted, as when the journal claimed "more than one hundred thousand readers in various parts of the United States" (5 September 1846). Finally, the *Police Gazette* argued that its contents were accorded special attention by readers: "there are but few of the many thousands who receive it, who do not retain it on file for perusal and reference" (24 January 1846).

These were among the factors that may have justified the increase in the advertising rates and the change in policy in June 1846. Now the *Police Gazette,* emphasizing its "limited space for advertising," increased charges to ten cents a line "for each and every insertion" (27 June 1846). This gesture of confidence was followed by a retail price drop from five to four cents a copy and by more claims about increasing circulation (10 October 1846). "Without fear of being considered exaggerative, we state that the reading circulation of 'The Police Gazette' is equal, if not superior, to any other paper in the country" (17 April 1847). The extremely fragmentary evidence available after September 1847 indicates that success probably continued. In 1848 the *Police Gazette* touted its commercial distribution system, allowing that "the *Herald,* the *Ledger,* the *Police Gazette,* and other papers, are as local in New Orleans, or Cincinnati, or Boston, as in the cities of their publication" (28 October 1848). At the same time the *Police Gazette* declined to make any further yearly contracts with advertisers; no advertising runs longer than a month would be accepted, it insisted, and rates again increased (ibid.). The *Police Gazette* now became a full-sized, four-page folio newspaper, edited and published by George Wilkes alone, and, at the beginning of its sixth year, claiming a circulation of "over 40,000" (2 November 1850). For the years with which we are concerned, the *Police Gazette* may be characterized as a blossoming commercial concern.

If the last three pages of the *Police Gazette* were devoted mainly to advertising, the first two invariably flaunted the journal's prized feature—serialized criminal biographies that constituted "The Lives of the Felons."

Here, as we shall see in detail in chapter 5, the causes, character, and consequences of crime were evaluated and condemned. A woodcut of varying quality appeared on the top of page one and usually illustrated a scene described in the text of the series. The middle three pages of the *Police Gazette* contained extensive trial reports, paragraph-length news items detailing recent offenses committed around the nation, and a contemporary version of an editorial page. Whether two sentences or several columns in length, editorials were in fact written by the editors and were used to focus attention on particular points and to expand on the theory of American political institutions or social life. The stories that received special play in the middle sections of the *Police Gazette* emphasized crimes against persons more than did either "The Lives of the Felons" series or the brief news accounts. In the latter, property crime was singled out for special attention. The impression is strong that, insofar as crimes against persons are notably displayed, criminal violence involving both sexes—in murders, rapes, and incest—is stressed. The middle pages of the *Police Gazette,* and especially the editorial page (as we shall see in chapter 4), also underscored corruption in the state.

Perhaps the most notable feature of this journal, when looked at today, is its flexibility: when a good murder or a salacious incest case appeared, the *Police Gazette* cut back on other features (the short news items were the most likely target) to make room for courtroom testimony and trial developments. Usually an essay on the editorial page would explain and justify any idiosyncratic features of the new edition.

A Transcendent View of an Objective World

As was the custom whenever a new journal found its way across the nation through exchanges sponsored by the post office (newspapers were subsidized so that news might travel efficiently from place to place), the *National Police Gazette* prompted other journalists to testify to its merits, such as they might be. Testify they did, and they lingered in their comments over the especially appreciable veracity of the journal.[3] The editors of the *Police Gazette* were quick to print their praise. "Founded entirely on truth," said the New Haven *Democrat* (4 July 1846); "pictures of reality, not of fancy," applauded the Providence *Herald* (8 November 1845); and the Louisville *Daily Democrat*

3. The following testimonials, although taken from the pages of the *Police Gazette*, do not thereby lose but indeed may gain in validity, by virtue of the selection presumably made by the journal's editors. The testimonials become, thus, evidence for what the editors understood as their own proper role.

added that the *Police Gazette*'s biographical series entitled the "Lives of the Felons" was "authentic, derived from reports of legal proceedings, and the confessions of the criminals themselves" (5 September 1846). When these "Lives" were reprinted in a separate volume, the New York *Globe* stated: "It will be read with great interest, it being unlike works of fiction, founded upon facts as they have actually occurred" (4 July 1846). Still another paper underscored the *Police Gazette*'s employment of "documentary proof" of crime and corruption (5 September 1846); and the Rondout (New York) *Freeman* signified that the *Police Gazette* had achieved a place within the state apparatus when that paper called it "an important element in the police system of the country":

> It disseminates accurate information of the rogues and rogueries to every village in every state in the Union, and villany [*sic*] finds itself marked and detected at every turn. Nor is its influence in keeping the police of the cities from the corrupt practices which have at times rendered them public nuisances, the least of its merits. (8 August 1846)

From these statements I conclude that, although a study of journalistic objectivity within a single newspaper will inevitably be limited, such an investigation may not be quite so restricted in significance as might be thought. The *Police Gazette* spoke for itself, to be sure, but its voice was accepted and even applauded by many others within a developing journalistic fraternity.

The *Police Gazette* formulated its overriding concern with accuracy and veracity in direct opposition to partisan political activity, for "a man is never so apt to commit errors of fact . . . as when under the influence of heady passion" (21 February 1846). This concern fitted snugly with the journal's chosen subject, for criminality transcended party affiliation. It did not matter, thus, whether the malefactor were "whig or loco foco," because in either case he would deserve "the same measure of punishment" (ibid.). Objectivity was welded to the American state as a whole. When defense counsel in an incest case challenged the *Police Gazette*'s right to report the proceedings, the editors complained: "We regret this particularly, as it has forced us to assume a position which makes us look as if we were taking sides" (16 May 1846). "A Landlord and Tenant" acknowledged, in a letter to the editors, "that your Journal is destined to pursue a neutral path." Therefore, he continued, his remarks would be addressed "to every citizen of this city, without reference in the slightest degree to politics" (19 December 1846).[4]

"Truth is strange," stated the *Police Gazette* in a much repeated phrase, "stranger than fiction" (24 January 1846). The journal went to some length to emphasize the veracity of its news reports in explicit fashion. A correspondent's letter provoked the editors to announce that they had "satisfied" themselves "of the accuracy of the main points of its information. . . . We herewith give it a place in our columns" (8 November 1845). "Correspondents cannot be too cautious in preparing their communications," said the editors (10 July 1847); letter writers were requested "to stick strictly to the relation of facts" (21 February 1846).[5] In a trial report, justice demanded nothing less than "a full and accurate report of all the testimony for the prosecution and defence" (16 January 1847). Thus, the news was elevated above partisan interest, both within the courtroom and in the class-stratified world that it dramatized: "we are merely stating facts, and if truth, will not, chamelean [*sic*] like, alter its complexion because of a gentle neighborhood, we are not called upon to apologize for its rough realities" (24 January 1846). The *Police Gazette,* counterpoised to all private interest, was "only bound to make true statements" (16 May 1846). As the journal put it, waxing poetic in its "Annual Address of the Carriers of the National Police Gazette to Their Patrons" on 9 January 1847:

> To read these deeds, and feel and know,
> That they have been and must be so,
>
> . . . .
>
> What mischiefs dire! what murders black!
> What corpses lie along your track!
> What fiendish rapes! what beastly acts
> Stand ranged in rows of stubborn facts!

It was the avowed intention of the *Police Gazette,* from the first, to display "more of the philosophy of character" of crime and criminality than could be found in any other source (16 October 1845). The word *philosophy* is significant, for in contemporary usage it was the normal equivalent of *science; philosophy* thus has been defined by a historian of science of this era, George

---

4. See also *National Police Gazette,* 21 August 1847.
5. From a stylistic point of view, correspondents were to narrate facts according to the rules of everyday speech. According to the *Police Gazette,* "the only safe rule for a young author is to *write* nothing that he would not *say* in conversation" (21 February 1846). The same admonition carried with it a moral caution, evinced in the journal's account of an incest case: "The report has been very carefully taken, and with the exception of some of the grosser details of the offence, is laid before our readers exactly as it transpired before the magistrate" (13 February 1847).

Daniels, as "those principles of reasoning and fundamental assumptions upon which scientific investigations are carried out" (1968:246). The series "Lives of the Felons," in particular, was eminently scientific in a formal sense: the character and qualities of particular species—pickpockets, counterfeiters, burglars, murderers—of the genus criminal were listed and analyzed. It was only appropriate that this explicitly scientific intention should be animated by the objectivism that characterized contemporary science and, above all, by the incessant preoccupation of science with the facts.

The extent of this reverence seems almost incredible by more modern standards. At one point the journal stated, "we have reduced the size of our reading type to Minion, in order to give our readers the additional space required by our extensive correspondence and the increase of wickedness and crime" (3 January 1846).

The *Police Gazette* reiterated its concern for objectivity in varied contexts, for instance, in its comments about the engravings that embellished its front page each week. Often these illustrations were portraits of a criminal or a government official. Repeatedly, the *Police Gazette* claimed that such portraits were "correct and perfect" (20 December 1845), or "faithful likenesses" (21 February 1846). The paper's "likeness of the negro Freeman, now in prison at Auburn for the horrible murder of the Van Ness family, was taken by a superior artist, and will be found remarkably faithful, as well in the peculiar expression of the monster's countenance, as in accuracy of delineation" (11 April 1846).

The major criterion of accuracy was immediate and universal recognition. The *Police Gazette* boasted of one portrait that it "will be found so truthlike that recognition follows at a glance" (20 December 1845).[6] From the perspective of the *Police Gazette,* recognition of criminals served a useful purpose, and the journal was quick to point out that its engravings of the pickpocket Billy Fish had been instrumental in his arrest in New Orleans (11 April 1846). Indeed, the *Police Gazette* argued that its serialized rogue's gallery "had the effect of making the originals hide and burrow in their dens,"

6. This criterion, which opened up appraisal and evaluation to anyone who could claim familiarity with the subject of illustration, was not confined to portraits. An advertisement for a "Grand View of the Battle of Buena Vista," an engagement in the ongoing Mexican–American War, noted that this lithograph print was "from a sketch taken on the spot." Its accuracy was "vouched for by the gallant Colonel May" and by "William H. Woods." The latter, claiming to have been at the battle, stated, "I, unqualifiedly, state the view of the Battle Ground is correct in every particular, and the troops—as far as my position would enable me to judge—are correctly posted" (28 August 1847).

for, should an offender break prison or remain at large, the journal's likeness would "inevitably secure his re-arrest." The scheme would be best served by utilizing "the art of the daguerreotype . . . in taking the likenesses of notorious felons, for distribution among the police" (ibid.). If immediate recognition was the desired standard, it might be achieved by adhering to the newly incumbent general standard of visual truth—photographic realism. The *Police Gazette* accordingly mentioned often that its "faithful copy" was "drawn from a superior daguerreotype" (28 February 1846).[7] Editors Camp and Wilkes apparently made special attempts to obtain daguerreotypes of criminals, as in the case of the highwayman Adams, whom they induced "to accompany us to Plumbe's daguerrian rooms, where, with his steel hand-cuffs on, Adams sat for the likeness which is to be found on our first page" (12 September 1846).[8] Other newspapers were duly impressed by this practice. The New York *Morning News* praised the *Police Gazette* for its series of portraits, "which, as wood engravings, are beautiful specimens of the art— the last, that of Mayor Mickle, being a most perfect likeness" (*Police Gazette*, 22 August 1846).

The unitary, universally appreciable world of fact to which the photograph attested was expressed and validated by recourse to professionalism, situated language, and verification of source reliability and news authenticity.

Professional Appraisal of the Facts

With its insistence on the universal recognizability of the facts, the *Police Gazette* laid repeated claim to its professional right of access to the pertinent facts about crime and criminality. Because it was believed that "the facts" were transparent and accessible, in principle, to anyone with a requisite familiarity, the *Police Gazette* was able to claim special competence by virtue of its proprietors' carefully displayed knowledge of the underworld. Restated, once accuracy became merely a matter of access to a seemingly uniform world rather than a matter of adherence to a defining point of view, the way was open for professional specialization itself to become a feasible defense of validity and reliability. The *Police Gazette* took great care to accent its unique

7. See also *National Police Gazette*, 1 August 1846 and 29 August 1846.
8. Observe that the translation of daguerreotype to newspaper is stripped of mediating features —it is, so to speak, invisible. In actuality, however, lacking halftone or other mechanical photographic reproductive technologies, the photograph had to undergo particular and definite substantive translation by way of an engraver, as is indicated in the next quotation. Jussim's (1974) important book takes up this question in detail.

privilege of access to the special province of crime and criminality: our modern Eyewitness News is actually almost a century and a half old. An apparently reformed felon, for example, was said to have committed a grand larceny "on a Sunday morning" in July of 1843 "as is well recollected by the writer of this article, who was an eyewitness of the affair" (1 November 1845). The journal also vouched for the governor's behavior in pardoning an unjustly imprisoned man: his action "was induced by incontrovertible facts," and his "careful investigation" bore the knowledgeable testimonial of "the writer of this paragraph [who] reported the original trial, and has been acquainted with every subsequent step in the proceedings which led to the prisoner's discharge" (22 November 1845).

The *Police Gazette* also relied on "private information from our correspondents" as a means of furnishing "the most full and particular history of the case yet given to the public" (1 November 1845). Occasional mention of facts "which have been in our sole possession for several weeks, but which we found it prudent to conceal" (15 November 1845), or of informants who "communicated the above circumstances to us personally" (13 December 1845), bolstered the *Police Gazette*'s authority while also underscoring the reliability of its information. The journal also took pains to accentuate its arduous, empirical, and expensive search for the facts:

> We direct the attention of the public, and of police officers in particular, to the following minute personal description of Albert J. Tirrell, the supposed murderer of Mrs. Bickford, at Boston, which we have obtained at considerable trouble, and which is the only correct one that has been given to the public. We take this opportunity to direct our correspondents to send us, in all cases of crime, a full description of the criminal.[9] (1 November 1845)

Recounting the recent depredations of Reed and Charley Webb, the editors emphasized the effort expended in bringing such information to light: "The greater part of these extraordinary events have, up to the present moment, been shrouded in the tenacious obscurity of interested officers' bosoms, and have only been obtained by us at the outlay of immense exertion, and also

---

9. There followed the description of Tirrell, which served to apprise readers of the features of competent correspondence as well as to alert them to the physical characteristics of the suspect: "Albert J. Tirrell is about 22 to 23 years of age, stands six feet and half an inch high, but stoops so that he does not appear to be more than five feet and eleven inches, dark complexion, very dark featured, high and prominent cheekbones, slight in frame, dark hair; his beard is dark in color, but thin and light. He wore at the time of his escape thin mustachios" (1 November 1845).

of considerable expense" (1 November 1845). Finally, in justifying a price rise, the editors explained that "the expenses of a paper whose contents must be collected by the personal inquiries and efforts of its editors and repertorial [*sic*] attaches, and which is devoted entirely to the recording of facts, is greatly beyond any other description of publication, and therefore cannot be afforded at the same prices as sheets of an inferior size, which can be 'written up' in a single afternoon without the editor moving from an arm-chair for reference. Our duties are of an arduous character" (22 November 1845).

Empirical fact-finding backed by lavish expenditure provided the access to the criminal world that, in turn, justified the *Police Gazette*'s claim to specialized competence and authority. Explanations that clarified the meaning of otherwise obtuse or inexplicable criminal activities both signaled and cultivated this role. The *Police Gazette,* for example, climaxed one of the felon Murrell's horrific murders on the Mississippi River as follows:

> There was but one measure more to take to finish the business with professional perfection, and that was to conceal the body. This was done in an instant by ripping open the belly* with the dexterity of a butcher, and tumbling it into the stream to find the bottom. (31 October 1846)

The asterisk directed the reader to the bottom of the column, where he read:

> *This is the invariable practice of river pirates and assassins, to conceal the bodies of their victims. It prevents the decaying corpse from collecting those gaseous humors which would bring it to the surface.[10]

Professional competence was nowhere more evident, though, than in reports of new or noteworthy criminal procedures. These might evince great sensitivity to language and technique, as the following paragraph shows.

10. Such specialized knowledge also applied to less spectacularly vicious activities. Another installment of Murrell's career footnoted the miscreant's claim that a stray horse was, indeed, the one he had lost. "This is a common trick among horse thieves, who not only steal outright all the animals they can lay their hands on, but thus manage to obtain possession of all strays that fall within their knowledge. In pursuance of this system, some of the party examines the stray books regularly, and whenever there is a record of an animal of any value found, get the complete description, and secretly communicated [*sic*] it to several of the clan or gang in different points of the surrounding neighborhood. As soon as any of these rogues hear of the animal being picked up as an estray, they send two accomplices who are strangers in the place where the horse is detained. One of these then claims the animal and the other proves the property, and the prize is soon borne out of reach, for the common benefit of all" (21 November 1846).

PICKING POCKETS.—The mode adopted by thieves to pick a pocket book from the pantaloons, or *"kick,"* as it is called, is as follows: —They mostly travel in gangs of from three to five. When in a crowd, that is landing from a Steamboat or entering a Car, one thief will step on each side of the person designated, and press against him, and at the same time raise his arms up, so as to "wing him." The most expert one of the gang is placed behind, ready to put his hand into the pantaloons pocket, and if successful, passes the book directly to his "pal," who stands in the rear of him, and who makes off at once, with the "dummy" or pocketbook.[11] (12 September 1846)

By way of authoritative, reiterated reports from an otherwise obscure and inaccessible criminal world, the *National Police Gazette* announced its specialized capacity for objective news accounts.

The *Police Gazette* used a second, related convention—situated language—to support its claims to professional competence and verisimilitude.

Situated Language

Situated language has been defined as the attempt to comprehend language "as pertaining to cultural and personal occasions which invest discourse with part of their meaning and structure" (Hymes 1974:100). The phrase was developed in the study of conversational speech. Here I understand situated language to be writing that attempts to locate itself—and the reader—in recognizably conversational contexts; it is writing in which the author conventionally attempts to approximate the speech of everyday life.[12] When, as with the *Police Gazette,* the everyday life that is signified is dominated by criminals and police and by illegal activities and law enforcement, situated language may often emphasize thieves' cant, slang, and the argot employed by criminals and police (Halliday 1976). Situated language thus may coincide with the cherished hope of photographic realism to reflect the exact texture of everyday life. At the same time, it may reinforce the specialized knowledge that alone permits translation of such language into lay terminology. Situated language also reinforced the *National Police Gazette*'s enactment of news objectivity as, through translation of such language into a more standard English, the journal displayed its professional expertise.

The *Police Gazette* used slang, cant, and argot regularly but strategi-

---

11. See also *National Police Gazette,* 21 November 1846.
12. It must be recognized that newspaper language is "situated" in a second sense as well, according to which the newspaper itself is read in different contexts.

cally, both during and after our period. Interest in such terms apparently was high, for a notice to correspondents informed readers that the editors were contemplating a column devoted to defining items of slang (21 March 1846). Somewhat later, the *Police Gazette* did initiate a column of "cant phrases and terms used by persons engaged in crime in England and in this country" (9 January 1847). This column was stopped after three issues for unspecified reasons, but the weekly continued to lace slang and cant terms throughout its news columns.

It is worth observing, parenthetically, that George W. Matsell, longtime Police Chief of New York City and, after 1857, owner of the *National Police Gazette*, prefaced his cant dictionary in terms that again stressed a professional commitment to the special language of criminals:

> The rogue fraternity have a language peculiarly their own, which is understood and spoken by them no matter what their dialect, or the nation where they were reared. Many of their words and phrases, owing to their comprehensive general meaning, have come into general use, so that a Vocabulum or Rogue's Lexicon, has become a necessity to the general reader, but more especially to those who read police intelligence. . . .
>
> To the readers of the *National Police Gazette*, the oldest and most reliable criminal journal published in the United States, this work will prove invaluable, as it will enable them to understand and fully comprehend language that the editors and correspondents are frequently compelled to use in order to convey the idea as understood by rogues in general.[13] (1859:iii–iv, vi)

Employment of thieves' cant usually was followed by translation into more respectable English, either parenthetically or in a footnote. "CHARLEY

13. It is suggestive that Matsell purchased the *Police Gazette* in view of its evident institutional impact on the police department of the city. I could find no records detailing this transaction.

Slang and cant almost certainly helped to separate the *Police Gazette* from classes more concerned with establishing and upholding "decency." Impure language awakened "licentious purposes," wrote William Alcott in his popular advice book (1839:333). And the Washington, D.C., *National Intelligencer* cautioned that the "cant term of 'Lynch Law'. . . ought not to find a place in the columns of a newspaper, nor in the conversation of men, any more than the illegal doings which it involves, should find perpetrators or abettors in civilized society and in a country of law" (29 August 1835). At the other end of our period, New York *Tribune* editor Horace Greeley found himself severely rebuked by Henry Raymond of the *Times* for having called the governor a "liar." Raymond stated that such language "shocks the taste, the sense of propriety of every man. It is coarse, brutal, and it is used only by coarse and brutal people; and the reason why they use it is because it corresponds with the coarseness and brutality of their natures" (in Hudson 1873:636). The sociolinguistic character of news, historically considered, is a matter of prime interest but little exact knowledge.

ROPER, the 'knuck,' 'gonnauf,' or 'pickpocket,' " stated the *Police Gazette* in characteristic form, "is also among the recent arrivals" to New York City (8 November 1845).[14] " 'Well,' " asks a felon of his compatriots, " 'what has been done in the way of "bogus," and "queer"?'*"; and, at the bottom of the page: " 'Bogus,' is base coin; 'queer,' is counterfeit paper" (9 January 1847).

Translation could also entail greater complexity. When Henry Thomas attempts to rob a well-dressed gentleman he meets on the road, the latter responds: " 'I've got five hundred dollars about me . . . and you are welcome to it if you think its [*sic*] right to levy on a brother of the "cross"*.' " The asterisk led the reader to a note:

> * "Of the *cross,*" is synonymous with—of the thievish profession. The word *"crossman"* is a general term for felons of all descriptions, whether pickpockets, burglars or highwaymen.
> He's a *"family-man,"* or "one of the *family,*" though commonly used in society with more creditable definitions, are understood by thieves in the same sense. (18 April 1846)

As if to sustain the linguistic point that professional or even familial camaraderie prevailed among thieves "of all descriptions," the paper reports that Thomas refuses to take the young man's money.

Another significant social relationship, this time between thieves and police, was animated through the language employed by a Philadelphia correspondent. "We have had quite a *stir* and a *split* among several *cross* women, and their husbands-in-law (a name given to police officers, and others who *take care* of cross women, while their husbands are in prison)" (28 August 1847). The ambivalence expressed here is at the center of the infamous identity of interests between criminals and police that the *Police Gazette* exposed. A more prevalent estimate of the police is that dramatized by the translation appended to a passage describing the attempt by members of New York's finest to induce a drunkard associate of a dangerous gang "to *'come it,'** on the whole business. It was decided, therefore, that he should be remanded, and kept on meagre food, and entirely without drink, to bring him to the desired condition.**"

14. For other examples see *National Police Gazette,* 8 November 1845; 15 November 1845; 6 December 1845; 21 February 1846.

* To reveal to officers, or to become State's evidence.

** This method of conquering the contumacy of hard drinkers, who refuse to testify, is called, in the peculiar parlance of the police, "putting them down to soak." This would be a paradox in any other system, but it is very properly applied, where every thing else is hind side before.[15] (21 March 1846)

Perhaps the most forceful and conscious instance of police corruption animated through language, which at the same time was used to dramatize the journal's objectivity, occurred in a story headed "A TREMENDOUS PRONOUN":

Alfonso Schmidt, *alias* Joseph Mallard, being overhauled on last Tuesday morning, by a gentleman connected with the police department of our office, exclaimed, in a tirade of complaint at the pain of his exposure, —"Ah, you tink your paper break up de old police—eh? You cannot do it sar! No sar! You cannot do it sar! You cannot break US (!) up, sar!"

Here is a pronoun of tremendous force, because it involves a tremendous fact, and we advise all old police officers to *decline* it. If the public wants any stronger evidence of the congenial interests of these two branches of society, let them ask for it. (15 November 1845)

Situated language was also used to create an analogy between business, particularly finance, and crime. At a trial of two men for conspiracy to defraud the public by passing counterfeit money, numerous letters found on their persons are read in evidence. The letters relate mainly to the purchase and sale of counterfeit money and are "perfect curiousities of their kind":

One of the gang in Virginia, writes to a comrade, that he has on hand a quantity of "No. 5 Indiana Tobacco:" also some "No. 1, 3 and 10, Kentucky Tobacco, which he will sell at 30 per cent." He also has "oats worth 14 cents per bushel," but presumes they are not "good enough for the market." Some other commercial expressions of a similar character are made use of in the correspondence, showing that the gang, which appears to be an extensive one, has a "slang" language of its own. (11 April 1846)

Again, the *Police Gazette,* in its thorough account of the felon Murrell's nefarious schemes, refers to his "extensive correspondence with the influen-

15. See also *National Police Gazette,* 15 August 1846.

NEW-YORK, SATURDAY, DECEMBER 26, 1846.

The New-York "Divers," or Street Thieves, at Work.

National Police Gazette, 26 December 1846. Criminals. The moment of depredation captured in exemplary snapshot form. Use of slang or cant acquainted the reader with the texture of criminal culture; translation revealed its character and underscored the authoritativeness of the journal's presentation.

tial speculators* who were the recognized heads of the marauding clans." A footnote added: "We should have mentioned before that the term *'speculator'* was, at the time we speak of, the common and comprehensive term used among the marauders of the west, to distinguish all who were devoted to dishonest courses" (14 November 1846). Here was a prominent ambiguity, or perhaps an implied identity, for the *Police Gazette* itself employed the term speculator in a different sense to include Wall Street stockjobbers (29 August 1846) as well as avowed criminals.

Finance and crime were identified even more closely in a discussion of pickpockets and their affinities. On pickpockets, the journal commented: "Most, if not all of . . . the fraternity are Whigs, being naturally forced to that course of policy by the strenuous opposition of the Democratic party to Banks and paper currency" (17 January 1846). Then, mobilizing the voice of the notorious pickpocket, Jack Gibson, the *Police Gazette* ironically added that the Democratic position

> "must prove deeply injurious to us, for if it should succeed, we shall have no more 'jugs' to 'crack,' and instead of *'dummies'* (pocket-books,) with several thousands in *'flimsies'* inside of them, we shall not be able to get a 'skin' (purse,) with more than $100, in 'blunt.'" (Ibid.)

Among the interesting implications of this statement is the evident belief that political interest is maneuvered ("naturally forced") by a pecuniary logic derived from economic imperatives. More significant for present purposes is that the Whigs and the banking interest are placed in league with open criminals.

The *Police Gazette* was quite careful to make explicit how it obtained conversational speech. In an early issue the journal recounted a conversation between thieves in which they agree to send evidence concerning an unjustly accused man, Redmond, "to Redmond's *'black-box'* (lawyer)" (11 October 1845). At the conclusion of this slang-filled conversation between the three felons, Sutton, Stevens, and Holdgate, an asterisk takes the reader's eye to the bottom of the column:

> *As the above conversations may be attributed to the imagination of the writer, it is proper to state that they were among the revelations made by Stevens after he had become State's evidence against Sutton and Holdgate. (Ibid.)

In accrediting the reliability of its evidence, the veracity of its sources, and the accuracy of its information, in this and other instances the *Police Gazette* made perhaps its most visible attempt to sustain news objectivity.

News Authenticity and Source Reliability

In a general appraisal of its weekly "Lives of the Felons" series, the *Police Gazette* observed that official records, private police memoranda, criminal confessions, trial reports, "and even, at times, the prison conversation of felons (as overheard by keepers and others) have contributed to perfect these narratives" (20 June 1846).[16] Later, these biographies were begun with a brief, standard statement such as: "Compiled from the public records, the secret correspondence of Helen Jewett, the recollections of her acquaintance and of the police, and the journal of Robinson" (28 October 1848). Sensitivity to evidentiary claims—to the believability of news—was a vital concern of the *National Police Gazette.* In denouncing false reports and rumors while simultaneously assuming that, in principle, news accounts were to be treated as fact, in explicitly mentioning its sources and obtaining testimonials to the authenticity of their information, and in discussing what ought to constitute acceptable evidentiary criteria, the *Police Gazette* continuously monitored its own reliability.

In reporting a case of robbery, the journal took the opportunity to proclaim its methodology: "rejecting every thing that was visionary, we determined to content ourselves with nothing else but facts, and to form our opinions upon their legitimate deductions. What then were these facts?" (24 January 1846). The *Police Gazette* did not deign to publish rumors or hearsay, so it said (29 November 1845); and the paper took the trouble to denounce occasional "false reports" circulating in other newspapers:

> OUTRAGEOUS FABRICATION.—The article going the rounds of the papers, headed 'Atrocious murder of a woman and two children'

16. The journal continued: "Through these various sources, and through the information which officers frequently gain from secret emissaries of police among criminals themselves, the authors have obtained in many cases even the dialogue which took place among certain rogues, while in the meditation of perpetration of particular crimes. These they have occasionally given to the reader to relieve the monotony of the details, as well as to show the peculiar bent of the character under development. Though, to some, these conversations may not appear to be consistent with the gravity of the central design, the majority of the intelligent will doubtless gain from them a more profound knowledge of human nature, and more pungent lessons of philosophy, than are to be found in the less characteristic portions of the mere narrative" (20 June 1846). For an example of a police officer as chief source, see *National Police Gazette,* 15 November 1845.

... is a pure fabrication from beginning to end. It was got up by George Washington Dixon, somewhat famous for bloody flights of the imagination.[17] (27 December 1845)

Rumors might be exposed by contrasting the supposedly polluted source with one purported to be more reliable. Reprinting an article from the Boston *Post,* a sketch of the life of the murder victim Mary Bickford, the *Police Gazette* echoed the charge that accounts published in other newspapers were "erroneous in point of fact." The "reliable source" who had prompted this conclusion was "Mr. Bickford himself," and he testified that the "paragraph, which is going the rounds of the papers, is untrue in every particular," and offered up his own, presumably more credible, version (6 December 1845).

Although the *Police Gazette* carefully exposed and corrected other newspapers when their accounts did not mesh with the *Police Gazette*'s own knowledge, news in any newspaper was more routinely classed as history, and hence other newspapers were cited regularly as sources of unimpeachable factual evidence (15 November 1845). The realities of the exchange system, which supplied a major portion of most newspapers' accounts, were probably crucial to this practice. Thus it was exceptional when, under the umbrella of this mutually derived and respected facticity, the *Police Gazette* contrasted its reports with those provided by other journals. News objectivity, developing as a convention embracing many newspapers, was gently clarified and enumerated in such innocuous interchanges as the following. After giving an account of a forgery committed by John Reed and Charley Webb, the *Police Gazette* observed:

It will be seen that the above statement conflicts with the testimony taken in the recent examination of Reed in London, which will be found on another page, as extracted from the London Times of October 10th, but we will be found to be correct. (1 November 1845)

Occasional refutations of accounts in other newspapers discharged the *Police Gazette*'s specific commitment to facticity. On the whole, however, newspapers implicitly accepted that objectivity was becoming a universal journalistic ideal and, therefore, they were more likely to borrow from each other than to challenge each other.[18]

17. For other instances see *National Police Gazette,* 1 November 1845; 8 November 1845.
18. It might be said that, within news organizations, this mutual and evolving regard for procedurally stable facticity might now animate journalistic professionalism; for, unlike political party battles, objectivity permitted horizontal movement from one journal to another to the

What was the substance of this ideal? What was the concrete character of this language of fact? We may rephrase this as, Who vouchsafes and defines the facts around which news reports were based? What was the character of reputable sources, and what was thought to be authentic evidence, in the *Police Gazette*'s presentation?

Attesting the accuracy and authenticity of information was, first, the criminal himself. Usually his account was in the form of a confession, made to a clergyman shortly before his execution (28 March 1846). De facto censorship by authorities doubtless exacted a toll in this case. Thus, in a final confession the felon might be said to have "disregarded a sincere ingenuousness in the relation of some of his exploits"; nonetheless, such an account was accorded "altogether a tolerably truthful guise . . . deserving of the superior attention we have paid to it over the other communications which have been sent to us on the same subject" (11 July 1846). As an expert in the field, the *Police Gazette* was qualified to make such judgments.

Especially atrocious events, however, might be omitted from confessions. When Murrell mechanically murders a man for his horse, without even allowing him a moment's prayer, a *Police Gazette* footnote was appended to ensure belief in this heinous crime. "Murrell did not make these cold and daring confessions after his captivity, but related them to a supposed accomplice, who had joined the clan for the purpose of delivering him up to justice" (21 November 1846). The words of the criminal, then, could be used if handled with appropriate care, and clergymen and agents of justice frequently assumed the necessary intermediary role.

Even under these conditions, the *Police Gazette* found it expedient to interpose a disclaimer if the criminal's testimony assumed fantastic or supernatural qualities. After committing a robbery, Joseph Hare has a terrifying vision of a "pure white horse," which, although an "apparition," successfully blocks his path—causing him to be arrested. Hare explicitly informs the reader that, although he has been told that "these things were mere chimeras of a feverish brain . . . I know better, for I subsequently experienced similar forewarnings and forerunners of misfortune . . .*" The *Police Gazette* countered this superstitious interpretation with the designated footnote:

---

extent that it derived from common, practical ethics. Also, it should be added that the realities of the newspaper business and, particularly, general dependence on the exchange of news through the mails materially reinforced the journalistic commitment to cooperation.

*The above incident is in Hare's own language almost word for word. It was related by him within a few hours of his death, and, therefore, though extravagant in the extreme, it is interesting as an evidence of the strange vagaries which can gain a foothold in an otherwise substantial mind. (17 July 1847)

Under the strain of approaching death, the *Police Gazette* argued, Hare's testimony could not be disdained: "we are obliged, while we withhold from it our belief, at least to credit the absolute sincerity of the relator" (24 July 1847). Authenticated information might be disbelieved, but if it commanded the belief of the criminal, it was, nevertheless, worth the attention of a more substantial and authoritative rationality.

The authenticity of information could also be substantiated by an appeal to recognized authorities. When the *Police Gazette* printed an indictment against Charles Hilson for burglary, it added the official seal of certification of the New York Clerk of the Court of General Sessions

> that the annexed is a copy of an indictment now on file, in my office, and that the same has been compared by me with the original, and is a correct transcript therefrom, and of the whole of such original. (8 August 1846)

A letter written by a felon to obtain illicit evidence for his defense was accorded a similar notarization by the Circuit Court Clerk, who had marked it as evidence in the case (30 January 1847).[19] During a murder trial, the *Police Gazette* published passionate correspondence between a man and his lover as evidence of their illicit union; the accompanying comment was a blunt admission that "the letters are genuine, having been proved, on trial, to be in the handwriting of the parties named" (24 October 1846). The credibility of evidence, therefore, was most often established by agents of the state.

The officials' occupational and institutional access to the world of crime and punishment made them and their testimony invaluable for the construction of objective news accounts. The *Police Gazette* commonly emphasized its reliance on such sources. In compiling the life of the rogue Henry Thomas, for example, the *Police Gazette* acknowledged its debts to the recorder of Thomas's confession, to the prosecuting attorney at whose hands Thomas had been convicted, and to a police officer "for an account of the arrest and for other information relating to the criminal in question" (20 June 1846).

19. For other examples see *National Police Gazette,* 7 November 1846; 26 December 1846.

When the journal began to publish items from the London *Police Gazette,* the editors stated unequivocally that "the descriptions can be relied on as accurate. The London Police Gazette is publishing by the authority of the Government, and at Government expense," they explained (20 December 1845). When two counterfeiters were arrested in Iowa by High Sheriff John H. McKenny, the *Police Gazette* boasted that its eyewitness account was "received . . . from Sheriff McKenny himself" (20 December 1845). And in another affair the journal relied explicitly upon a Deputy United States Marshal, arguing, moreover, "that this circumstance is positively true we therefore cannot doubt" (20 December 1845). The inside accounts of police were even solicited by the *Police Gazette:*

> All officers whose names are mentioned, or whose exploits are referred
> to . . . will have a respectful attention paid to their suggestions, should
> they feel disposed to communicate to us upon the subject.[20] (21 February
> 1846)

The *Police Gazette*'s "reflection" of the world of crime, therefore, betrayed a well-marked reliance on standard, selected sources, and hence the hierarchical social relations that confounded the *Police Gazette*'s vision of an honest state dispensing equal justice paradoxically were incorporated into the newspaper itself. The journal attempted to make the best of this situation in a rare, but still tacit, confession that it did indeed exist:

> Acknowledgement should be made to those magistrates, officers, com-
> missioners of prisons and members of the bar, who contributed their
> personal information or their memoranda to this compilation; and it
> may here be necessary also to remark that the occasional developments
> of departmental and professional mysteries to be found in the work, are
> instigated by no motives of ill will but are given for the purpose of
> making the public familiar with the *modus operandi,* the aims and
> tendencies of a disputed system, that they may be enabled, at need, to
> make a practical application of the knowledge, to the present and future
> agitations of police reform. (20 June 1846)

In his important study of English crime reporters, Chibnall states that the history of crime reporting has been characterized by "an increasing reliance on one major institutional source—the Police" (1975:51). In the American

20. For other examples see *National Police Gazette,* 11 October 1845; 29 November 1845; 20 June 1846; 1 May 1847.

context, we find the *National Police Gazette* attempting to preserve an uneasy and never directly acknowledged balance. We shall find that the paper was critical, sometimes even stridently so, in its reporting of the mechanisms of law; on the other hand, to maintain its fundamental commitment to objectivity in the news, the *Police Gazette* found itself compelled to accept as authoritative and convincing the testimony of the specific persons who *were* the active, functioning agents of American law. Evidenced here was a longstanding journalistic predicament: the legitimacy of the American state was presumed at the same time as the particular corruptions of its officers were assailed.

The fundamental purpose of the journal was to assume the state's responsibility for defining the public good; the *Police Gazette,* therefore, made much of its own contribution to the discourse on evidence. The "intelligent citizens" who conduct the American newspaper press, stated the editors, "from the very nature of their vocation are obliged to read and weigh with care every tittle of the evidence" given in courts (11 April 1846). In particular, the *Police Gazette* was disturbed by the admission of imprecise or incompletely proven scientific evidence into the courts. Resentment surfaced, for instance, in the trial of Tirrell for the murder of Mary Bickford in April 1846. The suspect's defense rested on his purported state of somnambulism when committing the murder; and medical witnesses were called to testify to somnambulism's unpredictable and uncontrollable effects. Calling the jury that swallowed such "nonsense" "credulous" for its acquittal of Tirrell, the *Police Gazette* lashed out at this failure of justice:

> As long as the rules of common sense and justice are violated by the introduction to a case, in the shape of *evidence,* of all the vagaries and prejudices of professional visionaries, we shall have just such acquittals as that of the murderer of Maria Bickford. (4 April 1846)

The focus of the paper's grievance was "the impropriety of the introduction of medical evidence in relation to a disputed principle or science" (18 April 1846). Anything less than positive knowledge, in brief, should be held at arm's length by positive law. Herein there lurked, apparently, not only a pragmatic awareness that legal forms permitted extensive sleight-of-hand but also a mistrust of the medical science that so impressed the court: "Anything can be proved if you get witnesses enough, and we know of nothing that is attended with a greater effect before a jury than the scientific testimony of medical visionaries" (11 April 1846).

Again, when a fornication charge was brought by a woman who claimed to have given birth 313 days after the purported act to a healthy, normal child, medical witnesses testified that such a long gestation period was "rare and improbable . . . although some of them did not deem it impossible." The jury, remarked the *Police Gazette* in irony, "rejected the overwhelming common sense probabilities in favor of the defendant, and found him *guilty* on the learned Judge's scientific *possibility*" (13 June 1846). Once more, the democratic antiprofessionalism so common to the 1830s chafed at the "visionary" science of a suspect court. To be valid, scientific evidence had to be invariant and exact—that is, "scientific"—or common sense should serve. The *Police Gazette* held to direct knowledge as the litmus test and therefore grumbled over the criminal statistics for policy gambling offices—the numbers racket —included in the chief of police's annual report to the mayor:

> These statistics are very imperfect, as they include but little more than half the number of some of the offenders. The Mayor and Chief must compel the Captains and Policemen to do their full duty, as official statistics are calculated to mislead and deceive, unless strictly correct. There are nearer 1500 than 160 policy offices in this city. (12 June 1847)

Firsthand knowledge of the facts afforded more accurate assessment than that which emanated from a less than dutiful police force, but, as we have seen, the *Police Gazette* was accustomed to depending on police and other state officials for many of its facts. Such sporadic checkups as the one above, then, perhaps underlined the journal's distance from corrupt individuals in government, while also legitimating its routine dependence on state information.

If exact and direct correspondence to reality constituted an abstract test of evidence, the *National Police Gazette*'s way of passing this test with flying colors was indubitably concrete. The empirical standard that the *Police Gazette* both proposed and, apparently, met at once accentuated the journal's stewardship of public good and its participation in developing a "web of facticity": "The faithfulness of our report of the trial of Parkinson is fully evidenced by the fact that the counsel on both sides of the present case use our paper for reference in all disputed points of the testimony" (20 December 1845). In the face of consensus by mutually antagonistic parties, the paper preserved its commitment to equal justice and simultaneously cultivated an irrefutable objectivity. Lauding the "masterly accuracy" of its reports of the trial of the abortionists Costello and Mason, the *Police Gazette* pointed happily to the fact that these accounts "were used successively by all the counsel in preference to their own notes" (21 February 1846). The same standard apparently sufficed to allay the anxieties of at least one other paper, the *Christian Advocate*, which called the *Police Gazette*'s report of one trial "the best account of the whole affair. . . . The report is authenticated by the counsel on both sides, and by the Court itself" (*Police Gazette,* 27 February 1847). Similarly, the *Police Gazette* boasted that another of its trial reports had been "endorsed and certified by the presiding Judges of the Courts, by the District Attorney, and by all the counsel employed in the case" (13 February 1847). By inducing recognized state authority to validate its coverage (cf. Tuchman 1978b:110), the *Police Gazette* asserted and celebrated its successful penetration of institutional life. Here was a measure of objectivity that seemingly resisted charges of bias from other, opposed interests.

Through claims to a universally appreciable facticity, the *National Police Gazette* first demonstrated its concern for objectivity. Objectivity took the form of a broad convention according to which information was presented as a democratically accessible, value-free entity. To prove the truth of this convention, routine attempts were made to tell the reader periodically what he was looking at, how reliable it was, how it had been obtained. The origins of information were made to appear as direct and clear-cut as possible; if readers could not inspect the facts themselves, they might know the sources of information that supplied these facts. By means of situated language, the *Police Gazette* brought the reader closer to a purported criminal world, utilizing its specialized, privileged status as a professional eyewitness to confirm the objectivity of its accounts. Finally, though, in emphasizing the reliability of its news, the *Police Gazette* found it necessary to invoke concrete —normally implicit—evidentiary standards. Because the most trusted sources were those with a special or legitimate access to criminal affairs, it was convenient for the journal to turn to criminals and, more important, to officers of the state, for authoritative pronouncements on its veracity. Those with access to the facts, as institutionally defined, thus became those with power to appraise and validate them. The papers developed a system for verifying the contents of their news reports, which depended crucially on certified information sources, on state agencies (Hall et al. 1978:57–60), and, finally, on the threshold of proof authorized by the social hierarchy itself. This development was vital because it implied that commercial journalism's periodic account of reality would systemically echo the judgments and perspectives of the power elite.

Objectivity developed together with the commercial press's enveloping, transcendent defense of natural rights. In the following chapters I investigate this defense in greater detail by analyzing the *National Police Gazette*. The latter brought to a new height the penny papers' use of exposure and crime news to dramatize their independent and impartial pursuit of public good. The *Police Gazette*'s continuous attempt to shore up a sacrosanct state sphere thus may illuminate the social status and cultural form of the commercial press as a social institution of a new kind.

5

Defending Public Good:
The Critique of State Corruption
in the *National Police Gazette* 1845–1850

Penny editors of the 1830s saw themselves in a new role—that of "social reformers and defenders of the rights of common men" (Gordon 1977:43). Investigative exposure, especially in conjunction with crime news, was the basis for this defense. In this chapter I begin a systematic appraisal of exposure in the young commercial press through an analysis of its development in the *National Police Gazette.*

Some may object that the *Police Gazette* is not a fair index of tendencies in mainstream commercial journalism, but this, I think, is not the case: the *Police Gazette* merely raised the tactic of exposure of civil and criminal corruption to a new level of prominence. In common with the commercial press generally, the *Police Gazette* invoked objectivity, as we have seen; also common to the commercial press was the attempt to appropriate journalism's new institutional role as the enlightened protector of natural rights. Where the *Police Gazette* became distinctive was in its vigorous, sometimes searing, exposures of violations of public good and in its consistent attempt to link legal abuses to emergent class divisions in society. Even in its radicalism, however, the *Police Gazette* shared with the penny papers a fundamental belief in the analytic and moral primacy of natural rights. Examination of the *Police Gazette,* therefore, may tell us a good deal about the paradigmatic limits of commercial journalism in its early years.

The Self-Consciousness of the National Police Gazette

The *Police Gazette* punctuated its weekly accounts with comments that express a self-conscious sense of its journalistic endeavor. In the view of its proprietors, the *Police Gazette* was part of a long historical process by which the absolute monarchy of earlier centuries was gradually divested of power. Crucial to this process was the stripping away of the king's right to exclusive legitimation of acts of state, a right manifested in a variety of controls— licensing, taxes, outright suppression—over the press (Siebert 1952). In the struggle for "freedom of the press," the newspaper and its precursors and descendants seized the institutional capacity to define the context in which actions of the state might occur.[1] This development arced across the Atlantic to the colonies and thence to republican America.

The *Police Gazette* cited the New York *Sunday Mercury* approvingly in elaborating the tradition it thus claimed to extend:

> Within every other legal sanctuary which the wisdom of our English ancestry has handed down, the bosom of reform has obtained at some period or other, an entering wedge, and, once there, the press as the representative—the fourth Estate, as it is termed in England—of the people has boldly claimed its rights, and had its claims allowed. The star chamber first, the court of chancery next, and finally the houses of parliament—have had to succumb to the press. (24 July 1847)

Journalistic exposure of unequal justice in the state and of the emasculation of public good in society did indeed extend the power of the press. The rationale for exposure offered by the *Police Gazette* was that enfeebled and corrupt state officials were rapidly corroding the republic constituted as the United States. Because the state was derelict in superintending the public good, the commercial press would assume this vital and substantive function. Far too many social abuses were "beyond the reach of palsied authority"; unscrupulous pursuit of private interest infused the state with corruption; and, symptomatic of this malaise, criminals were able to "laugh at and despise the powers of the law." In such circumstances, rogues would dread only "the penetrating search and untiring pursuit of the press. From this they must not be suffered to escape, whatever other punishment they may evade." Exposure was, literally, "the only means of redress which society has left" (16 October 1845). In contrast to the government, the newspaper would speak

---

1. This is why the party system and the newspaper press were so intricately intertwined and why, also, the party press was so bitterly disliked by those who were largely removed from its interests.

for "society" as a whole. If criminals did not fear the arm of the law, argued the *Police Gazette,* "we will make them feel the searching, withering, blasting force of public condemnation" (15 November 1845).

More particularly, the *Police Gazette* stated in its prospectus that it would be devoted "to the interests of criminal police":

> The necessity of such an instrument to assist the operations of the department, and to perform that species of service which does not lie within the scope of the present system, will make itself apparent at a glance. (16 October 1845)

The *Police Gazette* was conceived of as an alternative agency for the protection of a concrete public good. The nation was swarming with thieves, burglars, pickpockets, and swindlers, of whose character the community was perilously ignorant. "Until a system be adopted which will effectually hold [them] up to public shame and irrevocable exposure, the public will still remain at the mercy of [their] depredations" (ibid.).

Plan after plan to reform the crime problem had been devised, claimed the editors; yet instead of resulting in the adoption of "new, bold, and original measures," they had resulted merely in the remodeling of the police department (in 1845). "The press—the mightiest conservator of social welfare—has been left from the category of appliances, while every other branch of civil polity feels the force of its protective surveillance" (ibid.).

Whereas in the nations of continental Europe "gigantic and penetrating systems of police, the regulation of passports, and the continual surveillance of a numerous and energetic *gens d'armes*" made journalistic exposure gratuitous, in England "a more liberal system of civil regulation rejects such checks upon the freedom of the subject." There, the government found it "politic, nay necessary . . . to maintain an organ of their own" with "extensively beneficial influences" throughout the realm. Following the English model the *Police Gazette* would function as "an untiring and ubiquitous minister of public justice," exposing rogues to the public gaze "until they become powerless from the notoriety of their debasement" (ibid.).

Exposure was equally formidable when it reached directly into the arena of state power. Wilkes and Camp fumed, "it is of little use for public journalists to expose the fraud, corruption and infamy of public officers, without the addition of political power to make the exposition felt." Therefore, the *Police Gazette* now would "closely canvas" candidates for public office, regardless of party affiliation. The *Police Gazette* simply would not tolerate "cunning, scheming politicians" pursuing "their private ends." The time had gone by, the journal assured its readers, "when a knot of mutton-heads can secure, by nomination, the election of a clique candidate and then govern him to answer their private ends, regardless of public good" (7 August 1847).[2] Thus, admitted the *Police Gazette*, "we have been compelled, at various times, to point out the evils existing in the administration of justice by persons selected as public agents." Yet, "wherever public duty has prompted such exposition, our motives have been impugned by the parties arraigned in order to hide their violations of the trust reposed in them." Indeed, said the journal, "our most bitter opponents—not even excepting thieves—have been those connected with the administration of the laws" (24 January 1846).

Exposure was a forceful, institutional expropriation, and it was resented by those on whom it encroached. In turn, the *Police Gazette* had no illusions about the source of its power—publicity. When some members of the bar organized "a regular warfare against the press, for its interference with their interests, and for its exposure of their peculiar hocus pocus in juggling knaves through the meshes of the law," the *Police Gazette* advised the bar to desist:

> It is especially foolish to attempt to wage the warfare by splutterings in a court room. The whole effect of their idle diatribes are [*sic*] confined to the few hearers within the circle of a wooden railing, while the influence of the power they attack, is "as broad and general as the casing air," and speaks in every car. (10 January 1846)

Unlike its English namesake, the *National Police Gazette* was a privately owned, commercial undertaking. It was therefore patently untrue that its sole motive, as its editors boasted, was "the protection of the public against public wrongs" (21 November 1846).[3] Nonetheless, the *Police Gazette* successfully

---

2. This rhetoric of private interest versus public good found a lasting place in commercial journalism and, thus, transcends the idiosyncratic character of the *Police Gazette*. When, in 1902, Joseph Pulitzer drafted a confidential memorandum in which he set down his thoughts on establishing a school of journalism at Columbia University, he argued that "to differentiate between Journalism as an intellectual profession and as a business must be a fundamental object" (in Baker 1954:23). "My point of view," stated Pulitzer definitively, "is that a great newspaper must be a public institution for the public good, although incidentally and inevitably it cannot help also being a business" (ibid.:23–24). This viewpoint echoed James Gordon Bennett's: "I have entered on a course of private enterprise, but also of public usefulness" (*Herald*, 2 March 1836).

3. The mechanism through which the *Police Gazette* claimed to have attained such utility is of interest: "every man who reads is made an officer, and every suspicious character is made the object of universal scrutiny" (1 November 1845). In other variants: "we place the whole country at once upon the watch, and convert every reader of the circumstance into the character of a police officer" (13 December 1845); the *Police Gazette* "has made voluntary policemen of a great

equated mass circulation with its license to speak in the name of the people. The journal expressed this in a remarkable analogy:

> It is as much at violence with the whole theory of the law and institutions of this country to exclude the Press which represents The People, from a court-room, as it would be in a monarchy to exclude the king, from Courts which are held in the king's name. (24 April 1847)

In support of its appropriation of vox populi, the *Police Gazette* made efficacious use of a dramatic technique. When the mayor of Pittsburgh refused to allow the press into court to cover a trial, for example, the *Police Gazette* lashed out: "If the Press of Pittsburgh submit to his Imperial edicts, they are *not* an 'Independent Press,' and are untrue to the great social interest of which they should be the guardians" (24 April 1847). Again, when Enoch Camp was held in contempt of court for his unfriendly questions concerning a judge's lenient bail of a suspect, he filed a civil suit against the judge for false imprisonment, which could then be publicized in the *Police Gazette* (17 January 1846). There was "no principle more incontrovertible than that The People have a right to hear and to know all that is done in their name"; therefore, no judge had the right to prescribe a rule "which makes a distinction between that portion of the community in actual attendance on their court, and those outside" (27 June 1846). Both the inevitable selectivity exercised in presenting to the public events "done in their name" and the role of the commercial press in making such selective publication serve the purpose of private profit were thereby obscured.

As we shall see in more detail below, exposure both drew on and cultivated a powerful reformist impulse. The libel law—to choose an instance of immediate consequence for journalists—placed an evident limit on the power of the newspaper. Wilkes himself had earlier stated with regard to judges and legislators: "As public men, they naturally dread a power which can hold their conduct to the light, and therefore feel concerned in the maintenance of a rule which protects them when wrong from public exposure and execration. Such is the libel law; such its origin and such the influences which sustain it" (1844:2). When quoting the *Journal of Commerce,* the *Police Gazette* drew on its position as protector of the public good in protesting the law of libel:

---

portion of our country population, who, with our paper in one hand and a stout stick in the other, scrutinize every stranger who comes within their limits" (21 February 1846).

The public are suffering severely for their severity toward the newspapers on the subject of libels. There are a multitude of frauds which the newspapers would readily expose were it not for the apprehension of illiberal verdicts. Many of them are proper subjects for newspaper animadversion; yet such is the tenderness of public sentiment toward the personal rights of notorious villains, that the newspapers do not deem it safe to guard the people against them. The editors may all know that some sign hung out in Broadway is only a decoy to robbery, yet the only way is, to be quiet, and let the people be robbed until they learn to protect, more liberally, those who would protect themselves. (3 October 1846)

Here and throughout, the *Police Gazette* banished any distinction between the people and the press, their most loyal representative, and utilized this raucously announced alliance to cultivate its status as a powerful social institution. Let us turn now to the record, to the substantive and concrete exposures of state corruption that constituted the *Police Gazette*'s protection of the public good.

The Critique of State Corruption

The most crucial duty of the state, in the *National Police Gazette*'s view, was the defense of public good—of individual rights to life, liberty, and property, for all citizens. These were *natural* rights, prior to and transcendent of any political obligation owed to the state. The obligation to the state took the form of a contract by which the citizen submitted to legal limits placed on the conduct of commercial and social life in return for the *"protection* which government affords us and our property," as Wilkes put it (1844:23). The voluntary nature of this compact was emphasized by a *Police Gazette* correspondent calling himself "Justice":

The object of law in civilized communities, is the protection of the honest from the arts of the designing, and the weak from the wrongful force of the strong. For this reason certain general rules are adopted by the great body of the people, and Courts are established for their enforcement. (17 January 1846)

As is implicit in this citation, one basic criterion permitted an appraisal of the state's efforts to defend public good: adherence to "impartial" or "equal justice." In a pamphlet, George Wilkes succinctly defined this standard. A rule or law, he wrote, is "oppressive and unjust, because its operation and result are unequal." The example Wilkes chose to illustrate his point is significant: "The rich offender pays his fine at once, turns on his heel as gay as a lark, and goes scott free of any real punishment; while poverty, terrible poverty, is made a crime, and its unfortunate victim is thrust into a prospectless confinement" (1844:31).

Unequal justice arose as a discretionary response by the state to property right; in turn, this connived at political entrenchment of nascent social class divisions. "Discretionary" or "arbitrary" or "partisan" practices were identified as the key sources of legal corruption by the *Police Gazette* because they lent themselves to the installment of permanent political inequalities. In organizing class difference into a dangerous encroachment on political rights, the state's discretionary exercise of power became "a treachery to the community, which goes very far to annul all obligations to obedience" (17 January 1846). In contrast, equal justice meant, for all citizens, *both* equal rights *and* equal access to the legal machinery of the state, which systematically defined the character of social relationships bearing on those rights. It was evident to the *Police Gazette,* as it had been to mechanics and artisans in the 1830s, that without this dual focus the tyranny of a corrupted state might exact a fearsome price.[4]

Equal justice was thus asymmetrical; natural rights were presumed to be respected until otherwise proven. The basis of the state itself, therefore, was never directly challenged, for a functioning republic was axiomatic to the *Police Gazette*'s endeavor. At most, the state's discretionary responsiveness to property might be publicly exposed and protested.[5] "The law is always more tender to property than to human life," admitted the editors in an unusual generalization (6 March 1847). If the state tended to defer to property right per se rather than to any prior concept of substantive justice, the *Police*

4. The *Police Gazette* granted a *natural* right to eat to two starving English children who had been imprisoned for stealing and eating six "small diseased turnips" (6 March 1847), and insinuated that it was the state's obligation to defend this substantive right. The journal disapproved of this "false system, which regards the rights of property as superior to the rights of nature. The property contained in those refuse turnips was considered as entitled to more consideration at the hand of the law, than the natural right which had been given these starving children by the Almighty God—the right to eat rather than die" (ibid.). The "false system," though, pertained to England—not to the United States. Moreover, it was precisely in the growing disjuncture between natural rights and property rights alone that the commercial newspaper sought and found its institutional impetus.
5. Even this, as we shall see in the following chapter, was not entirely unalloyed, for the *Police Gazette*'s portrayal of crime tended to support the state's.

Gazette attributed this mainly to derelict or corrupt officials and administrators rather than to the state as a social institution. Even so, things had to change.

Because revolution was unthinkable, massive reform was unavoidable, and reform would be engendered in and orchestrated by the *Police Gazette* itself. By exposing corruption and the arbitrary exercise of power, the journal would monitor and defend the substantive criterion of equal justice by which public good was gauged. The *Police Gazette*'s defense of "equal justice" was achieved, in the first instance, through repeated but concrete exposures of the legal system's subservience to property and private design.[6]

From initial arrest through trial, conviction, and incarceration, the system of criminal law, like the police department that formed one part of it, was "open to personal intervention and manipulation at every stage" (Richardson 1970:284). The *National Police Gazette* viewed this built-in discretionary capacity for "compromise" as a heinous violation of equal justice, and one which, further, both responded to and helped to solidify emergent social class divisions. "We are opposed to all descriptions of compromise," stated the editors. "We insist that this whole doctrine of compromise is wrong throughout." The "infamous custom of allowing a thief to buy out the law with a portion of the proceeds of the crime which outraged it" presented an illustration of this doctrine (27 December 1845).[7] The *Police Gazette* grounded its argument against compromise in "the spirit and genius of the law":

> The offence which a robber perpetrates when he despoils a victim, is committed upon the whole "people." In the eye of the criminal law, the pecuniary sufferer has endured no special wrong—is entitled to no special revenge—nor can he demand a particular redress; and the prosecuting officer who sacrifices the public interests of the whole community to the private interests of a single individual, no matter how hard the case may be, violates his oath and betrays the important trusts which have been confided to his care. (Ibid.)

Though never voiced in such overarching terms, the state, in this view, was a matrix of potentially corrupt institutions and practices, and its faithless

---

6. In the next chapter I shall have occasion to assess the journal's exposures of criminal infringements of natural rights in society. Surveillance of both state and society was essential to the commercial newspaper's transcendent defense of a unitary public good.

7. The *Police Gazette* went on: "and we present in the concluding chapter of the lives of the Webbs, and in the life of Geo. Howell, the pickpocket, in this day's paper, additional examples of its dangerous and demoralising effects" (27 December 1845). Here one can glimpse the mesh between what we now call news and editorials.

exercise of arbitrary power was manifested in the police force, grand juries, executive pardons, and throughout the criminal justice system as a whole. Through exposure of the facts of corruption, exposure heavily reliant on the conventions of objectivity in news discussed above, the *National Police Gazette* cultivated a position as a commercial protector of natural rights.

The *Police Gazette,* for example, gave continuing attention to the activities of the New York Police. The journal flagged all evidence of a spirit of partisanship or private interest within the force. General mockery of the police was accompanied by increasingly caustic analysis and exposure of the department's functioning and internal structure.[8] When William V. Brady became mayor in 1847, the *Police Gazette* anxiously warned that the recently constituted Municipal Police would face the vagaries of the spoils system, as the mayor "will have much to contend with to satisfy the demands of his friends." Urging Mayor Brady to "be governed by his well known liberality of principle and regard for justice," the *Police Gazette* charged that his actions in respect of the police "will mark precedent for his successor" (17 April 1847).

A month later the journal found growing cause for alarm in the tendency of the new police "to centralize itself into a dangerous political organization" —a tendency which, if not checked immediately, "will become its greatest aim and render the department a civil despotism, perfectly odious to every citizen whose suffrage is not hampered with the spoils of office." Codification of functions and duties was urgently needed to correct police partisanship; "clearly defined and stringent departmental regulations" could free officers to act "separately and independently," in keeping with their major responsibility to "The People." In contrast, if the police continued to be "at the mercy of Aldermen and Assistants," they would "wheel into every political campaign as the banded cohorts of those on whose favor they will have to depend" (15 May 1847).

Criticism of the police apparently stopped short of Police Chief George Washington Matsell, who was praised as the "efficient director" of "the excellent system" of policing the city (4 July 1846). Yet headlines such as "POLICE FAVORITISM" (14 November 1846), "PETTY TYRANNY" (12

8. An example: "GUM ELASTIC POLICE.—We understand that this title has been substituted for that of the 'Star Police,' as applied to the new municipal force. Whether it arises from the fact of their having adopted India rubber coats and shoes as their winter uniform, or from the supposed elasticity of their consciences, we are not able to say" (6 December 1845). In an earlier issue the journal had applauded enthusiastically a report entitled "Chinese Ideas on Police," which centered on how a stolen watch had been recovered in China by jailing 200 *police* (8 November 1845).

December 1846), and "CAPTAINS OF POLICE" (26 December 1846) hinted that the force's injustice and inefficiency were linked to its hierarchical order. Members of the "old police," or "watch," who had been retained in the departmental reorganization of 1845, still occupied "the best positions" in the force, said the *Police Gazette*. To make matters worse, the old police were indolent, corrupt, and unwilling to work at their duty (16 January 1847). It was the *Police Gazette*'s striking observation that such "difference in station is only instituted for the proper methodization of the department, not for the purpose of making distinctions of worth, or right, or privilege" (5 September 1846). Public good was not to be subject to the internal imperatives of hierarchical, government bureaucracy, for public good was the common property of all citizens.

The complaints of policemen that their long workday interfered with effective action found strong support in the *Police Gazette*. The split-shift workdays, reportedly of sixteen or even eighteen hours a day, demanded "a prompt reform," because such a system furnished "an example and a warrant for the private taskmaster to wring the sinews of his laborers to immeasurable toil." Public good included government-initiated economic reform, and hence the editors also focused on this aspect of inequality: "The People do not understand the Economy that is only obtained by the oppression of the poor," the journal generalized.

> They are willing to give the laborer his hire, and in their adoption of the present police system, never contemplated the recognition of a principle which belongs to the dark ages, and to the tyranny of wealth and power. If a mechanic should work but twelve hours a day, a policeman or other public servant should work no more. If a private employer can make his interest concede to this rule, The People, as public employers, can afford to do the same. Nay, it is incumbent on the latter to set the humane example which shall protect labor from encroachment and oppression. (22 August 1846)

In short, "no mere notion of *Economy* should operate to the subversion of a great principle" (29 August 1846). The *Police Gazette* would support members of the police who agitated for shorter hours, and the journal told such men not to be deterred "by the apprehension of giving offence by these movements to those who exercise a control over them" (5 September 1846). All policemen were alike servants of public good.

Rampant economic self-interest within the force, however, was seen to sustain favoritism and partisanship. The old police especially were a target for bitter remonstrance. Many of the old police, the journal charged, "have been heard to declare that they would never bring in a thief, or point one out to a young officer, unless they could make something of it" (27 February 1847). The *Police Gazette* unsuccessfully tried to differentiate the old from the new police, claiming that under the new system it was in the interest of the policeman "to arrest old rogues and bring them in, for that gains them credit and keeps the rogues from troubling them in future" (29 August 1846). Yet the distinction between old and new occasionally collapsed. Both internal structure and efficiency in arresting crime were corrupted by monetary rewards to police. Such rewards sapped the force's independence and determined its organizational structure as officers competed for the most remunerative positions.

This system of "fraud, duplicity, secret compromise, and secret villainy, which is increasing with a stealthy and vicious thrift," exclaimed the *Police Gazette,* "threatens to exceed in evil consequences the worst practices of the old regime." The law permitted rewards to policemen from citizens for services rendered, contingent on the mayor's explicit assent, but this error in theory "stands natural sponsor to the present evils in practice":

> The pernicious principle which makes mere avaricious speculators of servants of the law should be abolished entirely, and the receipt by an officer of a single farthing beyond his stipulated salary made a penal offence. (24 June 1847)

Unless and until such a rule was established, wrote Camp and Wilkes, bribery, corruption, and "secret compromise, will infuse themselves through all the avenues of the system" (ibid.).

In the absence of such a law, the *Police Gazette* would direct its own energies at effecting a partial solution by exposing illicit payments to the police and by keeping a close eye on the operations of the force. Thus, the journal would utilize objective reports of police corruption to validate its own social role. The *Police Gazette,* for example, commented ironically that "the Tombs and the Chief's office are the whitebread and chickenfixens of the police service," and bitingly attacked disparities between old and new police:

> A citizen possessed of a foolish notion for *equality* in all public systems, might condemn this distinction between the old drones and the new workers in the common hive, as invidious and unjust, but as the positions and the profits of the snug stations seem to give full satisfaction to those who hold them in possession, such objections will probably be

condemned as the petulant opposition of some splenetic jacobin. (19 June 1847)

The *Police Gazette* asked citizens to notify the editors of rewards paid to policemen that did not appear in the weekly list it published, for these were illegal, being unapproved by the mayor. The journal even offered a reward of fifty dollars for legal testimony showing the receipt of unauthorized money or gifts by policemen (28 August 1847); and the editors then claimed to have sponsored "several interviews with persons who have been wronged, and we might almost add, robbed" by corrupt police (4 September 1847).

The journal's exposures only intimated the approach of an impending reform, whereby police corruption would be crushed by "the fatal grindstone of public condemnation" with the *Police Gazette* itself "at the handle" (15 November 1845). Similarly, this "death struggle between corruption and reform" was centered on the *Police Gazette*'s exposures of police abuse (29 August 1846). Information and hints to police on specific problems were common: "WHEREABOUTS OF THIEVES.—NEWS FOR POLICE OFFICERS" was the peremptory heading for such disclosures (10 January 1846).[9] An exemplary instance occurred when the *Police Gazette* advised Chief of Police Matsell to station some men in Broadway, "from the corner of Courtlandt street to Park place," because of the recent clustering of pickpockets around the area, lying in wait "to 'wing' every stranger that comes along" (20 June 1846). Here, the *Police Gazette*'s inside knowledge operated as a weapon in defense of the journal's own institutional role. In the same way, the editors used objective news accounts to attack police corruption:

> [Confessed thief Billy Cox] stated in bravado, that he knew there were several warrants "out agin" him, "but Thank God," added he, hauling out a handful of bills, "thank God I've got stuff enough to buy off all the police officers that can come to take me."
> We sincerely hope his case will be attended to; and attended to, moreover, by an officer who will act in the matter as the agent of the law, and not the servant of the thief.[10] (8 November 1845)

9. For other examples see *National Police Gazette,* 31 January 1846; 20 December 1845; 21 November 1846. The *Police Gazette* apparently organized its own independent police force, which would have interacted symbiotically with the journal's need for "inside information." Constituting an independent police force was in keeping with the journal's major intention of autonomously protecting public good, but to what extent it abused this position through "compromise" cannot be surmised. Such a force would certainly also have increased friction between the *Police Gazette* and the New York City Police. For comment on the *Police Gazette*'s police, see 18 October 1845; 1 November 1845; 13 December 1845; 26 July 1846; 15 August 1846.

10. For other examples, see *National Police Gazette,* 8 November 1845; 6 December 1845.

Vigilant oversight of police activities was a key aspect of the journal's role. For, in these and other ways, the *Police Gazette,* deftly created for itself a central position as "a new social institution" (Williams 1974:22).

The practice of executive pardons for criminals furnished another opportunity for exposure of the facts. Executive control of the pardon gave rise to evils that, in the *Police Gazette*'s estimation, had "become perfectly unbearable":

> No sooner does an old professional thief receive his sentence, than a movement is set on foot at once, by his outside accomplices, to obtain his pardon. Police officers are employed to intercede and make affidavits in his favor. . . . Nineteen-twentieths of the pardons that are made from the different prisons of the Northern States are granted in the cases of professional English and other thieves, and their interceders are in all cases Police officers, who have been paid for the disgraceful and dishonest service. (22 November 1845)

Particularly noxious were "conditional pardons," according to which the criminal, in return for his freedom, promised to banish himself from the state, or to hand back the undiscovered spoils of his last depredation. Such an "infamous system of compromise and pardon running through all the operations of the law" gave good reason for thieves to "stick by their trade, and rely upon the proceeds of their offences to buy their offences a license" (3 January 1846). Corruption in the state intersected with crime in society; conditional pardons did not befit "our republican system" (4 July 1846).

A report entitled "The Pardoning Power" gave a detailed, ideological outline of the position that determined *Police Gazette*'s exposures of unjust executive clemency. The justification for this article was that "in a Government professing to be equal in its distributions of the law to all, it is the peculiar privilege of the citizen to require a reason for every rule or restriction of which he is made the subject." The abuses to which the pardoning power evidently lent itself thus made it "our special duty to learn how and for what purpose the regulation originally obtained." What, then, were the facts? The history of the prerogative followed:

> The pardoning power is one of the imperative and arbitrary prerogatives of the English kings, and was adopted bodily into the system of our governmental economy with the mass of arbitrary statutes that fell upon us as an unfortunate inheritance from our English ancestors. (22 November 1845)

In England, under a monarchy, the pardon made logical sense: " 'All offences,' says Blackstone, 'are either against the king's peace or his crown and dignity. He is therefore, the proper person to prosecute for all public offences and breaches of the peace, being the person injured in the eyes of the law.' " The pardoning power was fitting in that " 'he only who is injured should have the power of forgiving' " (ibid.). In other words, as the journal later pronounced, "where all offences are committed against the King's peace and dignity, it is consistent with the theory to allow the supreme authority the privilege of pardoning offences against himself." On the other hand, the pardon "has no more business in a democratic scheme of government than the sceptre and the crown" (24 January 1846). Here, said the journal,

> the people are sovereign, and acting upon that there is no more reason that a President or a Governor should be clothed with this monarchial attribute, than that they should be invested with judicial functions in the first degree. (22 November 1845)

The facts of history and of current practice revealed that the executive pardon "is in derogation of the rights of the People, it is in violation of the spirit of our institutions, and it is demoralizing in influence and dangerous in practice" (24 January 1846). The pardoning power ought to be vested in the legislature—"the special representative and mouthpiece of the wishes of the PEOPLE"—argued the *Police Gazette,* because the legislature was less easily deceived, intimidated, or corrupted than the executive. Such a transfer would have the salutary effect of "debarring wealthy felons from purchasing out the law with a portion of the proceeds of their crimes" (22 November 1845).

But, in the interim period before this reform might be effected, the *Police Gazette* would expose abuses of the prerogative, endeavoring to demonstrate for readers the true "character" of pardons: "for the publicity of these transactions will be found the most effectual method of counteracting similar attempts in future" (22 November 1845). The *Police Gazette* therefore published statistics, purportedly from the secretary of state of New York, showing that whereas in 1840 Governor Şeward had pardoned 55 miscreants, in 1845 Governor Wright employed the pardon no fewer than 95 times (23 May 1846). Routine exposures of attempts to obtain pardons, some successful, others failures, also were printed. Characteristically, the journal would inform readers, for example, that "a movement is on foot to obtain a pardon for McQuade, the notorious receiver of stolen goods who was convicted last week." Because its special access to the facts permitted an informed judgment, it then would make its recommendation: "it is to be hoped that Governor Young will not suffer himself to be deceived by interested emissaries" (20 February 1847).[11]

The criminal justice system was similarly attacked and exposed. Within the courtroom, corrupt and ignorant judges compounded felonies by compromising with felons by lightening sentences in proportion to the amount of stolen property returned (27 December 1845).[12] Once more, property bought legal standing in disregard of substantive measures for public good:

> JACK GIBSON, the wealthy pickpocket of Philadelphia, has been granted a new trial by Judge Parsons of that city, and the same *justice* that produced that shameful result, will acquit him of the charge preferred against him. Let him pass—his money and industry entitles him to favor from Philadelphia officials. (24 January 1846)

The rules governing magistrates in setting and receiving bail also demanded reform in order "to place innocent poverty . . . on as fair a platform as guilty riches." As it was then administered, the bailing system afforded immunity to men of wealth: "Under the same rule the Devil himself would be discharged from custody if Mammon would 'go his bail,' while the angel Gabriel would be sent to the Tombs for want of wealthy friends." The *Police Gazette* recommended that, instead, "moderate, but good, surety" be demanded of all; and, in the case of "notorious offenders," that bail not be given without "full evidence" that it would be paid if forfeited (31 July 1847).[13] By the same token, the increasingly obtuse form of legal proceedings (in "open variance with the rules of common sense") called for immediate legislative action (7 November 1846). The courts, it was said, were "cramped by ridiculous technical restrictions," showing "the extreme necessity of a legal reform" (29 November 1845). Only a simplified system of practice, capable of protecting

11. For other examples of exposure of pardon abuses, see *National Police Gazette,* 25 October 1845; 1 November 1845; 15 November 1845; 10 January 1846; 28 March 1846; 27 June 1846; 23 January 1847. On several occasions the *Police Gazette* itself requested a pardon for an unjustly convicted criminal. The only suitable argument in this regard was, typically, the revelation of new and convincing facts capable of changing "the whole character of the testimony presented against him on the trial" and in the unique possession of the *Police Gazette* (15 November 1845). For other examples, see the issues of 14 February 1846 and 28 March 1846.
12. For other examples of judicial corruption, see *National Police Gazette,* 27 December 1845; 24 January 1846; 31 January 1846; 11 July 1846.
13. For other exposures of corrupt bailing practices, see *National Police Gazette,* 29 November 1845; 28 March 1846.

the rights of the commonwealth, would "also lend its service to the poor who seek a redress in civil jurisprudence" (7 November 1846).[14]

The lawyer, whose mediating role between society and the state made him peculiarly susceptible to corruption, received especially virulent criticism. The lawyer's "guilty but eventful career" developed inevitably, perhaps, from his livelihood, which in turn was gained, as an advertisement for a new novel pointed out, by living on "depredation and crime" (3 January 1846). "Legal skinners" (31 January 1846) and "corrupt alibi lawyers who consort with thieves" (29 November 1845) were the butt of ironic and revealing jokes:

> To hear some men at the bar, you would suppose that if they were held up by the feet the words would run out of their mouth by mere force of gravity, for a week at a time, without troubling their brains at all.[15]

Nowhere was the legal entrenchment of class divisions more savagely attacked by the *Police Gazette,* using the same techniques for the presentation of objective news, than in its portrayal of the institution of the grand jury. "Each invasion of a just principle or flaw in a just system, leaves the door open to the most dangerous practical evils," stated the *Police Gazette.* For this reason, "the secret and partial tribunal known as the Grand Inquest, calls upon every citizen to demand the eradication of its blemish from the face of an enlightened and liberal code" (12 June 1847). The grand jury was a "monstrous evil": "omnipotent in its power, secret in its operations, partial in its action, and not accountable for any of its acts" (17 October 1846). Without fear of challenge, the grand jury might impugn or even dispose of "the life, character, or liberty, of the most innocent citizen" (7 November 1846).

If the grand jury was so easily "accessible to the designs of private malignity" (18 October 1845), what was the basis of its existence in republican

---

14. Courtroom procedure was infamous for its complexity. At the arraignment of one Spencer, on indictment for the murder of his wife in Jersey City, the *Police Gazette* remarked: "the *substance* of the indictment was, as usual, so hid by the *form,* that the Attorney General thought it necessary, after reading the whole indictment over to the prisoner, to tell him verbally, in plain language, that he was charged with the murder of his wife by shooting her with a pistol" (22 August 1846).

15. "The house of Counsellor————was broken into and plundered. The following morning, in Court, Mr. Curran was asked if he had heard of Counsellor————'s robbery? 'No,' replied he, *'Who did he rob?'* " (21 August 1847). "A judge once said to a lawyer, who was more remarkable for the number of his words, than for the sense of his speeches, that he was 'very much like *necessity.'* 'How do you make that out?' inquired the loquacious attorney. 'Because,' said the judge, 'necessity knows no law' " (21 August 1847).

America? Could the grand jury be defended "with satisfactory reasoning" (14 November 1846)? No, answered the editors, looking to the history of the grand jury for justification of their response. Grand juries

> were established at an age, in monarchial England, when judges were creatures of the king, and where a check was necessary upon a committing magistrate who was not responsible to The People. Grand Juries were therefore established, and were made secret inquisitions, that the minions of power should not question their motives, or check their independent action. They were also made, *ex parte,* to secure this secrecy, and to further guarantee the main desideratum of their independence from extraneous influence, each grand juror was sworn not to communicate the proceedings of the sittings, and was held to be irresponsible for his acts. . . . Having been wrung from power as a boon, it continued to be regarded as a blessing even long after it had ceased to possess a virtue, and in this condition, without the slightest applicability to our institutions, it was imported bodily, with the executive prerogative of pardon, and numerous other inconsistent and uncongenial systems, and engrafted upon our policy and jurisprudence. But ever since its introduction, it has been at war with every portion of our republican system, and has encouraged and increased the evils which it is supposed to check. (14 November 1846)

The discretionary power of the grand jury was rooted not in respect for an abstract political theory alone, but in the facts of a concretely perceived inequality. Jurors, selected on the basis of a property qualification, "are but too apt to adjudicate according to narrow views, and invidious motives, instead of being guided by the broad and liberal principles of common justice" (5 December 1846). It would be next to impossible, declared the *Police Gazette,* "to stigmatise a bank director, or a bank president, through a grand jury composed of brokers and bank men, as has been proved invariably in this city" (22 May 1847). A correspondent, one "Probius," assumed an even sharper tone:

> So long as secret tribunals, composed mostly of wealthy financiers, intervene between responsible and elective magistrates, so long may rich offenders rejoice in an impunity from the stern visitations of the law, and so long will poverty or social obscurity writhe under their most pitiless enforcement. (3 July 1847)

The privilege of access to law, which class and the "faithlessness" of a corrupt state nourished, underlay the social drama of the grand jury.

Because class was generally viewed as a political rather than as a social product, the *Police Gazette* attempted a powerful remedial role through publicity and exposure, to redress the political corruption that led to permanent class divisions. This role drew heavily on the rhetoric of vox populi that infused the independent press: "in default of the entire abolishment of Grand Juries in criminal cases, we demand *open sessions,* that we may know hereafter how the fourteen hundred wealthy men in the city of New York, who alone are eligible to the service, deal with the lives, the liberties, and the sacred honors of the remaining quarter million of their poorer fellow citizens" (14 November 1846). There can be no imaginable form of judicial proceedings taken on behalf of the people, thundered the *Police Gazette,* that "The People have not a right to publicly inspect, and any rule, or scheme, or practice, or device, to the contrary, is in derogation of our rights and should not stand." Through open sessions "the penetrating eye of the Public" would monitor the acts of an otherwise tyrannical system (17 October 1846).[16] Implicit in all this was that the "eye of the Public" would be animated and focused by the *Police Gazette* itself. Exposure of abuses arising from the operations of the grand jury would act as a deterrent to the partiality inherent in that body.

The *Police Gazette* often printed the names of grand jurors when a new session opened and sometimes listed each member's occupation next to his name (8 November 1845). Liberally interspersed throughout the paper were ironic comments on the grand jury itself. When, at the October term of the Court of Sessions, the grand jury found 100 true bills of indictment and dismissed 96 complaints, the *Police Gazette* applauded:

> Their action has been most impartially divided, and protects them completely from any imputation of unfairness. . . . The present system is what gives rise to the flash expression of thieves, who say, when they fall fairly within the grip of the law, that they are *"tossed."* (1 November 1845)

Exposure also might focus on individuals. Shepherd Knapp and F. W. Edmonds, president and cashier, respectively, of the Mechanic's Bank, had been charged with compounding the felony of forgery. The charge then was rejected summarily by the grand jury, which, said the journal, was "indignant

16. The insidious power of the grand jury evidently was also observed in England; the *Police Gazette* cited an article from a London paper that argued that, through the grand jury, "power covers itself up with roses and smiles, and other soft methods of disguise" (12 June 1847).

at the arraignment of persons of such high respectability as the accused," and the jury therefore "apologized for the insolent interference of the law with the inviolability of a Bank President."

> All this is doubtless perfectly correct, and satisfactory to the public, and the proceedings furnish another convincing example of the priceless benefit of Grand Juries. Thank heaven, in this case there is no room for imputation of improper motives, as there were certainly not more than *three* Bank Presidents in the whole tribunal. The hope of "equal and exact justice", (sic) fading of late so fast from the minds of men, must now assuredly revive. (25 October 1845)

In another instance a wealthy young man, having learned to alter and pass bank notes, finally is apprehended, "and there was wo among the respectables of his respectable line." But grief, said the *Police Gazette,* "very seldom reaches the climax of despair with those who have money in their pockets, and the respectable friends of that highly respectable rogue bethought themselves of the deep sympathy which a respectable Grand Jury could be made to feel for the disgrace of such a family as theirs." The youth's bail is quickly paid, a lawyer is hired to obtain in advance of the session a list of new grand jury members, and friends and relatives then apply personally to these men. The case is called and proof against the young man is irrefutable; yet though the grand jurors are "acting in the name of The People . . . there were no vulgar rabble to supervise their conduct and hold them accountable." The felon is set free. The *Police Gazette* then appeals to the reader directly, asking if, upon his "calm review" of these facts, he is willing to endure a judicial institution "before which penniless or friendless innocence may be condemned for hatred and for malice, with the same facility as wealthy villany [*sic*] may be acquitted for sympathy and for favor" (19 June 1847).

More generally, the *Police Gazette* focused less on the grand jury and more on attempts by wealthy and respectable felons to flout the law and argued that "it is high time that all distinctions should be abolished between criminals" (7 February 1846).[17] The malefactor, claimed the editors, "is the property of the people"; thus, "the feelings of rich relations are no equivalent for the defeat of justice" (14 March 1846). Another journal, whose laudatory comment was published as a testimonial in the *Police Gazette,* stated that a major aim of the latter journal was

17. For other examples, see *National Police Gazette,* 29 August 1846; 27 February 1847; 27 March 1847; 28 August 1847.

> to bring about such a reform in criminal proceedings, that great scoundrels as well as little ones may be punished. The net of the law is now only strong enough to hold minnows and such small fry—the great leviathans rush right through the frail web. (3 October 1846)

Indeed, if "a man need but to be possessed of money to be aloof from the restraints or terrors of the law," publication of the facts of legal abuse was the only available remedy. The problem was severe, for, stated the *Police Gazette,* the wealthy rogue "has but to bring his gold into the market, and he can buy up the minions of justice, almost from the highest dignitary down to the meanest tipstaff, as a knacker would buy rotten sheep from the shambles. . . . Vice loses its hideousness under the glitter of marketable gold, and the sense of profit which its display inspires, absorbs the sense of duty which should insure all the severities of impartial prosecution" (14 August 1847).

In the face of a corrupt legal system, the *Police Gazette* held fast to the belief that there are "no distinctions in respectability that are made by money" (7 February 1846). The journal disdained to use the "obnoxious term" of "lower classes" to designate the poorer strata of artisans and workingmen (17 October 1846). Concomitantly, laws that helped to solidify class boundaries were to be avoided. The *Police Gazette* complained, for example, of the "anti-republican, restrictive," and "invidious distinctions" that the license laws made between trades and callings, by acting as a tax on labor rather than on property (3 April 1847). Licensing officials were arbitrarily empowered, in this view, "to sentence a hard-working man to starvation, and to decree that he shall henceforth be a vagabond on the face of the earth" (11 April 1846). Again, with a referendum over the proposed establishment of a public college to be funded out of public monies (for children who had passed with honor through the lower public schools) drawing near, the opposition argued that public schools "already furnish all the education required by the poorer classes." The *Police Gazette* swiftly condemned this argument as "insolent." "It not only tells Poverty that it must never aspire above the destiny of labor, but it virtually impugns the intellectual capacity of the masses for the higher branches of improvement, and consequently excludes its claim to the emoluments of social and civil honors which naturally fall to cultivated minds." Such an alliance between property and culture, in short,

> draws the line between the classes as distinct as any which separates the rich and poor in any portion of monarchial Europe, and confers, as they

do, upon Wealth the sunshine and showering honors of the state, while Poverty drudges out its doom upon the other side without one single ray of hope. (5 June 1847)

The upcoming referendum thus would decide a much deeper issue than the establishment of a public college: *"the great question of intellectual equality between the classes"* (ibid.).[18]

The favoritism that allowed certain felons to escape justice and that led to the entrenchment of social class divisions, in actuality, said the *Police Gazette,* disclosed a dire warning to the gentle classes: "They must beware how they help precipitate a reckoning between the two extremes, whose terrible realities may be too fearful for the contemplation" (21 February 1846). It is vitally significant that the *Police Gazette* apparently could not speak in the terms employed by one of its editors, George Wilkes, in his earlier pamphlet critique of American law:

> The poor man is the slave and tool—the rich man the pet of government, of the laws and of society. . . .
>
> I begin to have serious doubts whether prisons ought ever to be built, and whether one set of men, entertaining one set of views, should have entire control and sway over those who differ with them. In short, I doubt whether it is right that Wall street brokers and pettifogging lawyers, who steal and extort by cunningly devised systems, should have the power to lock up their simple and unscientific disciples who steal outright. (1844:24, 36)

In omitting such sentiments, the *National Police Gazette* stopped one step short of viewing property right as incompatible with the other natural rights to life and liberty. Similarly, the journal could view social class as the result, but never as the cause, of political inequality and corruption.[19] Although increasingly defensive, perhaps, the *Police Gazette* held to its fundamental goal of sustaining an inviolate state sphere, whose rigorous duty it was to

18. The terms culture and intellectual equality were to be defined according to well-understood types of activity, whose supposedly universal and self-evident qualities obscured recognition of their own social patterning.

19. On the other hand, recognition of a causal nature in social class frequently seems to lurk just beneath the surface of reportage. Even in Wilkes's earlier pamphlet, though, class receives less attention than legal injustice; and the latter is said to be corrected by means of a quite conventional technique: "There are partial remedies . . . and one is to entrust these tremendous powers only to men of high character, benevolent hearts and enlightened minds, and not to wretches of narrow abilities, narrower hearts and meaner attainments" (1844:7–8).

oversee and protect a substantive public good. This demanded constant vigilance in watching for infractions of public good, wherever they appeared, and in reporting the facts of such abuse to a politically active and responsible public.

"Mock merchants," swindlers who supplied references from business-men in league with them and then absconded after purchasing goods on credit, were denounced (16 October 1845). Banks were a focus of heavier attack. When the president of the New England Bank, Philip Marett, was accused of having defrauded the bank of $60,000, taken from interest charged by the bank, the *Police Gazette* stated:

> It is simply a quarrel between a corporation of rogues and an individual rogue about the appropriation of plunder. . . . We define the crime committed by Philip Marett . . . to be simply this: He was guilty, while president thereof, of compelling the New England Bank to be an honest law-abiding institution.—Further than this he appears to be no more guilty than any other broker. (29 May 1847)

Unsealed weights and measures were attacked (19 June 1847), as were "coal swindlers" who sold short loads (28 October 1848). Spurious tickets sold to immigrants by men who falsely represented themselves as steamboat agents were exposed (24 July 1847). Obscene books were noticed as a social evil (15 November 1845); and prostitution was castigated as a contributor to "the increase in rents in the lower part of our city":

> Many of these dens of iniquity, or ordinary capacity, located in Reed, Duane, Church, Leonard, Elm, &c., rent for nearly double their actual value, and the wages of prostitution is [*sic*] thus rolled into the lap of grasping landlords, while honest tenants, with respectable families, are forced into garrets or to the outskirts of the city. (1 May 1847)

Once again, the facts pointed to the need for a remedy; and the remedy the *Police Gazette* proposed neatly combined concern for the public good with a dramatic use of journalistic exposure: "This is the publication of the names of all persons *owning* houses in the city that are leased and occupied as houses of ill fame, with the prices of the rents received. Thus the community can recognize at a glance, the source of income of many who profess to be good citizens" (ibid).[20]

New criminal techniques were exposed—in the varied realms of the

20. For another example, see *National Police Gazette,* 27 June 1846.

pickpocket (21 March 1846); the counterfeiter (25 October 1845); and the swindler (25 October 1845). To render the journal "of absolute necessity to the whole business community," lists of counterfeit bank notes were published regularly (25 October 1845).[21]

Pawnbrokers were singled out for chastisement as "a striking example of the unjust and cruel distinctions which selfish legislators are continually drawing between Rich and Poor."

> The wealthy representative, in horror of the sin of the demand of an extra one per cent. upon the hypothecation of his lands or stocks, protects himself from the extortion by making the charge of more than *seven per cent.* against *his* interests, a crime punishable with a felonious incarceration in the State Prison; while he arms a horde of extortioners with a statutory warrant to pluck the destitute, at *twenty-five per cent. He* gives in security for his loans a fluctuating pledge at the sacrifice of less than *one fourteenth* of the the sum obtained; while the sweating mechanic leaves his jack-plane, the starving mother her smoothing iron, or her scanty apparel, at the loss of *one quarter* of its value. Is this Justice?[22] (11 October 1845)

Lottery policy gambling—the numbers racket—was labeled a "social leprosy" for its reputedly deleterious effects on the laboring poor, who, by its means, were said to be reduced to crime to pay for their lottery tickets (13 June 1846).[23] In response, the *Police Gazette* printed the names and addresses of the biggest policy dealers, calling on the police to "do their duty" and arrest them (9 May 1846).[24]

As a final illustration of the range of the *Police Gazette*'s criminal concerns, we may consider the journal's attacks on receivers of stolen goods as a major social evil. Many of these receivers, announced the editors, were old thieves who "through their dishonest gains have managed to acquire a political influence which intimidates the elective and political changeling of office." By liberal use of their ill-gotten money, receivers managed to avoid punishment, "while those who are merely laborers in the field of crime, are

21. For other examples, see *National Police Gazette,* 25 October 1845; 12 December 1846.
22. For other examples, see *National Police Gazette,* 25 October 1845; 15 November 1845; 21 February 1846; 28 February 1846.
23. The pernicious influence of the lottery grew from its capacity to generate in all players a relentless need to pursue unearned wealth: "Its deluded and infatuated victims, unable to satisfy its exhorbitant demands by their legitimate earnings, yield to its corrupting influence, and commence pilfering from their employers" (16 October 1845).
24. For other examples, see *National Police Gazette,* 23 May 1846; 30 May 1846; 20 June 1846; 27 June 1846.

sentenced over and over again for the very offences on which the receiver is again and again released" (11 April 1846). This commercial metaphor was extended significantly when the *Police Gazette* called the attention of authorities "to the great increase of manufacturers of thieves, better known, perhaps, as receivers of stolen goods." Most receivers, said the journal, were "unknown to the police"; furthermore, "in nine cases out of ten, they are engaged in business that has the appearance of respectability, which is assumed as a cover to their infamous practices" (28 November 1846). How could the community come to know and guard against such infamous men? In answer, typically, the *Police Gazette* presented, "by way of a singular contrast to Beach's list of rich men, the following list of rich thieves who reside in the city" (8 November 1845).[25]

In all likelihood, the *Police Gazette* lay at the radical end of the journalistic spectrum in that its cumulative critique of law held that property and class status commanded far too much control over the shape and functions of the legal apparatus. In the *Police Gazette,* it was clear that footing lawyer's fees, buying off police, compromising with judges, wielding influence with the governor to obtain a pardon, and exercising arbitrary power in other ways all returned at once to the cardinal issue of privileges for those with property. Property per se in turn suggested a strong affinity between the wealthy criminal and the gentleman, both of whom were afforded special access to law.

But the adversary relation between the *Police Gazette* and the government, although quite real, did not openly dispute the legitimacy of the state. In much more prominent display was the journal's contribution to an expanding arena of reform, in which forces like the *Police Gazette* contended against corrupt officials in protecting the rights of man. Grounded in enlightened reason and natural right, reformism nonetheless had a dark side, which was manifested in a pervasive belief that equal justice was unraveling, leaving in its stead not a face-off between capital and labor, but the terrifying prospect of a Hobbesian state of nature. When, in one of the *Police Gazette*'s richly textured criminal biographies, concerned citizen Virgil Stewart tries to befriend the felon Murrell in order to catch him unawares and bring him to justice, he says to the malefactor: "In this world every man must take care of himself. Some do it by siding with the majority, and by helping to enforce

25. For other examples, see *National Police Gazette,* 21 February 1846; 9 January 1847; 28 August 1847.

set-laws while they violate higher moral obligations without scruple, and a smaller portion despise hypocrisy, and set themselves in open opposition to the rest. . . . I believe, sir, in respect for the law, when the law takes care of all alike, but when war is open between classes of society, I say let the hardest fend off" (19 December 1846). State officials' evident disdain for equal justice vindicated an uncontained assault on civil society by predatory individuals seeking self-aggrandizement without regard for others' natural rights. Again, society's only hope of salvation lay in the commercial press and, specifically, in the *Police Gazette*.

6

"Let the Hardest Fend Off":
Rogues and the Rights of Men

The assimilation of crime news into the newspaper was eased by the popularity of crime accounts in ballads, broadsheets, chapbooks, and, in a somewhat different form, earlier newspapers themselves.[1] Unquestionably, too, the convenience of the police court as an "information-gathering system" also played a part (Given 1907:69). The New York *Transcript* referred to the police court as "the grand focus for obtaining important and correct local intelligence," and, like the Philadelphia *Public Ledger,* the *Transcript* boasted of its full-time police reporters (23 June 1834). The courts, easily accessible, became an important source because they encompassed a type of highly stylized events that might be quickly transcribed to meet periodic deadlines. Yet, I contend, both the penny papers and the *Police Gazette* in the mid-nineteenth century chose to focus on and cultivate in their crime news the widespread anxiety over the legal system's increasing capacity for state corruption. It was in accounts of criminal violation, again, that the newspapers' commercial defense of natural rights was developed and enlarged.

In the stylized world that the *Police Gazette* created, easily recognizable felons routinely pursued standard patterns of behavior in more or less rigidly preconstructed life histories.[2] Yet the journal's characterization of the crimi-

1. Kunzle (1971, 1973) discusses the history of pictorial crime narrative in premodern Europe; Foucault (1977) and Rediker (1978) explore the "discourse" on crime in different contexts; Peterson (1945, 1950) focuses on English crime pamphleteers of the eighteenth and early nineteenth centuries; Nordin (1977) concentrates on "sensational" accounts in eighteenth-century Boston newspapers.
2. In their contemporary study entitled "The Representation of Criminal Events in Houston's

nal raised profound questions about the nature of society, questions fully in keeping with a class-accented perception of the primacy of natural rights. In particular, because individual property right was accepted (because all upstanding men should be acquisitive), how was it possible to distinguish felonious interference in given property relations from legitimate pursuit of gain? Where was the line between crime and business to be drawn?

To answer these questions, I analyzed all available issues of the *Police Gazette* from its first issue in 1845 until 4 September 1847, an unbroken run of 101 issues, after which only scattered numbers of the journal have been preserved on microfilm.[3] I limited my analysis of the patterning of crime largely to the prominent weekly series called "The Lives of the Felons," which occupied the first and very often the second page as well, thereby taking up between one-eighth and one-fourth of the total space available in the *Police Gazette.*

The series was separately bound and sold after publication and was said by the *Police Gazette* to form "a standard history and record of the great criminal offenders of this country" (7 February 1846)—a native Newgate Calendar. These biographies "of notorious professional offenders" were to focus on what the editors called "the philosophy of character" (16 October 1845). According to a testimonial, the series was important because it was "unlike works of fiction, (being) founded upon facts as they have actually occurred" (4 July 1846). Other papers characterized the lives as "authentic" (5 September 1846), and "founded entirely on truth" (4 July 1846). The series was the *Police Gazette*'s most prized feature; it was embellished with a relevant woodcut nearly every week, reprinted in book form, and referred to as exemplary of the path of crime. "The Lives of the Felons" was too important, both for the *Police Gazette* and for comprehension of nineteenth-century crime news, to disregard.

Because the individual "Lives" vary greatly in length—ranging from about 68 column inches to over 3,400—it might be argued that there is little comparability between the biographies. Yet the *Police Gazette* testified that

---

Two Daily Newspapers," Antunes and Hurley conclude that "the daily press presents the public with a small sample of crime events which are specifically selected for publication on the basis of criteria which make them unusual or different from the preponderance of local crime" (1977:760). In particular, they report that murder, which constituted less than one-quarter of one percent of crimes known to the police, accounted for 39.5 percent and 50 percent of the crime news offered by the two newspapers they analyzed (ibid.:759).

3. Numbers one through four of the *Police Gazette* unfortunately are not extant; however, an abridged but apparently otherwise unmodified condensation of these first four issues, dated 16 October 1845, is available. This condensation included the important "Lives of the Felons" series, but excluded other material. I have treated it as a single issue.

the histories were appreciated in holistic terms, as organically unfolding stories: "Some of our readers complain at having the story so lengthened out, but if they will devote a moment's reflection to the subject, they will see that a story so crowded with interest and complicated mystery could not be unravelled in a smaller space" (11 October 1845).[4] Analysis of entire life histories permitted meaningful inference about the criminals' full careers.

For the period under investigation the histories of thirteen felons were isolated; but these thirteen offenders committed well over 200 crimes, and their felonious careers exemplified a repetitive cycle of criminal behaviors. The lengthy description and psychological and philosophical speculation common to these accounts may appear to be unrepresentative, in a narrow sense, of the *Police Gazette*'s portrayal of crime, but the journal itself considered the series to be its definitive statement on the subject. For the analysis of crime and criminality in the *National Police Gazette* these biographies offer in toto a coherent and valid sample.[5] Reference to other felons, mentioned outside the context of the series, fleshed out the analysis.

In approaching the "Lives" series I looked to Lowenthal's classic study (1968) of biographies in popular magazines. Lowenthal examined public figures whose lives were popularized in *Collier's* and the *Saturday Evening Post.* He discovered a seminal contrast in these biographies between the spheres of production and consumption. In 1940, thus, the great majority of "heroes" are found in the arena of consumption—in sports, entertainment, consumer services. Yet Lowenthal finds that at the turn of the twentieth century, far more of these success stories emanated from business, labor, and politics—the sphere of production.

Lowenthal's major intention is to comprehend public glorification in its benign aspect: he wants to reveal the composition of "success" as defined in popular media. Lowenthal's "mass idols" are the lucky ones; success awaits the "well-trained employee from a well-disciplined lower middle-class family" (1968:129); and Lowenthal acknowledges briefly a need to discuss "when and how the failures stopped"—and how success began (ibid.:127). The pre-

4. The journal went on, concerning the life of Bob Sutton: "We shall endeavor to close it up in our next number, and pass on to another, but should we find that that cannot be done with fidelity to our purpose, we will extend it for another week, and not sacrifice its completeness to a visionary idea of dispatch" (11 October 1845). The strong objectivism in this paragraph is self-evident. I have already mentioned the iterative character of reading the *Police Gazette.*
5. It is possible that, had the entire text of each issue of the *Police Gazette* been scrutinized, crimes against persons would receive slightly heavier emphasis than they do (as we will see). In my estimation this would not qualitatively alter the findings. Moreover, I found no evidence in other sections of the journal that would tend to contradict either the sequence or substance of the causes, motives, character, and consequences of crime.

sent investigation reverses these priorities. "The Lives of the Felons" may be understood to pose a more repressive, even a savage, question: When and how did the failure begin? How did the *Police Gazette* perceive the character and result of criminal deviance?

Crime in Context

The *Police Gazette*'s felons animate and extend the editors' fear that society was reverting to a Hobbesian state of nature, to the war "of every man, against every man," with "continuall feare, and danger of violent death" (Hobbes 1968:185–86). In their attack on natural rights, in their social character, and in their corruption of the state, felons embodied and actively contributed to the breakdown of the republic. I begin with the social identity of the criminal heroes in "The Lives of the Felons" (table 1).

Some outstanding biographical features become clear at once in table 1. All the felons are white males. This is curious and significant. Women and most blacks in the 1840s were unenfranchised, barred from citizenship, and therefore incapable in principle of independent participation in political society; consequently, blacks and women seemed to pose a mere external threat to public good. White men who turned to a criminal life challenged the very state they were in part constituting. Hence, their deviations were significant and became a major focus of those who would protect the state.

These are, further, mature criminals, whose commitment to their calling merits the label "professional." As noted, the *Police Gazette* was cognizant of the professional character of these offenders, even drawing attention to it. These hardened felons, steeped in the habits of crime, collectively furnished a pool of life histories out of which the definitive causes, motivations, and consequences of criminal deviance could be extracted. They constituted a reservoir from which the *Police Gazette* hoped to pump the "philosophy of character" that underlay criminality (16 October 1845).

Half of these felons are English, while not one is a native New Yorker. Again, a provocative finding; for, as Rothman shows, the inmates of penitentiaries changed markedly in nativity between 1830 and 1860 (1971:254–55). Between 1830 and 1835 New York's Auburn prison housed about 50 percent New Yorkers, 30 percent immigrants from other states, and 20 percent foreigners. By 1850 the foreign-born confined to Auburn, Sing-Sing, and Clinton penitentiaries made up 32 percent of the total inmate group; and by

TABLE I

Demographic Features of Criminals in
"The Lives of the Felons"

	Felon	Sex	Race	Nationality[a]	Age[b]	Column Inches
1	Robert Sutton	M	W	near London	55	751
2	James Smith	M	W	London	50	126
3	Charles Webb	M	W	London	51	599[c]
4	James Webb	M	W	London	49	599[c]
5	George Howell	M	W	Philadelphia	?	68
6	Thomas Conroy	M	W	American	36	110
7	James Downer	M	W	London	35	226
8	Lyman Parkes	M	W	Massachusetts	55	830
9	Henry Thomas	M	W	Middle States	31*	1,601
10	George B. Harvey	M	W	London	50*	567
11	John Washburn	M	W	North Carolina	26*	247
12	John A. Murrell	M	W	Mid-Tennessee	41*	3,402
13	Joseph T. Hare	M	W	Chester, Pa.	38*	2,132

[a]Nationality is calculated in terms of place of birth, listed here.

[b]Age is calculated either at time of writing or at time of death. Deceased felons are marked with an asterisk.

[c]The Webbs were brothers whose lives were written as one account. I counted it twice to obtain column inches.

the Civil War they constituted 44 percent of all prisoners.[6] While not initiating this social trend toward defining the criminal as foreign-born, the *Police Gazette* unquestionably accentuated and cultivated it. For the years from 1845 to 1847 almost half of the *Police Gazette*'s felons are foreigners; the other half are out-of-staters. Thus if crime threatened public good from within, it was defined demographically as a special bonus of transnational and internal migration to the booming commercial port of New York.[7] It is interesting that in this respect the *Police Gazette* itself hoped to effect an actual physical

6. Rothman argues that this tendency was not unique to New York, nor even to the East, but that it was representative of the nation as a whole (1971:254).

7. The *Police Gazette* was careful to publish "voluminous lists of escaped convicts from the English penal settlements" (31 January 1846); and five out of six artisans in my sample were English. Nonetheless, the journal did not evince any virulent nativism (11 July 1846).

displacement of criminality, "to drive all resident rogues to a more safe and congenial meridian, and to deter all floating tribes of vagabond adventurers from embarking to a region where an untiring and ubiquitous minister of public justice stands ready to hold them to the public gaze" (16 October 1845).

What was the occupational and class character of the felon as depicted by the *Police Gazette?* The data are slightly less conclusive, but only slightly so. Six felons, we are told, were bound out "at a proper age" as apprentices —to a morocco dresser, a wheelwright, a glass cutter, a gun finisher, an upholsterer, and a marble cutter (1, 2, 3, 4, 7, 8).[8] Two others were put out to work on farms (9, 11). One had "extensively connected" parents, whose "correct habits and comfortable circumstances" may have elevated him somewhat above the others. Even in this case, however, the future felon (13) is from the beginning "irritated that . . . he had so long remained in want, when miserable drones around him lived in splendour and enjoyed the luxury of ostentatious waste" (1 May 1847). Inattendance to proper education in a trade is instrumental to the careers of the remaining four felons. The father of one has taken no pains to instruct him in a calling (10); the parents of another set him "a sad example," so that he "commenced his apprenticeship at pilfering at a very early period of life" (5) (27 December 1845); another "very early entered into crime" (6) (3 January 1846); while the last (12), whose father, though poor, "bore a good reputation," is taught to be "an expert professional thief" by his coarse and "licentious" mother (12 September 1846). Almost to a man these are children "of virtuous and respectable" tradespeople (24 January 1846) whose proper station in adulthood would have been that of an artisan, mechanic, or farmer.[9] Criminals are apprentices gone wrong.

Two features of this definition bear further comment. First, wayward apprentices and servants had long been the recipients of this sort of cautionary advice, often in much more openly admonitory tones. An instance is provided by a broadside printed in 1733 in Boston, occasioned by the execution of "Poor Julian" for murder. The broadside was said to be "Very proper to be Read by all Persons, but especially young People, and Servants of all Sorts," and it included a verse demanding "That Children and all Servants they / Would in their Stations all obey, / Parents and Masters every

---

8. Numerals inside parentheses refer to individual felons as designated in table 1.
9. Rothman states of penitentiary prisoners: "the overwhelming majority of inmates stood toward the bottom of the social ladder." Ordinary laborers dominated the group; and the total number of "professionals, merchants, shopkeepers, and farmers, in a sample of some eighteen hundred convicts in 1849 was less than three per cent" (1971:252).

one, / And not to do as he ("Poor Julian") has done" (in Winslow 1930:83).

Second, although the *Police Gazette* echoed in these personal histories a long tradition of advice to artisans' apprentices, the meaning of the caution was dramatically changed. No longer constrained by the preacherly style of the earlier narratives, the fear that young miscreants might become articled to crime now ballooned outward into society, where it implicated state officials and bankers, masters and men.

According to the *Police Gazette,* discontent initially drove the felon to crime; the discontent was expressed in such phrases as a "growing dislike to his honest labor" (8 November 1845). Again and again the refusal to labor is equated with the preeminent decision in the life history of the rogue. Crime is opposed directly to the sometimes not so honest world of gainful work, and it is the rejection of honest labor that opens Act One of the life of the criminal.

Henry Thomas and his cohort, Ike Jarvis (a minor character), temporarily take separate paths when Jarvis, an ex-convict, balks at the prospect of returning to a life of crime. Thomas burglarizes a house to obtain fine clothes and money, returning thence to confront his pal humbly laboring in an employer's shop:

> "Well, damn honesty, now and forever," exclaimed Jarvis bitterly, and throwing down his hammer. "I've been at work, like a dog, for the last three days; and, from what I've learnt on the character of my employer, I'm not only likely to be cheated out of my wages, but to be turned out of the shop with disgrace—for I believe they already begin to suspect where I came from. (2 May 1846)

In this complex depiction it is important to bear in mind that Jarvis's employer may be as hungry for gain as the criminal Thomas—a similarity discussed in chapter 5 and again explored in greater depth below. Nonetheless, in the crucial scene Jarvis is said to have "renewed his identures with the Devil" (ibid.).[10] The felon is set qualitatively apart by his utter rejection of honest labor. The same theme runs forcefully through the life of George Howell. To cloak his activities as a thief, Howell begins to manufacture mineral water for bars and finds his small experiment unintentionally burgeoning into a "rapidly growing business" yielding "very heavy profits":

> He could afford to be honest, but integrity being no part of his system or calculations, he paid no attention to the invitation which success held

10. On the status of artisans in this era, see above, chapter 1; Laurie (1980); Wilentz (1980).

out to him to reform his life, but still kept dabbling into felonious enterprises, and at length becoming disgusted with the methodical regularity of his existence he resolved to discard an uncongenial industry altogether, close up his business, and take to downright "clyfaking" [pickpocketing] again. (27 December 1845)

Once more, the extremely atypical commitment of the rogue and counterfeiter Lyman Parkes on the activity of work itself was employed by the *Police Gazette* in a powerful and disturbing contrast with corrupt state officials. Thus, the journal depicted a network of police informers working to entrap Parkes, while the "perverted artisan" himself labored "over his criminal task." Said the editors about "the morality of the contrast":

the spectacle of his conspiring betrayers driving with their gay equipages in luxurious summer afternoons past the lonely residence where sat the patient, unconscious and self-sacrificing devotee over his weary task, affords anything but a gratifying contemplation for the mind. (7 March 1846)

Labor was a positive force in its own right, and hence even the labor of the criminal assumed a painfully praiseworthy aspect when compared with the useless indolence characteristic of corrupt justice or with the cut-throat world of business.

On the other hand, the felons understood that laboring at a respectable employment was essential to avoid detection, and they recognized also that "character" was contingent on steadfast pursuit of legitimate business. Charles Webb, for instance, consciously determines "to commence proceedings by earning a character," and therefore "he opened a glass-cutter's shop, and for some months devoted himself apparently most assiduously to his trade" (8 November 1845). Pressed hard by police, the old criminal Thorpe (a minor character) asserts in his own defense that he has a fifteen-year-old son: "He's bound out, and is a good honest boy as ever lived" (21 March 1846). Putting the boy out as an apprentice here served to reenlist Thorpe himself within decent society by demonstrating that he respected and subserved his proper place.

More frequently, felons are made to regret their unuseful lives in execution speeches or in final confessions. Henry Thomas, for example, says, "Had I went to work at an honest calling, I might have been in easy circumstances and duly respected" (11 July 1846). Hare admits, supposedly for the benefit of "those who are wedded to viscious [*sic*] schemes of life" but actually for the readers of the *Police Gazette,* that the "six months of honest labor which I spent in the saddler's workshop, was the happiest portion of my life" (31 July 1847). Later on he expands on this judgment: "I have followed the highway for seventeen years," he says, thereby substantiating an implicit claim to professional expertise and knowledge, "and have also engaged in all other branches of the robber's art." "More successful than any robber that ever was in this country," Hare nevertheless claims to have been extremely poor for two-thirds of the time, and for almost half of it he has been "the degraded and wretched tenant of a felon's cell." Then, the main point: "The meanest trade at the smallest wages would have been preferable to my dashing career, for there I should have always been my own master, as God intended man to be; I should never have been entirely destitute" (21 August 1847). The robust and ambitious individuals who populated the criminal world forfeited their personal independence through crime. "The dullest rogue alive," expostulated the journal, "by comparing the happiness of the poorest laborer with his own, should be able to discover the utter folly of a life of crime, and to shun it as a leprosy, for with its stripes and chains, it also (except in very few instances) curses its miserable victims with an inevitable and continuous poverty" (11 July 1846). In short, there could be no excuses made for one who forsook gainful employment to follow a life of crime, because "in our prosperous country" any person "with habits of industry, had it in his power, at all times, to maintain himself and his family, by the honest labor of his hands" (28 August 1847).

We can not adequately comprehend this obviously idealized portrait without remembering that labor was generally considered a form of property in its own right. The felon's refusal to labor was in itself a rejection of property and, as we shall see, one that was completely in keeping with his subsequent attack on others' natural rights. For Act Two of the criminal drama, in which the rogue disputed the sanctity of natural rights by preying on others' property and thereby launched a civil war within society, directly followed.[11]

Crime, in this series, is defined overwhelmingly in terms of acts taken against individual rights to property (table 2). In this respect the *Police Gazette* may have both borne out the resentment of artisan-readers and paradoxically echoed and amplified the definitions of other legal agencies.

---

11. In refusing to labor within the sphere of the market legally defined, the criminal, because he was already defined as a working man, effectively renounced the single interest in political society that was granted by elite political theory to the unpropertied classes.

The journal cited a study of "Sing-Sing Prison Statistics" (18 October 1845) that found that, of the 800-odd convicts housed in that prison, only 115 or 14 percent had committed crimes against persons, while 671 or 84 percent had committed offenses against property.[12]

Even these figures, however, do not do justice to the preponderance of crimes against property recorded in "The Lives of the Felons." Of crimes against persons (n = 24), two-thirds (16) occurred only in conjunction with a simultaneous felonious attack on property. A full fifteen of the sixteen murders recorded in the entire series occurred in this way. Murder was atypical of the sample as a whole; similarly, it was unusual within the careers of criminals. Only three of the 13 (9, 11, 12) committed murder, two (11, 12) more than once. Very rarely do crimes against the person stand by themselves; of the eight remaining crimes of this class (two assaults, two attempted murders, one murder, and three attempted or successful suicides), three are committed to evade jail and three are committed as the result of imprisonment.[13] This leaves only two crimes against persons per se—an assault against a pugilist who publicly mocks Hare (13), who in turn retaliates; and a murder of a criminal who insults Murrell (12) in the presence of women. Even in its prospectus the *Police Gazette* had articulated its special province as the depiction of "the modes and means in continual operation against . . .

TABLE 2

Criminal Acts in "The Lives of the Felons"

Against Persons[a]	Against Property[b]	Other[c]	Total
24	211	7	242
10%	87%	3%	100%

[a]Includes: Assault and Battery; Attempted Murder; Murder; Attempted Suicide; Suicide; Rape

[b]Includes: Pocket Picking; Burglary; Forgery; Theft; Robbery; Sale of Stolen Goods; Fraud; Counterfeiting

[c]Includes: Jailbreak; Impersonation; Criminal Conversation

12. Rothman lists figures for state prison inmates but includes burglary and robbery within his category "crimes of violence," making it difficult to ascertain what proportion of malefactors served time for crimes against persons. Rothman claims that grand larceny accounted for the largest single group of offenders (1971:248–49).
13. One assault is provoked when a felon is escaping arrest (7), and the two attempted murders involve a key witness for the prosecution against Murrell; two rogues try suicide when they are imprisoned (9, 10); one is successful (10) in a second attempt.

NEW-YORK, SATURDAY, OCTOBER 24, 1846.   FOUR CENTS A NUMBER.

MURRELL AND CRENSHAW ROBBING THE MAIL.

The *National Police Gazette,* 24 October 1846. Criminals. A moment of crime illumined. Notice the gentlemanly dress of the two miscreants.

property" (16 October 1845). For these felons, in short, crime *is* the unauthorized interference with individual rights to property and its exchange through lawfully regulated markets.

The Third Act climaxed the criminal drama with an ostentatious display of riotous extravagance and waste. Here the felon used his ill-gotten money to pursue an aristocratic life of ease—drinking, gaming, and mingling incognito with society's bona fide upper class. For instance, Charles Webb turns thief, and "a year and a half's success in this line seduced him from his labor, and, closing his shop, he removed to Paulus Hook, hired a handsome residence, and celebrated it by a splendid entertainment" (8 November 1845). James Smith, initially "disposed to frolic," soon acquires "settled habits of enjoyment," which impel his life of crime (16 October 1845).[14] James Downer cultivates a predilection for "evening promenades, a Sunday drive to Greenwich in a one horse chaise, and creams and syllabubs in Kensington Garden" —the expenses of which "soon ran beyond Master Miller's little income" (10 January 1846). Henry Thomas is thought to have grown up "with false notions" of his "position in the world" (11 July 1846); George Barnes Harvey's "fashionable pretensions" lead him among the "gayest and most fashionable throngs at opera, masquerade, or on the pave" (8 August 1846). John Washburn frequently indulges in "every coarse and demoralizing pleasure"; his life of "utter dissipation" revolves around roulette and gaming—until, finding his stock of cash dwindling, he is obliged once more "to turn to business" (29 August 1846).[15]

Phrases drawn from the world of legitimate business were not gratuitous. Language posited a homology between business and crime, as when the *Police Gazette* referred to an old gang of criminals in Philadelphia, "known as the firm of 'Whitehouse, Slappy, Simpson, & Co.' ":

> This firm being shrewdly acquainted with the conditions of the markets for plunder, and finding that our system of weekly exposure and continual pursuit had rendered the old workmen here perfectly useless, withdrew the worn out hands to other quarters, and sent . . . fresh emigrants among us in their places. (10 April 1847)

The Webbs' "riotous extravagances" are similarly responsible for their initial attempts to find illicit means of "ministering to their disgraceful pleasures" (8 November 1845). Felonious and legitimate activity have become almost indistinguishable.

There are moments when the criminal becomes part of high society itself. Joseph Hare's first theft affords him the means to plunge into "excesses

---

14. The history of the purported murderer Tirrell (which appeared in the news columns) was said to "present another awful monition to the minds of youths of both sexes, whom a course of dangerous enjoyment and vicious reading are luring step by step through progressive experiments upon the passions" (13 December 1845).

15. The journal's view of gambling again was based on a broader view of the business world: "The scope of all laws against gaming should be confined to civil remedies for the recovery of money lost—except when fraud is exercised by the winner. This makes his operations *criminal* and should subject him to the punishment of *crime*. While men are allowed to wager by insurance, to gamble in stocks, and to speculate in flour, it is not consistent for the law to restrain them from any contingent investment, the operations of which is [*sic*] open to public scrutiny" (17 July 1847).

NEW-YORK, SATURDAY, NOVEMBER 7, 1846.

BUTLER&STRYPE

THE LAND-PIRATE TURNED PREACHER.

The *National Police Gazette,* 7 November 1846. Criminals. Disguise and symbolic inversion were constant and striking features of crime reporting, as also of much popular literature of the 1840s. Here the rogue Murrell demonstrates an enthusiastic Methodist religiosity, while through the engraver's art the reader is transformed into a vicarious witness.

of the most disreputable character" (1 May 1847); a few installments later, Hare's band of highwaymen obtains $39,000 through a series of robberies, prompting the journal to reflect:

> This little fortune for each in his own right of course inspired ideas of importance and desires of indulgence, and Dan declared that he'd be d——d if he'd live any longer like a miser, he was able enough to live like a gentleman. (29 May 1847)

"Showing plenty of money," says Hare, "I found no difficulty in getting into society" (ibid.). Again, the felon and the scion of wealth and fashion rubbed shoulders: "we felt a desire for relaxation and enjoyment . . . as is always the case with men of our vocation after a successful exploit has filled our pockets . . .":

> We therefore entered into the most expensive luxuries of the place, and allowed none of the fashionables to outdo us in our style of living. We gambled at nine pins, at billiards, and at cards, and we even got up scrub races on the road as an additional pastime and mode of laying wagers. We were thought the two gayest and pleasantest fellows at the place. (7 August 1847)

And, by the same token, the conspicuous consumption of the upper class determines the felon's behavioral cycle; for, when the money is gone, the profligate "despoiled of every dollar by these conjunctive wastes" is "driven, by actual necessity, into active crime again" (3 October 1846). The corrupt embrace of crime and illegitimate but pleasurable consumption sharply differentiates the felon from those who live in the idealized, virtuous world of useful labor.

Thus the rogue's initial rejection of useful labor triggered activities that related to other targets of the *Police Gazette*. The felon's assault on others' property, which in turn afforded him the means to engage in conspicuous consumption, made distinctions between the rogue, the speculator, and the banker difficult. Radically uncontained, predatory and felonious behavior might be commonly found throughout society. Nor was the state itself unaffected, for the criminal's attack on the natural right to property was matched precisely by the state's corrupt deference to property. And, as we shall see, the state was thus apparently incapable of punishing what it had helped to nurture.

Crime was both consolidated and compounded by the state's haphazard

NEW-YORK, SATURDAY, MARCH 6, 1847.

FOUR CENTS A NUM

MORNING SCENE AT THE POLICE OFFICE, IN THE TOMBS.

National Police Gazette, 6 March 1847. Justice. The bowed heads and supplicatory gestures of the young men before the bench contrast markedly with the admonishing hand of the magistrate. The Tombs housed a prison as well, in which editor George Wilkes spent thirty days in 1844 after being convicted of libel.

dispensation of justice; in "The Lives of the Felons" the legal system is shown to be riddled with corrupt and iniquitous practices. Punishment of these hardened offenders either was ineffectual or rested on practices that reduced the state to the level of the felon. Ghastly as they were, the facts of crime became still more devastating in light of the state's seeming decrepitude, for absence of punishment in turn dramatized the state's evident inability to superintend a unitary public good. Crime and corruption in the state intertwined in their threat to the republic.

The "inevitable destiny of crime," that is, "doom and death, within the walls of a State prison" (10 January 1846), is shown in "The Lives of the Felons" to be far from inevitable. Moreover, when the law does take its toll, justice may still be defrauded. "The Lives of the Felons" displays a legal system rife with corruption, locked in step with crime itself, that may not bring the criminal to justice until after he has lived a full lifetime of crime.

Henry Thomas, John Washburn, and Joseph Hare (all of whom were hanged, in 1846, 1837, and 1818, respectively) can be said to exemplify ultimately the full life-cycle of the criminal, as described by Thomas himself:

> When [committing a crime] is once done, the person generally abandons himself to this course of life, growing worse and worse, until like myself, he comes, perhaps to an unhappy end. (28 March 1846)

Such an end should be the natural and just denouement to a violent and base career: "I wish to tell the jurors that I have no unkindly feelings towards any of them," says Thomas benevolently, after his murder trial, "for I think they could'nt [*sic*] have given any other verdict on the evidence which they had presented to them" (11 July 1846). Washburn's hanging for murder also properly climaxes a "journey of life which was doomed to run through a road of blood, and to end only on the gallows" (29 August 1846).[16] Hare, though active for years as a highwayman, never took a victim's life, but when hanged, he is turned into a victim of "the corrupting influence of idle habits while a boy" (4 September 1847). Two murderers and a highwayman thus ultimately receive an exemplary punishment.

Within his career, on the other hand, Hare's life illustrates the problem of retribution. Early on, he finds it an advantage to enlist in the Louisiana Governor's Guard, an elite police force, where he is promoted to corporal for his "alacrity . . . and strict attention to duty" (1 May 1847). Under cover

---

16. The *Police Gazette,* however, opposed capital punishment as a matter of policy. See *National Police Gazette,* 11 April 1846; 25 April 1846.

NATIONAL POLICE GAZETTE.

VOL. I. NEW-YORK, SATURDAY, JULY 11, 1846. No. 44.

The National Police Gazette

BY ENOCH E. CAMP AND GEORGE WILKES,

CIRCULATION, 15,000 COPIES,

Is published every Saturday morning, at the low sum of $2 per annum, to mail subscribers, payable invariably in advance.

SINGLE COPIES FIVE CENTS.

☞ Agents supplied at the usual discount.

ADVERTISEMENTS—Ten cents per line for each insertion—payable in advance.

☞ All letters, to insure prompt attention, must be post paid, and addressed to CAMP & WILKES, Editors and publishers, 27 Centre street, New York.

Entered according to Act of Congress in the year 1846, by ENOCH E. CAMP and GEORGE WILKES, in the Clerk's Office of the District Court of the United States for the Southern District of New York.

LIVES OF THE FELONS.

No. 5.

CONCLUDED.

HENRY THOMAS,

Alias Dean, alias James Mitchell,

THE BURGLAR AND MURDERER.

The verdict—The philosophy of courage—The sentence—Its effect upon the prisoner—Visits of the clergy—The confession—Erection of the gallows—The night before the execution—The last attempt—Excitement of the populace of Chillicothe—The final summons—The dying speech—The expiation—Conclusion.

THE EXECUTION OF THOMAS, THE MURDERER,

At Chillicothe, Ohio, March 6, 1846.

National Police Gazette, 11 July 1846. Justice. Henry Thomas's dying speech on the scaffold before the crowd. Thousands of persons often attended public executions, where drunken revelry and popular culture collided with stern justice. The ritual speeches of the doomed were commonly printed in chapbooks and broadsides for sale to the public. Convicted persons were pressured by agents of the state to recant, often doing so by pointing to their own lives as instances of the just desserts of crime, before being launched into eternity. Public executions, however, were on the wane; laws abolishing such spectacles were promulgated throughout the United States in the antebellum years.

NEW-YORK, SATURDAY, SEPTEMBER 4, 1847.

THE EXECUTION OF HARE.

National Police Gazette, 4 September 1847. Justice. The death of Joseph Hare. The appearance of the militia as a barrier between the crowd and the scaffold was a visible reminder that justice would be defended by earthly sanctions.

of this ingenious, but in no way novel, blind, Hare revels in criminal pursuits. His assumption of a policeman's role illustrates the organizational flaws and discretionary practices that repeatedly permitted the state to defraud justice of its due. As it turns out, no fewer than eleven of our sample of thirteen felons pursued careers that are permeated with analogous examples of the state's malfeasance, of its incapacity to redress heinous crimes.

Bob Sutton, sentenced to life for forgery in 1828, finds emissaries to besiege the governor with "continual petitions," and he is pardoned in 1839. Indeed, at the time of writing, Sutton is suspected of many recent crimes (25 October 1845). James Smith, though now incarcerated on a charge of barge robbery, has already been the subject of three abortive bail attempts (16 October 1845). When he is finally convicted and sentenced to seven years at hard labor, which happens months after his biography has been completed within the regular news columns of the *Police Gazette,* the journal admits that this was rather unexpected,

> as the prisoner had all that money, great legal cunning, and the secret favor of that portion of the police who live by such rogues as himself, to aid him.[17] (31 January 1846)

James Webb gets ten years in 1841 but is pardoned in 1844, his present whereabouts being unknown. Even more fortunate, his brother Charles is safe in France, where he is secure "in the enjoyment of the vast proceeds of his successful villany [*sic*]" (20 December 1845). Throughout their nefarious criminal lives, both Webbs repeatedly buy out the law to retain their freedom (22 November 1845). George Howell now resides in Eastern Penitentiary for a two-year term, but the *Police Gazette* cautions that, quite possibly, he may "escape a portion of his term by pardon" (27 December 1845). Thomas Conroy, having cheated the law of its due, is at liberty "and almost every day pays a visit to Wall street . . . in a professional pilfering expedition" (3 January 1846). Lyman Parkes and John Murrell both are pardoned shortly before their sentences expire, the former to resume his trade as a stonecutter

---

17. Not infrequently, stories about criminals in "The Lives of the Felons" may spill over into the news columns of the journal after completion of the biographies. A cohort of Smith's, James Downer, gets off with five years in prison, which we are told after his biography is finished (13 June 1846). The biography itself ends with Downer's arraignment for the barge robbery, at which point the *Police Gazette* states: "we must therefore abandon here the thread of his career, and direct the reader for its continuation, to the current criminal department of our paper" (10 January 1846). When Downer is convicted and sentenced, the *Police Gazette* applauds its own part in the prosecution of crime: "On all hands the result is mainly attributed to us" (13 June 1846).

and farmer, the latter to work at blacksmithing (a trade he learned in prison) until his death.[18] George Harvey is betrayed by corrupt law officers (18 July 1846) and is given the maximum sentence after a promise of leniency in return for cooperation. This "dishonorable conduct of the authorities" leads Harvey to take his own life in June 1846. He has been abused, says the *Police Gazette* in a vital phrase, by "the faithlessness of power" (22 August 1846).

The state's "faithlessness of power" is clearly and amply articulated. Murrell's enormous conspiratorial band numbers many "who have been fortunate enough to obtain offices of honor and profit while engaged in a life of crime"—offices such as justice of the peace, deputy sheriff, and police officer (5 December 1846).[19] Murrell himself determines to "devote himself assiduously to politics," to gain standing in the dominant local party and thereby to cultivate "an influence which would above all others, protect him and his friends in case they should become openly obnoxious to the law." Seeking a life of apparently upstanding politics was a "frequent resource" of felons, the *Police Gazette* added (24 October 1846). In another instance a correspondent remarks that a "civil war" is raging in southern Illinois, between criminals and honest men, "the former to invade the laws, the latter to put them in force." Here the rogues accomplish their villainous design in a significant way: "Full one half the magistrates, constables, coroners, and other officers, were elected from this organized gang" (5 December 1846). Again, Joseph Hare finds that the property whose initial theft prompted his prison conviction in turn has been plundered by the *"respectable* magistrate

18. Parkes and Murrell present an intriguing contrast. The former, whose steady labor makes him an unusual and almost tragic felon, finally is arrested, but only through entrapment or, in the journal's words, by "an immoral and unworthy piece of treachery" (14 March 1846). His sentence is light because he reveals some of the secrets of the counterfeiter's art to bank officials. Indeed, the five years that Parkes serves resonate strangely against the *Police Gazette*'s characterization of his capture, which is said to lead to "the heaped-up retribution of many years of offence" (14 February 1846). In a final piece of symmetry, Parkes obtains a pardon at the application of no less a man than the banker Nicholas Biddle (21 March 1846). Parkes ends his criminal career and once again pursues a life of upstanding labor. After serving most of a ten-year sentence, during which he reforms and takes up religion, Murrell also obtains a pardon. His moral transformation, however, leaves him with a vitiated spirit: "Ambition had died within him, and resigning himself into the hands of his religious benefactors, he retired to a little piece of land . . . set up a forge and sought to gain a living by tinkering, mending ploughs and chance blacksmithing. . . . But his course was run," and soon Murrell is a dead man (24 April 1847). Throughout, Parkes is sustained by a fierce, almost Faustian, ambition, coupled with resolute labor. Murrell, on the other hand, is reformed so completely into "a meek and sighing methodist" that his leadership qualities and his ambition evaporate, leaving him only a speedy death (24 April 1847).

19. The organization of criminality could be very large. Murrell's "great project" of "exciting a rebellion among the negroes of the slave-holding states" necessitated the formation of what was virtually a national political organization (14 November 1846).

and constable" who arrested and sentenced him; he comes to the seemingly irresistible conclusion that "the world is made up mostly of rogues of various degrees" (24 July 1847).

To posit the state as the rightful agent to punish criminal violations of natural rights brooked an obvious contradiction: it was precisely the state's capacity to protect public good, and, conversely, the state's subservience to unequal market relationships, that at this juncture had become fundamental issues. The facts of crime and state corruption showed that continuing, comprehensive evaluation of the state's performance in the redress of crime was necessary to ensure that the state's supervision of public good indeed was scrupulously impartial and just. It was this task—surveillance of the state's appropriate functions—that defined the institutional role of the *National Police Gazette*. Like the commercial newspaper more generally, the *Police Gazette*'s fulfillment of this role involved it in the activity of governance itself.

Speaking in the people's name, the *Police Gazette* undertook to assume an omniscient viewpoint, from which it surveyed both state and society, exposing violations of public good. The conventions of objective news reporting, which it mobilized for this purpose, permitted "the facts" to speak for themselves; at the same time, the conventions enabled the *Police Gazette* to decide the nature of the facts that it dispensed. We have seen that the criteria the *Police Gazette* utilized challenged the state and infringed on the state's preserve only insofar as it was necessary to cultivate a new institutional role for the newspaper. In cultivating journalistic objectivity, on the other hand, the *Police Gazette* was in key ways ultimately dependent on the testimony of state officials.

In its portrayal of felons who challenged the public good, again, the *Police Gazette* engaged in an important norm-setting function. Here, its definition of crime, under the umbrella of objectivity, enabled the legal system to define as criminals lower-class, immigrant invaders of property instead of some other social group assaulting a different natural right. Crime news in the *Police Gazette,* thus, through accounts initially patterned to express the commercial newspaper's defense of public good somewhat ironically contributed to the state's greater deference to property alone. This norm found decisive support in the *Police Gazette*'s systematic attempt to define the sources of criminality. In the journal's complex discussion of the causes and motives of crime we find the same tensions and antagonisms that clearly marked other aspects of criminality. Throughout, the *Police Gazette*'s firm acceptance of the right to property intertwined with an apparent inability to show convincingly that the felon's attack on individual property grew exclusively from his own recalcitrant perversity.

When John Washburn was hanged for robbery and murder in 1837, his words on the scaffold were relayed through the pages of the *Police Gazette,* almost ten years after the event. Washburn, at 26, claimed to have "spent my brief existence in perpetrating damning outrages against my fellow men." There followed a typical warning: "Let all who hear beware of the means which led me to this end. The first step was intemperance, the next, bad companions. . . . Let my last words be a warning—Farewell" (5 September 1846). At the sentencing of another murderer, one Judge Edmonds asserted, "the want of proper early culture, your continual indulgence in the fatal use of intoxicating liquors, have brought you at this early age to an untimely end" (10 January 1846). Parental negligence reputedly exacted a price from seven of our felons (5, 8, 9, 10, 11, 12, 13), although its specific form varied. Involuntary negligence could be fatal, as is implied when both of Washburn's parents die, leaving him at the mercy of a "stern and rigorous uncle" (5 September 1846)—no substitute for the guidance of the nuclear family—and, in the more suggestive instance of Murrell, whose father's "timid and irresolute" character buckles in front of a corrupt and immodest mother. It is only after the father's untimely death, however, that young Murrell "reeled headlong into vice" (12 September 1846). Joseph Hare also is a product of maternal carelessness—but of mollycoddling rather than viciousness. The eldest of six children, he has the misfortune to be "the especial favorite, or pet, of an indulgent mother":

> Naturally wayward and self-willed, the undue favors of maternal fondness converted his tendencies into habits, and confirmed his impulses into passions, and at the age of sixteen, when his mother died, he stood the victim of a vitiated will, that was destined to be the tyrant of his future life. Left thus entirely free from the only influence that ever had restrained him, he plunged more deeply into the wild and vicious courses which he had before somewhat circumspectly followed. (1 May 1847)

A parent's death sealed the certainty that his or her life had first engendered in the offspring; biology and familial corruption or ignorance conspired to breed vice and criminality.[20] Parents might set a "bad example" merely from "their mode of life" (5) (27 December 1845); or allow too much discretion to their child in selecting companions (10) (18 July 1846); or even unknowingly

---

20. A clear instance of the biological origin of crime is Murrell, who "may be said to have drawn his barbarous and vicious nature from his mother's breast" (12 September 1846).

"misdirect the germ, which, had it been properly cultivated and directed, would have accomplished the highest flights of honourable art" (8) (24 January 1846). Or, like Henry Thomas, perhaps "the principles of religion and correct morals" were not enforced "by the kindly influences of parental authority." Or, finally, as the judge said as he passed sentence on Thomas:

> You may have been permitted to grow up with false notions of your position in the world, and you may have permitted yourself to indulge the harsh feeling that men and society were to some extent enemies to you, and in this have sought an excuse for the evil you might do. (11 July 1846)

What biology and family care began, alcohol and low companions consummated. "LIQUOR, BAD COMPANY, and the Devil" produced his own ignominious end, said a convicted murderer (29 November 1845). Of this triad, vicious companions seem to have been most effective; intemperance or habitual attendance at pubs claimed three victims (1, 2, 11), while "loose and dangerous companions" left their indelible mark on no fewer than eleven of our sample (16 October 1845). Evil companions normally were encountered early in life, either in joining a gang (1, 3, 5, 10, 13) or, less formally, through mere association (2, 4, 9, 11). Much less often, criminal associations took place in late youth or maturity, at which point they needed to command greater force in their attempt to convert the initiate or neophyte. James Downer, who was already picking pockets with dexterity on his own behalf in late adolescence, was recognized for his talent by omnipresent thieves. He "could not be long overlooked by the members of the swell mob of the metropolis," and it was decided (as if the criminals were some sort of functional decision-making organization) that one Charley Hawkins "should assume the responsibility of bringing the youthful 'gonnauf' in, and regularly inducting him into the association" (10 January 1846). Hawkins, a master pickpocket in his own right, catches Downer in the act and frightens him into joining up with threats of exposure. John Washburn finds his career decided for him when he meets the thief Sam Denny, who "determined to mold him for an associate" (29 August 1846). Lyman Parkes is entrapped; his deep knowledge of the chemistry and engraving of counterfeits prompts a felonious band to devise means "of corrupting him into their diabolical confederacy" (24 January 1846). Parkes's counterfeiting achievements excite "the universal and strong admiration" of the band that traps him, and this "lent a new impulse to his efforts, and in a short time reconciled him to their society. Operated upon by these influences, he at length caught the fascination of crime" (31 January 1846). Starting late did not lessen the bonds of criminal consociation, as the career of John Reed, a professional colleague of both Robert Sutton and the Webbs, made clear: "having been the associate of none but English thieves, from the age of eighteen until forty-six—a period of nearly thirty years—he had imbibed all their notions, acquired all their habits, and squared his moral doctrine by every proposition of the strictest code of the *'cross'* " (6 December 1845).[21]

The facts of criminal causation were statistically presented by the *Police Gazette* as well. An intriguing quantitative assessment of "the causes assigned by the convicts for the commission of the offences for which they are now prison [*sic*]" at Sing-Sing appeared in the issue of 28 February 1846 (table 3).

Biological inheritance, the example set by one's parents, proper child care and religious education, and instruction in a trade—at each level, as we have seen, vicious and criminal propensities might be unwittingly introduced. The inquiry summarized in table 3, however, adds another major dimension to our understanding of contemporary "causes" of crime. In its whole conception this inquiry centers on the premise that the criminal is a proper source, capable of yielding truthful or significant answers to the question: What causes crime? Only a small fraction of the criminals interviewed, moreover, "don't know the cause." Most important, a substantial number of miscreants assign as causes either willful motivations such as "temptation," "anger," "for gain," and "jealousy" ($n = 103$), or the *absence* of those very qualities that supposedly should have restrained criminal behavior—"conscience," "principle," sanity, and will ($n = 56$).[22]

Once natural and environmental damage was accounted for, in short, the active, willful spirit of the prospective felon took over. This independent, conscious, criminal will had to accede to improper social and natural causes for them to wield their dreadful power, and, in this vital sense, the felon's will was *constitutive* of criminality. As with Hare, the criminal fell victim to "a vitiated will" (1 May 1847), which, feeding off "the thousand misdirected feelings and passions, grown beyond restraint, that have pushed reason aside and silenced conscience" (11 July 1846), would tyrannize his future life. "Every departure from morality brings its penalty," commented the *Police Gazette* on the career of James Webb (8 November 1845). Now planted in the

21. Mingling with this mechanistic characterization of criminal socialization is a crude concept of subculture.
22. The letter n refers to the total number of self-reported causes of crime, as given in table 3, that can be classed in each of these two categories.

TABLE 3

Self-Reported Causes of Crime among Convicts

Want of protection in early life	9
Intemperance	150
" of their parents	2
Destitution	84
No conscience	2
Innate Depravity	8
Insanity	9
Weak Principles	31
Sudden Temptation	24
Anger	12
For gain	64
Self-defence	9
Evil Associations	195
Imbecility of mind	6
Jealousy	3
Don't know the cause	3
Innocent (as they assert)	165
Refused to answer any questions	14

Total 790

SOURCE: I have transcribed this table exactly as it appeared in the *National Police Gazette* (28 February 1846).

individual's will, the seed of criminality would mature into a hardy and noxious weed, crowding out good intentions and choking prospects of reform. In the introduction to the life of Lyman Parkes, the journal explicitly emphasized the fatal combination of objective circumstances and subjective will, which together launched the young felon on a life of crime:

> It has long been a mooted point among metaphysicians and general philosophers, how far man is a creature of circumstance or predestination, or the instrument of his own will and of his own acts. As yet it has not been definitely settled. . . . Unlearned as we are in the science of metaphysics, and simple as are our pretensions to a critical acquaintance with the moves and stops which urge or check the human destiny,

whether for good or ill, we still think we can venture to assert that Lyman Parkes was the victim of his own genius, and a combination of adverse circumstances over which he could exercise no control. That he could have closed his hand and turned his fate against the temptations which were so assiduously offered to his embarrassments and his ambition, at any period in his progressive descent into the abyss of crime, is most true; but we are nevertheless obliged to make a charitable contrast between inherent depravity and a forced obliquity of moral conduct. (24 January 1846)

If Lowenthal's popular heroes found success by good fortune, accident, and luck, the *Police Gazette*'s felons deviated through choice. An advertisement from the Boston *Temperance Washingtonian* for "The Lives of the Felons" left no room for doubt on this score: "There is no sickly sentimentality or false sympathy thrown around these Felons. . . . Their crimes are *crimes*, premeditated and predetermined, and not the 'effects of a long train of circumstances beyond their control.' Youthful delinquencies are shown to be the unerring source from whence spring crimes of a deeper dye" (*Police Gazette*, 11 July 1846).[23] Crime was undertaken by choice; the criminal, therefore, was a responsible and autonomous subject who arrogantly refused the halter of political obligation and who violated others' natural rights.

Although the *Police Gazette* sought to assess the vagaries of a specifically criminal character motivated by will, the criminal shared key attributes with the rest of mankind. "Vice stamps no special mark upon its followers," argued the editors; no matter how degraded, "thieves nevertheless are men" (2 January 1847). In almost Shakespearean terms the *Police Gazette* added that "the felon still retains the same pride, the same hopes, the same attachments, the same ambition to excel, and the same dread of sinking in degree, as ever" (16 October 1845).[24] The most loathsome felon could not be discarded "from the scale of human nature" (18 October 1845); and even the

23. Murrell's career is illustrative of the role of free choice: at a very early age he resolves to study law in order "to acquaint myself with all the dangers that laid in the way of success and escape" (12 September 1846).
24. There can be no question from a phenomenological perspective that the criminal's world bestowed its own accent of reality upon his self-understanding and behavior: "The classes which he has abandoned may sneer at and contemn [*sic*], but he will find lesser circles that will reverence and admire. The hatred of mankind may bar him out from general intercourse, but still he has his little outcast world that lets in its measure of Elysium. To the poles of its diameters he is a true man; beyond—a social Ishmael, bearing the mark and curse of Cain" (2 January 1847). Yet, as we have seen, the boundaries of the criminal world were sometimes indistinguishable from those of "general intercourse."

murderer was "human to the enticements of social joys" (24 October 1846).

Indeed, the independence and ambition that marked the felon were especially notable. Lyman Parkes, for example, "was ambitious, and a secret, burning pride, which is the natural offspring of an aspiring mind, made him look forward hopefully to a better destiny" (24 January 1846). Murrell is "strong willed," a "leader" of men (24 April 1847). We find positive qualities most evident in Hare, who, also a "leader" (1 May 1847), manifests "no grovelling spirit or dullness of ambition" (8 May 1847). On the contrary, Hare possesses a "natural personal pride and love of personal independence" (19 June 1847). With his "saucy animal pride" and his primordial autonomy— "an independence that cannot be conferred by political franchises, and which finds its chief pleasure in defying encroachment or invasion" (1 May 1847)— Hare embodies man in the state of nature.

Although the criminal might thus be endowed with positive qualities insofar as he acted as an agent of punitive justice against debased society, he could not be confined exclusively to such a role. Precisely because he was not so different from other men, the rogue acted, fundamentally, as a catalyst of social disorganization. His fundamental behavior was a stark assault on individual rights to property. In all other ways nothing less than a natural man, Hare is irrevocably "perverted to the last degree in relation to the rights of property" (8 May 1847). The Webbs are driven by "acquisitiveness" (8 November 1845); Murrell is a "cold hearted calculator" (24 April 1847). "Gold," generalized the journal, was the rogue's "only incentive" (16 October 1845). The felon's relentless acquisitiveness, his compulsive disrespect for property, crystallized in the active, willful, and concrete "discontent" described above. Lyman Parkes's superior genius is "dissatisfied and repined at the meagre limit and unworthy degree to which it had been consigned" (24 January 1846). George Howell is beset by "temptation" (27 December 1845); Hare is "discontent," a "leader without means." His "ugly and mischievous discontent," again, is "the sullen minister of all the dark and bloody deeds of time." The destruction of the sense of property right occurred within the felon's conscious will:

> Hare wanted money. He wanted it, because some of his companions had it, and he had none. . . . How do men get what they want? Some work for it; some scheme for it, and others—*take* it. This was a dangerous corrollary for a mind which had always gone direct to its will without regard to obstacles. How should *he* get money? By going where money was, and, by taking it. (1 May 1847)

The basic problem, once more, was that contemporary distinctions between "workers" and "schemers" and "takers" were not at all clear.[25] The rogue, concomitantly, was not easily set apart.

The difficulty was met also in phrenology, a precursor to anthropometry and an elaborately systematized attempt to explain behavior in psychobiological terms: phrenology had trouble isolating the criminal as a distinct type. First, phrenology distinguished the rogue by conferring upon him "perverted manifestations of acquisitiveness" (Fowler 1845:96), but to claim simply that a rogue was someone who was acquisitive would put the criminal and capitalist in the same category. Acquisitiveness was defined, in this standard phrenological text, as the love of money "*as an end,* and not as a means," and as a trait evidenced "in bold relief in the human character" (ibid.:89). Only in conjunction with other properties, therefore, such as "Combativeness" and "Destructiveness," could acquisitiveness separate the criminal's drive for gain from that of law-abiding citizens. Even here, however, maintaining the boundaries between the two groups was problematic. Fowler's popular handbook evidently did not rigorously distinguish the criminal from the taskmaster: "One having acquis. very large, with combat. and destruct. also large, and benev. [olence] and conscien. [tiousness] only moderate or full, will 'grind the face of the poor;' practice extortion; take every advantage of his fellow men; and is light fingered" (ibid.:93). This overlap was explicit in a work written by George Lippard, a best-selling writer and journalist of the era:

> Understand, Mr. Hicks was no peculiar character; it was the object of his life to make money, and to keep up a fine appearance with the world; he was just as good a man as hundreds whom you meet every day, on Third street, or in the Exchange, or in any other Temple of Scrip and Stock; and was, withal, no better than any ninety-nine out of a hundred convicts in the Penitentiary. Out and out, through and through, Mr. Hicks was a business man—a perfect business man. Could we say more? (1850:21)

If the businessman's proclivities and character wedded him to the rogue, it was nonetheless vital that a space be found between the two by insisting that the felon's perversion of property right occurred only in tandem with other, equally basic, psychological deformations. A phrenological examination of

25. Davis's study of homicide in American novels before the Civil War characterizes the *fictive* murderer as one who bore "personal guilt and responsibility" for being a "ruthless and immoral competitor" (1968:34, 124).

Murrell thus adjudged him "uncommonly forcible and executive. Is prepared to go through thick and thin to accomplish his purpose. . . . His Acquisitiveness is fully developed, giving rather a strong desire for property; yet it is not a ruling passion" (5 December 1846). Because in the *Police Gazette,* as in the penny press and among the public of the 1830s, acceptance of the right of individual property stood firm, the felon's characterization was a permanent problem.

The felon's perverse depredations dramatized a fearful symmetry between contemporary society and the state of nature. From the rogue's perspective, as, perhaps, from the reader's, it looked as if "all mankind are engaged in preying upon one another, and . . . they who get the most, are the furtherest removed from the common injustice of the world" (19 June 1847). The dimensions of criminality appeared to be coextensive with American society itself; individual delinquents and a corrupt state were locked in a foul embrace, spawning a cycle of escalating depredation and disorganization. Only the *Police Gazette,* by its account, with the press as a whole, stood above these Hobbesian waters, where big fish chased little fish, looking back at the receding shoreline of an ideal republic and forward to an emerging landscape of liberal reform.

7

Democracy and the News

Crime news served as a concrete indicator of the vitality of the principle of natural rights at a time of rising class tension. From the reports on the trial of Richard Robinson for the murder of Helen Jewett to the sustained, broad coverage of crime in the *National Police Gazette,* the young commercial newspapers continued to use this test and its results to cultivate a new social role for themselves as the foremost defender of the public good. The press owed most of its success in its new role to the acceptance of natural rights—in particular, the right to property—by the recently emergent public of journeymen and mechanics. Such acceptance lent the small papers crucial leverage in their earliest years. *Before* the antagonism between capital and labor took a modern form (*before* workers confronted capitalists as propertyless proletarians), the penny press acted as an authentic, albeit a fundamentally self-interested, voice of the artisan public.

Each New Year's Day, following a practice that reached back to the Colonies, newspapers of the antebellum era published broadsheet addresses to their patrons. These addresses might recapture important events of the past year, or present a more general statement of principles. The second course was chosen by the Philadelphia *Public Ledger* ("Address of the Carriers of the Public Ledger 1839"):

> How blest thy lot, to feel no bondage gall,
> No bigot's blighting breath, no despot's thrall!
> Whose laws, designed to fence the rights of man,
> Have ne'er been equalled since the world began!

. . . .
The press, designed for freedom's best defence,
And learning, morals, wisdom to dispense,
Perverted, poisoned, lost to honor's rules,
Is made the sport of knaves, to govern fools.

. . . .
Yet is this noble state by factions vexed,
On every side by demagogues perplexed.

. . . .
   How shall our city from these ills be freed?
How from this downward march of crime recede?
Sustain your laws! Let all their vengeance fall
On those who dare to mock them great or small.
No more rogues in ruffles flaunt secure,
While rogues in rags each penalty endure.

. . . .
We strike for right, and will not spare a blow,
In bold defiance still our ensign show;
All cliques, all sects, all parties we despise,
Above all partial motives proudly rise;
The laws our guide, the good of all our aim,
We yield no principles for transient fame.

With widening class divisions and the transformation of handicraft production, widespread hostility to elite mercantile and political papers found expression in an emergent labor press. The latter, an organizational forum for developing trade unions as well as for the education of the journeymen, did not, however, survive the hard times of the latter 1830s. In the interval between the founding and demise of the labor press, the commercial penny papers arose, boasting of their mass circulation and equating this with a successful defense of public good. If the journeymen complained of unjust monopolies in the three spheres of property, power, and knowledge, these penny papers spoke directly to their grievances. Against unjust concentration of power in the government, the commercial press poised itself as a watchdog in wait for corrupt judges, dishonest police, and venal officials. Against the pretensions to knowledge offered by the sixpenny press, the cheap papers offered "common sense," both popular and scientifically ordained. And, in regard to unjust monopolies of property, the penny press offered entrepreneurial equal rights and an unfocused suspicion of upper-class manners and airs combined with a steadfast commitment to individual property.

In support of its defense of public good, the cheap press invoked journalistic objectivity. It was able to do so successfully, indeed "naturally," because of the pervasive hold of science over the public imagination, a grip made firmer still by photographic realism. "Truth, public faith and science," to use Bennett's terms, commanded that the cheap papers prevail. With advertisers clamoring to take advantage of their exploding circulation, who could disagree?

Yet it is ironic that the American public sphere as it developed in these formative years was directed primarily at absolutist political domination and social privilege (cf. Hohendahl 1979:96–97). Monarchy and aristocracy were left behind forever in the War of Independence, but, in the 1830s, defense of natural rights, public good, and the republic appeared vital in halting a backslide into monarchy and special privilege. This legacy, as we have seen, suffused the young commercial press, especially the *Police Gazette*. It can be glimpsed everywhere: in railings against aristocracy, in hostility to vestiges of English monarchy, which had been smuggled illicitly into the law of the American republic, in generalized suspicion of arbitrary power, in the sustained focus on equal rights of opportunity—in politics, in the economy, and in the public sphere. Objectivity invoked alongside and in support of natural rights became coextensive with resistance to encroachment by longstanding European corruptions. With its universalistic intent, its concern for public rationality based on equal access to the facts, objectivity harbored a profoundly democratic promise. From the 1830s the informational system was not to be the exclusive preserve of a king, a baron, a president, or a class but rather, as it seemed, of the political nation itself.

The *economic* nation was continuing on its course of dynamic change. The public of artisans was gradually destroyed. Factories moved from rural and suburban rivers into the heart of the city; an unskilled work-force, fed by immigrants hungry for work, was created. Changes in urban spatial organization and in the supervision of public order also contributed to a transformation of artisan culture that paralleled the transition to a more fully industrial capitalism. Throughout this complex process, the characteristic tensions of the penny press—between recognition of class as an intrusive force and adherence to individual property, between constant anxiety over "faithless power" and support of the American state—were decisively inclined toward the progressive strengthening of the hand of capital. Technological improvement of printing processes, an extraordinary increase in capital costs, the broadening of the division of labor, and the widening of the market all changed the social constitution of the newspaper and, indeed, of "the facts" themselves.[1]

Some of the main features of the commercial newspaper's emerging role may be briefly outlined. In general, *formal* equality of access to news reports came increasingly to mask *substantive inequality* in public access to information. Members of the public were free to read what was in the paper, but what was in the paper was not to be decided upon by the citizenry or its delegated representatives. Purported equality of access to news concealed, and left to the discretion of news-gathering organizations, the question of which facts would take the measure of the world each day. "Public opinion" began to conceal the unequal strengths of entities in the marketplace of ideas. Individuals who were largely barred from substantive decisions about news were lumped together with governmental and corporate institutions that exercised a direct and powerful interest in the same sphere. News quickly became a language of power, an idiom through which the correspondence between the public truth of events and the social power of their perpetrators was routinely renegotiated.

The tacit formalization of reporting that occurred beneath this veneer of universal facticity deserves brief mention. So that their articles would not " 'clash' and be contradictory," wrote W. Shanks of the *Herald* shortly after the Civil War, journalists should be " 'well trained,' and have learned by long intercourse the ideas, and caught something of the peculiar style, of the Editor-in-Chief" (1867:521). Outlining his strategy for achieving such uniformity, editor Henry Watterson bluntly confirmed that "two minds are better than one if they can be made to go the same way" (in Wingate 1875:22). The advantage of habitually "discussing matters with my subordinates," Watterson found, was that "they get, somehow, into my own way of thinking." On the job training was best in inculcating what was widely termed "the news sense." "To make proper and pleasing selections," wrote a Western journalist, "requires a rare tact, a sort of sixth sense, which is acquired only in the school of experience" (King 1871:9). Organizational imperatives thus substituted for independent professional expertise. By 1906 the author of a textbook for aspiring journalists could charge reporters generally to "cultivate the friendship of influential citizens" (McCarthy 1906:14) and point out matter-of-factly that "rank and social position add to the importance of news." "The mere killing of a mechanic or day laborer seldom gets more than

---

1. This formulation is borrowed from James W. Carey (personal communication).

a paragraph unless the circumstances are extraordinary," he intoned, "but if the King of England or the German Emperor falls down and fractures the royal ankle the incident is worthy of note and is considered a good story. It is easy to see why this is so" (ibid.:16). This indifference to certain social groups was not idiosyncratic: hierarchical news-gathering routines "mirrored" hierarchical social relations; the news net was cast, and a day's catch reflected reality as it had been defined by powerful social actors. New York *Sun* correspondent Julian Ralph mentioned a negotiation between a journalist and an important official, who together decided "to publish or not to publish, as the two agree" (Ralph 1903:184). He conceded that a "beat," as an exclusive news story was often called, was "growing to be more and more a product of intimate acquaintance with public men, and less and less a result of agility of mind and body" (ibid.:193). The simile Ralph chose to illumine the practices of contemporary journalists is striking:

> No one looks for news anymore. That is an old-fashioned idea which outsiders will persist in retaining. News is now gathered systematically by men stationed at all the outlets of it, like guards at the gate of a walled city, by whom nothing can pass in or out unnoticed. (Ibid.:10–11)

Ralph's confident acceptance that news had been definitively nailed down was congruent, paradoxically, with an enduring and prevalent journalistic belief in crude objectivity, or what Schudson (1978) labels "naive empiricism." "Make rules for news?" queried the official biographer of the New York *Sun*. "How is it possible to make a rule for something the value of which lies in the fact that it is the narrative of what never happened, in exactly the same way, before?" (O'Brien 1928:156). Editor Charles Dana believed that "whatever the divine Providence permitted to occur I was not too proud to report" (1895:12). Sufficiently open-ended to give maximum flexibility to market-hungry journals, Dana's conception of news dovetailed with his notion that "there is no system of maxims or professional rules that . . . is laid down for the guidance of the journalist." News was to be a strict and universal reflection of an objectively visible world. Dana thus contrasted the journalist with the physician, with "his system of ethics and that sublime oath of Hippocrates," and with the lawyer, who "also has his code of ethics . . . and the rules of practice which he is instructed in," and noted that he had "never met with a system of maxims that seemed to me to be perfectly adapted to the general direction of a newspaperman" (ibid.:18). For the majority of journalists, or at least for those who found publishers for the autobiographies they also had time to write, objectivity and organizational routine were unproblematic synonyms. By 1900, however, this easy identification was beset by unprecedented problems and tensions. The society in which newspapers were published had changed radically, molding key aspects of journalism and creating dynamic issues and conflicts that the producers of any major public cultural form of necessity had to face.

Even by the 1870s, newspapers had become big business and remained so. Cochran observes that at this time the biggest dailies, reaching circulations of up to 200,000, were worth one or two million dollars—"amounts exceeded by only a few other manufacturing companies" (1975:156). In the mid-1890s Pulitzer's New York *World,* in the forefront of the cut-throat journalism of the era, was worth ten million dollars and brought in a million in profit annually (Emery and Emery 1978:231). A list of the 500 largest American industrial companies in 1917 includes Hearst Publications, the Chicago Daily News, and E. W. Scripps (not to mention auxiliary producers of basic newspaper needs like International Paper and American Type Founders, or the gargantuan electronics firms like General Electric, Westinghouse, Western Electric, and Marconi, which were shortly to launch broadcasting as a social and cultural form) (Navin 1970). "To-day a million dollars will not begin to outfit a metropolitan newspaper," wrote a founding pioneer of American social science, Edward Alsworth Ross (1910:303). The owner of the major urban daily, Ross claimed, was more and more frequently "a business man who finds it hard to see why he should run his property on different lines from the hotel proprietor, the vaudeville manager, or the owner of an amusement park." In contrast to the recent past, "now that the provider of the newspaper capital hires the editor instead of the editor hiring the newspaper capital, the paper is likelier to be run as a money-maker pure and simple—a factory where ink and brains are so applied to white paper as to turn out the largest possible marketable product." This accumulation of "ultimate control" by men with "business motives" Ross termed "the commercialization of the press" (1910:304).

The commercialization of the press brought in-house changes in its train. By 1891 the International Typographical Union had amended its constitution to authorize the issuance of charters to reporters and editors (Quinn 1940:5), and a wave of twenty-one short-lived locals broke and spent itself between 1899 and 1904. Although no truly successful national union was formed before the American Newspaper Guild in 1933, agitation for unions was sporadic on a local scale through the opening decades of the twentieth century. Aside from arduous, unpredictable, long hours and notoriously low pay, a major incentive for unionization was the concentration of ownership within the industry. After 1900, the number of newspapers in operation began a long-term decline; while chain-owned papers burgeoned from 10 percent of total daily circulation in 1900 to 43 percent in 1930 (Sterling and Haight 1978:83). Closure of newspapers and staff reorganization made work tenure precarious for some journalists (Quinn 1940:8; Perry and Perry 1963:210, 476–79).

The rise of mass consumer advertising (cf. Ewen 1976) also directly affected a brand of journalism that had never questioned the essential legitimacy of advertiser support. Whereas in the mid-nineteenth century relatively unorganized advertising by relatively small companies did not exert decisive control over newspaper content (Atwan 1979:16–17), by the turn of the twentieth century both the size and the increased expenditures of advertisers changed this. Estimated advertiser expenditures in 1890 accounted for some $300 million, but by 1909 they reached a billion dollars annually (Sterling and Haight 1978:121). Advertising revenues furnished proportionately more, too, of daily newspaper earnings; and public patronage was less vital now than public attention per se: "The readers are there to *read,* not to provide funds," wrote one observer (Ross 1910:304). To collar a share of growing advertising budgets, the newspaper was prepared to make concessions. Stunts, gimmickry, sensation, flagrant self-advertisement, aggressive investigative campaigns, and yellow journalism were used to wrest readers from other activities and to seize their attention for advertisers. Critics complained that news columns and editorial pages had been subordinated to the profitable sale of editorial space; therefore, wrote one, "it is strictly 'businesslike' to let the big advertisers censor both":

> The immunity enjoyed by the big advertiser becomes the more serious as more kinds of business resort to advertising. Formerly, readers who understood why accidents and labor troubles never occur in department stores, why dramatic criticisms are so lenient, and the reviews of books from the publishers who advertise are so goodnatured, could still expect from their journal an ungloved freedom in dealing with gas, electric, railroad, and banking companies. (Ross 1910:304–5)

The startling rise of huge industrial combines with their extensive consumer-demand management implied to critics that, in the news columns of the sheet "that steers by the cash-register," every concern "that has favors to seek, duties to dodge, or regulations to evade, will be able to press the soft pedal." Cross ownership and trusts also took their toll: "when the shares of a newspaper lie in the safe-deposit box cheek by jowl with gas, telephone, and pipe-line stock, a tenderness for these collateral interests is likely to affect the news columns" (ibid.:305).

Turn-of-the-century America was indeed a heady time for what President Grover Cleveland, in his annual message to Congress in 1888, called "aggregated capital"—the "trusts, combinations and monopolies," such as United States Steel, the Pennsylvania Railroad, or Standard Oil. We cannot linger on the massive and sudden centralization and concentration of capital that occurred around 1900 (cf. Chandler 1977). Nor can we adequately chart the rise of militant reaction, through unionism and radical politics, to what both President Cleveland and the socialist writer Jack London called "an iron heel" of unchecked corporate capitalism. It was a time of savagery in labor relations, when railroad magnate Jay Gould might boast "I can hire one half the working class to kill the other half" (in Boyer and Morais 1972:65). His sentiments and others of the same sort were not lost on many workers. Between 1897 and 1920 union membership expanded from 450,000 to five million. The American Federation of Labor led by Samuel Gompers numbered a million and a half workers by 1904. Not all unions were radical in their challenge to the American state, but the emergence of union power was itself unprecedented. It was also a time of bitter and well-remembered strikes, particularly as World War I drew nigh: strikes led by the Industrial Workers of the World in Lawrence in 1912, and at Paterson in 1913; the Ludlow Massacre in 1914; the Los Angeles *Times* protest, climaxing in the dynamiting of its building in 1910; the steel strike of 1919. Gains were registered by employees—workmen's compensation, laws for factory safety, legislation on maximum hours for women and children may be mentioned (cf. Derber 1970), but conflict continued to escalate. In 1915 1,246 strikes were called, affecting some 470,000 employees. In 1917, 4,233 strikes involved 1,200,000 workers. In 1919, when conflict reached fever pitch in the Pittsburgh area over the steel strike, 3,253 strikes shot through the lives of 3,950,000 workers (Bing 1921:293). It was the heyday of the Socialist Party; while, further to the left, the Wobblies waged free speech fights and attacked "the prostituted press" as a fearsome head of that Hydra, capitalism (*Solidarity,* 7 July 1917; in Bing 1921:256). In a context such as this, any account of working conditions or strike report in the metropolitan press was likely to be caught, framed, and illuminated by the stark contest between organized capital and organizing labor—with consequences to be explored momentarily.

From the vantage point of concerned journalists, advertiser control and the rise of public relations, set against the contrary notions of an often indignant and even militant public, were nothing short of catastrophic. Frank Cobb of the New York *World* stated in 1919 that

> many of the direct channels to news have been closed and the informa-
> tion for the public is first filtered through publicity agents. The great
> corporations have them, the banks have them, the railroads have them,
> all the organizations of business and of social and political activity have
> them, and they are the media through which the news comes. Even
> statesmen have them. (In Schudson 1978:139)

The "walled city" of which Julian Ralph had earlier written was creating problems of access in a society that protected those whose motivating princi-ple was self-interest and whose interests had grown into powerful institutions. Unless a reporter knew that news "almost always starts from a special group," warned Walter Lippmann in 1920, "he is doomed to report the surface of events. He will report the ripples of a passing steamer, and forget the tides and the currents and the ground-swell. . . . He will deal with the flicker of events and not with their motives" (1920:87). Intertwining with an informational system that followed the curves of social power, blind adher-ence to the earlier form of objectivity allowed the emergence and phenomenal expansion of what has since been termed news management (cf. Schudson 1978; Raucher 1968). The power of institutional sources to mold versions of events pushed or pulled into the public sphere had become glaringly appar-ent.

This was so evident by the turn of the century that a stream of harsh criticism began to descend on the practice of journalism. As early as 1890, an article entitled "An Inside View of Commercial Journalism" demon-strated starkly how Nebraska newspapers had uniformly consented to sell their news and editorial columns to advertisers (Bishop 1890). In the *Nation* and the *New Republic,* especially, complaints over the character of the chang-ing public sphere were loudly voiced. One article excoriated statesmen whose first thought was "not how can I keep this from becoming known, but how can I make it known so as best to work out to my advantage, or that of my party?" (*Nation,* 17 December 1908, p. 594). Hearst's papers were alternately condemned for a rampant lack of "accuracy" and for the mighty editorial and political clout they collectively exercised (*New Republic,* 5 June 1915, p. 105; *Nation,* 10 September 1908, p. 229). Long before communications researchers got wind of the idea, detailed exposures of the techniques whereby journalists were subordinated to private interest, through "the blue pencil" (*New Republic,* 14 December 1918, pp. 192–94), the bribe, and the sack (Sinclair 1919), were common. *Harper's Weekly* (25 July 1914) joined in with revelations about Hearst's brand of journalism; the *Atlantic Monthly* gave space to sociologist Ross's thesis entitled "The Suppression of Important News" (Ross 1910). In their widely remembered essay, "A Test of the News," Lippmann and Merz presented devastating evidence to support their conclusion that "from the point of view of professional journalism the reporting of the Russian Revolution is nothing short of a disaster" (1920:3). Why? Because the *New York Times,* the focus of their study, had been "seriously misled" in its reliance "upon the official purveyors of information":

> It indicates that statements of fact emanating from governments and the circles around governments as well as from the leaders of political movements cannot be taken as judgments of fact by an independent press. They indicate opinion, they are controlled by special purpose, and they are not trustworthy news. (Ibid.:41)

Men were wondering, Lippmann announced, "whether government by consent can survive in a time when the manufacture of consent is an unregulated private enterprise" (1920:5). "Not hyperbolically and contemptuously, but literally and with scientific precision," chipped in the gadfly Upton Sinclair, "we define Journalism in America as the business and practice of presenting the news of the day in the interest of economic privilege" (1919:222).

What had changed decisively over nine decades was the definition of corrupting private interest—it now stood revealed as "economic privilege." Such resounding denunciations brought the hopes and fears of the 1830s into a new time: "So long as there is interposed between the ordinary citizen and the facts a news organization determining by entirely private and unexamined standards, no matter how lofty, what he shall know, and hence what he shall believe, no one will be able to say that the substance of democratic government is secure" (Lippmann 1920:12–13). The language of public good against private interest was renewed and made ready for another round. "There is everywhere an increasingly angry disillusionment about the press, a growing sense of being baffled and misled; and wise publishers will not pooh-pooh these omens," Lippmann charged (ibid.:75–76). In turn, the newspaper, the journalistic occupation, and the conventional practice of objectivity were again transformed in a crucible of social conflict.

Lippmann identified a "crisis in journalism" (ibid.:5) that stemmed from a resurgence of open class antagonism in society. In testimony before the

Senate Commission on Industrial Relations, John L. Matthews, editor of the *Paterson Press,* conceded that passages such as the one below were common in his paper during the agitation in 1913 by the Industrial Workers of the World:

> Akron could not find a law to banish this dangerous revolutionist and his cohorts, but a citizens' committee of 1,000 men did the trick in short order. Can Akron accomplish something that Paterson, N.J., can not duplicate? This Paterson Press dislikes to believe it, but time will tell. (1916:3:2582–84)

The San Diego *Tribune* of 4 March 1912 was less restrained: "Hanging is none too good for them. They would be much better dead" (in Boyer and Morais 1972:173). When the I.W.W.'s Frank Little was murdered in Butte, Montana, the Boston *Transcript* said that it knew "of millions of people who, while sternly reprehending such proceedings as the lynching of members of that anti-patriotic society (the I.W.W.), will nevertheless be glad, in their hearts, that Montana did it in the case of Little" (in Bing 1921:249).

This list of vituperation might be expanded at will. More to the point is that such utterances as the ones just cited were "spread far and wide by the radical press" (Bing 1921:250). The Wobblies' *Solidarity* and the Socialists' New York *Call* devoted much space to reprinting and condemning the violent language of innuendo and outright incitement common to much of the commercial press. After a particularly flagrant instance of abuse by the commercial press in a full-page advertisement in the Seattle *Post-Intelligencer* on 18 November 1919, the employees of the paper met and refused to continue work until the advertisement was removed. The resolution of protest the employees adopted is worth reproducing:

> We have been patient under misrepresentation, faithful in the face of slander, long suffering under insult; we have upheld our agreements and produced your paper, even though in so doing we were braiding the rope with which you propose to hang us; day after day we have put in type, stereotyped, printed and mailed calumny after calumny, lie after lie, insult after insult. . . . So long as these things appeared to be a part of your unfair fight against organization—our organization and others— we have been able to endure them in the hope that at last truth must prevail. But there must be a limit to all things. In the page advertisement, purporting to have been written and paid for by one Selvin, but which had as well have occupied the position in your paper usually taken up by your editorial page, your utter depravity as a newspaper, your shame-

less disregard of the laws of the land, your hatred of opposition, your reckless policy of appeal to the passions of the citizenry, reached depths of malice and malignancy hitherto unbelievable. It is nothing less than excitation to violence, stark and naked invitation to anarchy. If your business management cannot demonstrate its capacity and sagacity, if your editorial directing heads must remain blind to the things they are bringing us to; if, together, you cannot see the abyss to which you are leading us—all of us; if you have no more love for our common country than is manifested in your efforts to plunge it into anarchy, then as loyal American citizens—many of us ex-service men who very clearly proved our faith in America and its institutions—we must—not because we are unionists, but because we are Americans—find means to protect ourselves from the stigma of having aided and abetted your campaign of destruction. (In Bing 1921:250–51)

We are once again in the midst of a fiercely conservative appeal to the common good. A similar spirit pervaded the *New Republic*'s critique of the *New York Times* (18 September 1915), when the latter supported the barring of I.W.W. speakers from strike-ravaged Paterson: "It [the *Times*] admits 'that free speech is a noble and indispensable right.' But in view of the fact that the I.W.W. speakers are 'spouters' and 'ranters' and 'rattlesnakes,' and because Paterson lost fifteen million dollars in the recent strike, the authorities are justified in breaking the law and violating the letter and spirit of the Constitution of the United States." The journal went on: "Is the *Times* in favor of the Constitution only when it protects property rights? Is it against the Constitution when it protects the rights of 'spouters' and 'ranters'?" The longstanding concern about private interest and monopoly, revised according to changing circumstances, now assumed a marked economic accent. And when newsstand distributors Ward & Gow broke their contract with the radical *Masses* magazine, the *New Republic* commented: "When a private corporation which monopolizes one important avenue through which news is distributed sets up a censorship it creates an intolerable condition" (29 January 1916, p. 319).

The critique of journalism as a class practice fanned out to challenge hierarchical news values. After the Industrial Relations Commission investigation of tenant farmers in Texas, the *New Republic* observed that only the Socialist New York *Call* had paid any heed to its report.

The other papers have evidently not regarded the plight of the tenant farmers as very important news. The vaudeville performance of Mr. Carnegie was worth columns of space and elaborate editorials. But the rural slums of the Southwest are not headline material. . . . And then people are distressed by agitators. (27 March 1915, p. 191)

One journalist felt threatened enough by the crisis in journalism to protest, in an article appropriately entitled "In Defense of Reporters," that the public must not think that the "fact-loving, truth-serving, intelligent reporter" was a thing of the past. *Publishers* with these qualifications, he admitted, were, however, rarely to be found (*New Republic,* 10 June 1916, p. 147).

Lippmann's argument that "the present crisis of western democracy is a crisis in journalism" (1920:5) was not a mere figure of speech. Escalating social conflicts were putting pressure directly on the practice and characteristic forms of commercial journalism. This is nowhere more obvious than in the analysis written by journalist M. K. Wisehart entitled "The Pittsburgh Newspapers and the Steel Strike" for the Interchurch World Movement (1921).

On 22 September 1919, launching one of the bitterest strikes of the century, 350,000 steel workers around the nation walked off their jobs. The reasons for their strike, the conditions in the steel industry, and the level of militancy among strikers have been discussed elsewhere (cf. Brecher 1972: 118–28). In western Pennsylvania, the heart of the industry, the strike met a particularly fierce response from employers. Pittsburgh newspapers were evidently deeply implicated in this reaction. Documenting his extensive critique with eighty-odd pages of examples taken from the press, Wisehart reached this conclusion:

> It is inconceivable that the public which relied on the Pittsburgh newspapers could, by any human method of reading newspapers and allowing both for exaggeration due to bias and inaccuracy due to haste, have understood either the causes of the steel strike or the significance of its incidents. (1921:147)

A "policy of antagonism to the strike" had been manifested and sustained in the press and related directly to its adherence to long-touted, standard reporting practices. The context of the strike was so highly charged as to make these standards dramatically inadequate. Wisehart claimed that the press's flagrant abuse had been occasioned

> (c) by silence as to actual industrial grievances and by publishing statistics in a misleading way.

· ·

(e) by accepting and publishing accounts of violence and disorder from the employers' and officials' point of view without investigation of such incidents.

. . . .

(g) by effectual suppression of news whose tendency would have been to inspire a fair-minded examination of repressive conditions in the Pittsburgh district. (Ibid.:147–48)

The only unprecedented feature of any of this was that in the pitched battle the conventions of objective reportage were shown to be glaringly inappropriate. "The newspapers accepted such accounts," stated Wisehart in retrospect "as were given by the police or other authorities" (ibid.:148). And it was even possible for this Church-sponsored investigator to charge that

> there were no headlines such as: "Steel Workers say they work 7 days a week"; or "Half the Steel Workers are on the 12-hour day"; or "Steel Common Laborers declare they cannot earn enough for families"; or "Workers demand right to hold union meetings." (Ibid.:153)

He continues in the older tradition of investigative journalism (and also in the more modern tradition of naturalist description in novel and drama): "And yet these things were facts, they were news, they constituted the news which explained the strike, they were the 'news peg' of daily happenings, and they were all more or less accessible to reporters." The most damning indictment that Wisehart could make was that "the essential facts, *which were found by others during the strike,* could have been gathered at the time by investigating newspapermen, if searching investigation had been what the newspapers wanted" (ibid.). In a context of apparent class war, objectivity was hidebound.

With conflict both so intense and so focused, it was not easy to hold, with naive objectivity, that the facts were unproblematic. During the steel strike, unions in Wheeling, West Virginia, resolved: "We have knowledge that the Public Press fear to be impartial in this strike and give an unbiased, true account of actual conditions" (ibid.:154). Immediately following the strike, which the employees lost in January 1920, labor unions made determined attempts to launch their own national news service and to establish their own daily press (ibid.:89). "I propose," declared Upton Sinclair, "that we shall found and endow a weekly publication of truth-telling, to be known as 'The National News' ":

This publication will carry no advertisements and no editorials. It will not be a journal of opinion, but a record of events pure and simple. It will be published on ordinary news-print paper, and in the cheapest possible form. It will have one purpose, and one only, to give to the American people once every week the truth about the world's events. It will be strictly and absolutely nonpartisan, and never the propaganda organ of any cause. It will watch the country, and see where lies are being circulated and truth suppressed; its job will be to nail the lies, and bring the truth into the light of day. (1919:438–39)

Here as virtually everywhere, even during the most polarized period of the early twentieth century, *the ideal* of unitary truth with universal application continued to be uncontested. Lippmann hammered home the same point in arguing that "opinion could be made at once free and enlightening only by transferring our interest from 'opinion' to the objective realities from which it springs" (1920:97). "The real enemy is ignorance," continued this advocate of refereed pluralism, "from which all of us, conservative, liberal, and revolutionary, suffer. . . . We must go back of our opinions to the neutral facts for unity and refreshment of spirit" (ibid.:98–99). His use of the first-person plural was revealing; ideological disagreement was contained only by the purportedly ideal neutrality of the facts: "In going behind opinion to the information which it exploits, and in making the validity of the news our ideal, we shall be . . . protecting for the public interest that which all the special interests in the world are most anxious to corrupt" (ibid.:70). Lippmann therefore again hoped for the formation of a news agency backed by "those whose interests are not represented in the existing news-organization" —"organized labor and militant liberalism" (ibid.:99, 101). The organization would be one "in which editorial matter was rigorously excluded" (ibid.:103; cf. Ross 1910:310–11).

In such proposals the ideal of a unitary and universal truth was used explicitly to cultivate a single community in the face of sustained discord. The long-declared commitment of institutional journalism to the segregation of fact from value now became the peculiar warrant of the journalistic *profession* (cf. Schudson 1978). "If the news agencies fell into the hands of pacifists the whole complexion of facts would be different," charged the *New Republic* (24 April 1915, p. 290). Such sentiments as this in no way undermined the ideal of objectivity but rather gave it a new twist. Because of social polarization, it was imperative that journalism become "a specifically trained profession, for in schools of journalism there is an opportunity to train that sense of reality and perspective which great reporting requires." Indeed, the journal continued,

> There is an opportunity to create a morale as disinterested and as interesting as that of the scientists who are the reporters of natural phenomena. News-gathering cannot perhaps be as accurate as chemical research, but it can be undertaken in the same spirit. (Ibid.)

Scientific expertise mustered in support of what Gans called "responsible capitalism" (1979:206) was hailed in journalism as well as in other spheres of Progressive reform (cf. Derber 1970). What the *New Republic* frankly recognized as "the fundamental conflict between the economic interests" of wage earner and capitalist could and should be tempered by organized "arbitration" (21 October 1916, p. 283). Otherwise, "class suspicion and hatred" would drive labor "to meet force with force" (ibid:285). As was plain to many, however, this "spirit of arbitration" had been betrayed repeatedly by press coverage of labor. "If the principle of arbitration is to prevail," the magazine asserted, "facts must take the place of special pleading." And, finally, "for help in the accomplishment of this great transformation," it was imperative above all "to rely upon the conscientious sobriety of the daily press," with its capacity to lead "an enlightened public opinion" (ibid.:283, 285). With science for its ideal, what Lippmann termed "a sense of evidence" and a pragmatic "working knowledge of the main stratifications and current of interest" would serve as the best method of journalistic practice (1920:87). When Joseph Pulitzer drew up plans to establish a school of journalism at Columbia University in 1902, he distinguished sharply between business and editorial imperatives and singled out "the Editorial point of view," with its special emphasis on accurate and reliable reporting, as the fundamental concern of the proposed academic venture (Baker 1954:23–24). In the divisive two decades that followed, Lippmann's belief that training for journalists must be so designed that "the ideal of objective testimony is cardinal" took clear shape (in Schudson 1978:152).

The ensuing subordination of journalists to an explicit objectivity established a new legitimacy for the entire news-gathering system in the form of a standard that implies in its application a probing of "the validity of the news." By charging individual journalists with responsibility for mistakes and prejudices, the systemic biases of news-gathering organizations (the actual weave of the news net, to invoke Professor Tuchman's [1978a] phrase) might be implicitly avoided and displaced. Journalistic professionalism, accordingly, now might assist in reclaiming the commercial newspapers' earlier role of the defense of public good by demonstrating that the century-old ideals of the commercial press were being adhered to.

The forces that made "the validity of the news" a major concern also brought about a major change in the definition of objectivity. Objectivity was now invested with widely discrepant meanings by different, or opposed, social actors. One catches a glimpse of this in the American Newspaper Guild's code of ethics, as stated in 1935 (during another wave of social turmoil) before the U. S. Senate Committee on Education and Labor; the Guild believed

> (1) That the newspaperman's first duty is to give the public accurate and unbiased news reports. (1935:727)

Thus the Guild enshrined its adherence to the ideal of objectivity. Yet its concern with "the validity of the news" was also given dramatic and substantial expression:

> (2) That the equality of all men before the law should be observed by the men of the press; that they should not be swayed in news reporting by political, economic, social, racial, or religious prejudices, but should be guided only by fact and fairness. (Ibid.)

More specifically, the union held

> (4) That the guild should work through efforts of its members, or by agreement with editors and publishers, to curb the suppression of legitimate news concerning "privileged" persons or groups, including advertisers, commercial powers, and friends of newspapermen. . . .
> . . . .
> (6) That the news be edited exclusively in the editorial rooms instead of in the business office of the daily newspaper. (Ibid.)

In two codicils the Guild added to its challenge of established practices a dual condemnation:

> (1) The carrying of publicity in the news columns in the guise of news matter.
> (2) The current practice of requiring the procuring or writing of stories

which newspapermen know are false or misleading and which work oppression or wrong to persons and to groups. (Ibid.:728)

Yet, hearing this code of ethics read out, Senator Clark of the Committee asked blandly: "As I understand, that requires that they tell the truth?" "Yes sir," responded Newspaper Guild Vice President Robert M. Buck, tersely switching codes, "that is it, Senator" (ibid.). My point in elaborating this exchange is that objectivity had become polysemic: its universality as an ideal might shield open disparities in its application and interpretation. Objectivity was now nothing less than a socially patterned and stratified cultural resource. The captains of the newspaper industry were thus able to invoke the same ideal to a very different end when they attacked the Newspaper Guild's stand in favor of a closed shop. The Guild, said *Editor and Publisher* in its issue of 3 March 1934, "would defeat the right of the public to enjoy the interests of free, non-partisan disinterested news reporting":

> It is a simple minded notion that reporters and editors, sufficiently imbued with class conscious spirit to join a union and affiliate with other unions would continue to treat news from the viewpoint of impartial observers. They sacrifice neutrality and admit partisanship by their very act. (In Quinn 1940:48)

It was the journalist's job, the publishers insisted, to report controversy "not as a partisan but as an objective observer" (in Schudson 1978:157). In the 1830s apparent class divisions had led the penny papers to claim a universal truth based on natural right. A century later class divisions highlighted the boundaries of objectivity. The practice of objectivity had become open to fundamental dispute.

Disagreement over the substantive character of objectivity itself, however, has tended to be sharply limited. Instead, social conflicts have been disguised, contained, and displaced through the imposition of news objectivity, a framework legitimating the exercise of social power over the interpretation of reality. Those without institutionalized resources have, time and again, found themselves pilloried and marginalized in the press, while crucial issues have been amplified in such a way as to lead the general public to accept institutional control. McCarthy and his heirs found the press a willing partner in the adroit manipulation of the public (cf. Caute 1978:446–56). Routine reliance upon accredited sources permitted news management of the Vietnam war to sustain what may be termed "public opinion from above" (cf. Chomsky and Herman 1979). Today, the horrific and still largely untold story of nuclear power furnishes yet another dramatic example. Keller (1980) quotes ABC's Vice President for Program Development, Av Westin, as saying that, for years before Three Mile Island, "a general good will existed between the nuclear industry and the network news departments, whereby we all accepted the initial safety arguments for nuclear energy." The consequence of this friendly feeling, which was buttressed by expensive public relations efforts, was that for subjects critical of nuclear power a higher standard of proof came into play. In Westin's terms, those who opposed nuclear energy "were forced to prove their case more than those who supported it" (ibid.:16). This sort of abuse occurs, not through the mistakes or biases or corruptions of individual reporters, but because the press is institutionally placed to be used in this way. It is objectivity that protects journalists in their role as "the strongest remaining bastion of logical positivism in America" (Gans 1979:184), and whose scientistic aura sets up a formidable barrier to comprehension of actual news values. News remains credible in its insistence that, in ideal principle, it animates and displays no values whatsoever.

Scholars as well as lay activists also continue, on the other hand, to pierce objectivity's scientistic veneer and have amply demonstrated the social, organizational, ideological, and occupational constraints on the press and its invisible frame. Their critique points to renewed understanding of our common need for democratic public information, an ideal that returns at once to what is still valid and useful in the historic birth of the popular press. We must redeem the democratic promise that has, since the 1830s, been latent in the American information system. We must strive for a public sphere in which the people themselves rather than undelegated groups from their midst will be lord of the facts.

BIBLIOGRAPHY

Contemporary Publications

1839   Address of the Carriers of the Public Ledger. Printed for the Carriers by Wm. F. Rackliff, South-West Corner of George and Swanwick Streets.

Alcott, William A.

1839   *The Young Man's Guide.* Boston: Perkins and Marvin.

Ames, Mary Clemmer

1874   *Ten Years in Washington: Life and Scenes in the National Capital, as a Woman Sees Them.* Hartford: A. D. Worthington.

Austin, John M.

1838   *A Voice to Youth: Addressed to Young Men and Young Ladies.* Utica: Grosh and Hutchinson.

Bell, William H.

1850–51 *Diary.* New-York Historical Society Manuscript Collection. Microfilm.

Bing, Alexander M.

1921   *War-Time Strikes and Their Adjustment.* New York: E. P. Dutton.

Bishop, J. B.

1890   "An Inside View of Commercial Journalism." *Nation,* 12 June 1890, pp. 463–64.

1842   *The Boy's Manual, Comprising a Summary View of the Studies, Accomplishments, and Principles of Conduct Best Suited for Promoting Respectability and Success in Life.* New York: D. Appleton.

Dana, Charles A.

1895   *The Art of Newspaper Making.* New York: D. Appleton.

"The Decline of the Novel."

1868   *Nation,* 14 May 1868, pp. 389–90.

Foster, George G.

1850a   *Celio; or, New York above Ground and under Ground.* New York: Dewitt & Davenport.

1850b   *New York by Gas-Light.* New York: Dewitt & Davenport.

1854   *Fifteen Minutes around New York.* New York: Dewitt & Davenport.

Fowler, O. N.

1845   *Fowler's Practical Phrenology: Giving a Concise Elementary View of Phrenology.* 22d ed. New York: O. S. and L. N. Fowler.

Given, John L.
    1907   *Making a Newspaper.* New York: Henry Holt.
Godkin, E. L.
    1865   "The Newspaper and the Reader." *Nation,* 10 August 1865, pp. 165–66.
Greeley, Horace (ed.)
    1853   *Art and Industry as Represented in the Exhibition at the Crystal Palace New York 1853–4.* New York: Redfield.
    1872   *The Great Industries of the United States.* Hartford: J. B. Burr & Hyde.
Grund, Francis
    1837   *The Americans in Their Moral, Social, and Political Relations.* Boston: Marsh, Capen and Lyon.
Hammond, Jabez D.
    1842   *The History of Political Parties in the State of New-York.* 2 vols. Albany: C. Van Benthysen.
Hone, Philip
    1835–36   *Diaries.* New-York Historical Society Manuscript Collection. Microfilm.
Hudson, Frederic
    1873   *Journalism in the United States: From 1690 to 1872.* New York: Harper and Brothers.
Ingersoll, Lurton D.
    1873   *The Life of Horace Greeley.* Chicago: Union Publishing.
Kennedy, Joseph C. G.
    1862   *Preliminary Report on the Eighth Census.* Washington: Government Printing Office.
King, Henry
    1871   *American Journalism.* Topeka, Kansas: Commonwealth State Printing House.
Levermore, Charles H.
    1901   "The Rise of Metropolitan Journalism, 1800–1840." *American Historical Review* 6 (3): 446–65.
Lippard, George
    1850   *The Killers: A Narrative of Real Life in Philadelphia.* Philadelphia: Hankinson and Bartholomew.
Lippmann, Walter
    1920   *Liberty and the News.* New York: Harcourt, Brace and Howe.
Lippmann, Walter, and Merz, Charles
    1920   "A Test of the News." *New Republic,* 4 August 1920, pt. 2, 1–42.
Martin, Edward Winslow
    1868   *The Secrets of the Great City.* Philadelphia: National.
Matsell, George Washington
    1859   *Vocabulum; or, The Rogue's Lexicon.* New York: G. W. Matsell.
McCarthy, James
    1906   *The Newspaper Worker.* New York: The Press Guild.
Morrow, John
    1860   *A Voice from the Newsboys.* New York: Published for the Benefit of the Author.

North, S. N. D.
    1884   *The Newspaper and Periodical Press: A Special Report for the Tenth Census (1880).* Washington: Government Printing Office.
O'Brien, Frank M.
    1928   *The Story of the Sun.* New York: Greenwood Press.
    1845   "Periodical Reading." *The United States Magazine, and Democratic Review,* New Series, 16 (79):59–61.
Paine, Thomas
    1967   *The Writings of Thomas Paine.* Ed. Moncure Daniel Conway. 4 vols. New York: AMS Press.
Pray, Isaac Clark
    1855   *Memoirs of James Gordon Bennett and His Times.* New York: Stringer and Townsend.
"The Press."
    1811   *The Port Folio,* new series, 5 (6):522–38.
Quinn, Russell
    1940   *History of the San Francisco–Oakland Newspaper Guild.* Works Projects Administration 10008 San Francisco, August. O. P. 665–08–3–12. (History of San Francisco Journalism Series, vol. 3, E. L. Daggett, Supervisor.)
Ralph, Julian
    1903   *The Making of a Journalist.* New York: Harper and Brothers.
Robinson, Richard P.
    1837   *A Letter from Richard P. Robinson, as Connected with the Murder of Ellen Jewett, Sent in a Letter to His Friend, Thomas Armstrong, with a Defence of the Jury.* New York: Sold Wholesale at 29 Ann-Street.
Ross, Edward Alsworth
    1910   "The Suppression of Important News." *Atlantic Monthly* 105 (March):303–11.
Shanks, W. F. G.
    1867   "How We Get Our News." *Harper's New Monthly Magazine* 34 (March):511–22.
Sinclair, Upton
    1919   *The Brass Check.* Pasadena: Published by the Author.
    1836   *Sketch of the Life of Miss Ellen Jewett. By One Who Knew Her. Who Was Murdered in the City of New-York, on Saturday Evening, April 9, 1836.* Boston: J. Q. Adams.
Skidmore, Thomas
    1829   *The Rights of Man to Property!* New York. (Republished by Burt Franklin, 1964.)
Smith, Matthew Hale
    1868   *Sunshine and Shadow in New York.* Hartford: J. B. Burr.
    1854   *Statistical View of the United States.* Washington: A. O. P. Nicholson.
Tocqueville, Alexis de
    1961   *Democracy in America.* 2 vols. New York: Schocken Books. (First American Edition 1838.)

United Kingdom. Parliament. House of Commons
    1851   *Report from the Select Committee on Newspaper Stamps.* London: H. M. Stationery Office.

United States. Congress. Senate
    1885   *Report of the Committee of the Senate upon the Relations between Labor and Capital, and Testimony Taken by the Committee.* 5 vols. 48th Congress. Washington: Government Printing Office.

    1916   *Final Report and Testimony Submitted to Congress by the Commission on Industrial Relations.* vol. 3. 64th Congress, 1st Session. Document no. 415. Washington: Government Printing Office.

    1935   *Hearings before the Committee on Education and Labor on S. 1958.* pt. 3. 74th Congress, 1st Session. Washington: Government Printing Office.

Wilkes, George
    1844   *Original Work: The Mysteries of the Tombs; A Journal of Thirty Days Imprisonment in the New York City Prison: For Libel.* New York: n. p.

    1849   *The Life of Helen Jewett.* New-York: For Sale By Booksellers Generally.

Williams, Edwin (ed.)
    1834   *New-York as It Is, in 1834; and Citizens' Advertising Directory.* New York: J. Disturnell.

Wilmer, Lambert A.
    1859   *Our Press Gang; or, A Complete Exposition of the Corruptions and Crimes of the American Newspaper.* Philadelphia: J. T. Lloyd.

Wingate, Charles F. (ed.)
    1875   *Views and Interviews on Journalism.* New York: F. B. Patterson.

Wisehart, M. K.
    1921   *Interchurch World Movement Report on Public Opinion and the Steel Strike.* New York: Harcourt, Brace & Co.

Newspapers

Albany
    Daily Albany Argus (1835)
Baltimore
    Niles' Weekly Register (1834–35)
London
    Cleave's Weekly Police Gazette (1835–36)
    North Briton (1762)
    Police Gazette; or, Hue and Cry (1826)
New York City
    Evening Post (1836)
    Herald (1835–36)
    Man (1834)

National Police Gazette (1845–50)
New York Mechanic (1834)
New York Times (1851)
Subterranean (1845)
Sun (1833–34)
Transcript (1834)
Tribune (1845)

Philadelphia
Philadelphia Times, Mechanics' Free Press and Working Man's Register (1828)
Public Ledger (1836)
Spirit of the Times (1842)

Utica
The Mechanics' Press (1829–30)

Washington, D.C.
National Intelligencer (1835)

Magazines
Harper's Weekly (1914)
Nation (1865, 1870, 1890, 1908)
New Republic (1915–20)
The New World (1843)
Scientific American (1845)

Secondary Works

Ames, William E., and Teeter, Dwight L.
  1971   "Politics, Economics, and the Mass Media." In *Mass Media and the National Experience,* eds. Ronald T. Farrar and John D. Stevens, pp. 38–63. New York: Harper and Row.

Antunes, George E., and Hurley, Patricia A.
  1977   "The Representation of Criminal Events in Houston's Two Daily Newspapers." *Journalism Quarterly* 54 (4):756–60.

Atwan, Robert
  1979   "Newspapers and the Foundations of Modern Advertising." In *The Commercial Connection,* ed. John W. Wright, pp. 9–23. New York: Delta.

Auerbach, Erich
  1953   *Mimesis: The Representation of Reality in Western Literature.* Princeton: Princeton University Press.

Bagdikian, Ben H.
  1971   *The Information Machines.* New York: Harper and Row.

Baker, Keith Michael
  1975   *Condorcet; From Natural Philosophy to Social Mathematics.* Chicago: University of Chicago Press.

Baker, Richard Terrill
  1954   *A History of the Graduate School of Journalism, Columbia University.*
          New York: Columbia University Press.
Barthes, Roland
  1975   *Mythologies.* New York: Hill and Wang.
Benjamin, Walter
  1973   *Charles Baudelaire: A Lyric Poet in the Era of High Capitalism.* London: New Left Books.
Bessie, Simon Michael
  1938   *Jazz Journalism.* New York: E. P. Dutton.
Blankenburg, William B., and Walden, Ruth
  1977   "Objectivity, Interpretation and Economy in Reporting." *Journalism Quarterly* 54 (3):591–95.
Bloomfield, Maxwell
  1976   *American Lawyers in a Changing Society 1776–1876.* Cambridge: Harvard University Press.
Bosco, A.
  1978   "Lectures at the Pillory: The Early American Execution Sermon." *American Quarterly* 30 (2):156–76.
Boyer, Richard O., and Morais, Herbert M.
  1972   *Labor's Untold Story.* New York: United Electrical, Radio and Machine Workers of America.
Brecher, Jeremy
  1972   *Strike!* Boston: South End Press.
Breed, Warren
  1955   "Social Control in the Newsroom: A Functional Analysis." *Social Forces* 33:326–35.
  1958   "Mass Communication and Social Integration." *Social Forces* 37:109–16.
Bruchey, Stewart
  1968   *The Roots of American Economic Growth 1607–1861.* New York: Harper and Row.
Callcott, George H.
  1970   *History in the United States 1800–1860.* Baltimore: Johns Hopkins Press.
Capp, Bernard
  1979   *Astrology and the Popular Press.* London: Faber and Faber.
Carey, James W.
  1969   "The Communications Revolution and the Professional Communicator." In *Sociology of Mass Media Communicators,* ed. Paul Halmos. *The Sociological Review Monograph Number 13:*23–38.
  1974   "The Problem of Journalism History." *Journalism History* 1 (1):2–5.
Caute, David
  1978   *The Great Fear.* New York: Simon and Schuster.
Chandler, Alfred D., Jr.
  1972   "Anthracite Coal and the Beginnings of the Industrial Revolution in the United States." *Business History Review* 46 (2):141–81.

1977   *The Visible Hand.* Cambridge, Mass.: Belknap Press.
Chaney, David
1977   "Communication and Community." Working Papers in Sociology, no. 12. Mimeographed. Department of Sociology and Social Administration, University of Durham.
Chibnall, Steve
1975   "The Crime Reporter: A Study in the Production of Commercial Knowledge." *Sociology* 9 (1):49–66.
1977   *Law-and-Order News.* London: Tavistock.
Chomsky, Noam, and Herman, Edward S.
1979   *The Washington Connection and Third World Fascism.* Boston: South End Press.
Cochran, Thomas C.
1975   "Media as Business: A Brief History." *Journal of Communication* 25 (4):155–65.
1977   *200 Years of American Business.* New York: Basic Books.
Commons, John R.; Phillips, Ulrich B.; Gilmore, Eugene A.; Sumner, Helen L.; and Andrews, John B.
1958   *A Documentary History of American Industrial Society.* Vol. 3. New York: Russell & Russell.
Comte, Auguste
1970   *Introduction to Positive Philosophy.* Ed. and trans. Frederick Ferre. New York: Bobbs-Merrill.
Daniels, George H.
1968   *American Science in the Age of Jackson.* New York: Columbia University Press.
Darnton, Robert
1975   "Writing News and Telling Stories." *Daedalus* 104 (2):175–94.
Darrah, William Culp
1964   *Stereo Views; A History of Stereographs in America and Their Collection.* Gettysburg, Pa.: Times and News.
Davis, David Brion
1968   *Homicide in American Fiction 1798–1860.* Ithaca: Cornell University Press.
Davison, W. Phillips; Boylan, James; and Yu, Frederick T. C.
1976   *Mass Media Systems and Effects.* New York: Praeger.
Dawley, Alan
1976   *Class and Community: The Industrial Revolution in Lynn.* Cambridge, Mass.: Harvard University Press.
Derber, Milton
1970   *The American Idea of Industrial Democracy 1865–1965.* Urbana: University of Illinois Press.
Douglas, Ann
1977   *The Feminization of American Culture.* New York: Alfred A. Knopf.
Dudek, Louis
1961   *Literature and the Press.* Toronto: Ryerson and Contact Press.

Edel, Leon
    1974   "Novel and Camera." In *The Theory of the Novel: New Essays.* ed. John Halperin, pp. 177–88. New York: Oxford University Press.

Emery, Edwin
    1972   *The Press and America.* 3d ed. Englewood Cliffs, N.J.: Prentice-Hall.

Emery, Edwin, and Emery, Michael
    1978   *The Press and America.* 4th ed. Englewood Cliffs, N.J.: Prentice-Hall.

Ernst, Robert
    1949   *Immigrant Life in New York City 1825–1863.* Port Washington, N. Y.: Reprinted by Ira J. Friedman.

Everett, George
    1972   "The Linotype and U. S. Daily Newspaper Journalism in the 1890s: Analysis of a Relationship." Ph.D. dissertation, University of Iowa.

Ewen, Stuart
    1976   *Captains of Consciousness.* New York: McGraw-Hill.

Ferguson, Eugene S.
    1977   "The Mind's Eye: Nonverbal Thought in Technology." *Science* 197: 827–36.

Feyerabend, Paul
    1975   *Against Method.* London: NLB.

Fiske, John, and Hartley, John
    1978   *Reading Television.* London: Methuen.

Flaherty, David H.
    1971   "Law and the Enforcement of Morals in Early America." In *Perspectives in American History,* vol. 5, ed. Donald Fleming and Bernard Bailyn, pp. 203–53. Cambridge, Mass.: Harvard University Press.

Flaubert, Gustave
    1962   *Sentimental Education.* Trans. Anthony Goldsmith. London: J. M. Dent & Sons.

Foner, Eric
    1976   *Tom Paine and Revolutionary America.* New York: Oxford University Press.

Foner, Philip S.
    1947   *History of the Labor Movement in the United States.* vol. 1. New York: International Publishers.
    1975   *American Labor Songs of the Nineteenth Century.* Urbana: University of Illinois Press.

Foucault, Michel
    1977   *Discipline and Punish.* New York: Pantheon Books.

Fox, Celina
    1978   "Political Caricature and the Freedom of the Press in Early Nineteenth-Century England." In *Newspaper History,* ed. George Boyce, James Curran, and Pauline Wingate, pp. 226–46. Beverly Hills: Sage Publications.

Francke, Warren T.
    1974   "Investigative Exposure in the Nineteenth Century: The Journalistic

Heritage of the Muckrakers." Ph.D. dissertation, University of Minnesota.

Gans, Herbert J.
1979   *Deciding What's News.* New York: Pantheon.
Geertz, Clifford
1973   *The Interpretation of Cultures.* New York: Basic Books.
Gerbner, George
1964   "Ideological Perspectives and Political Tendencies in News Reporting." *Journalism Quarterly* 41 (3):495–508.
1973a   "Cultural Indicators: The Third Voice." In *Communications Technology and Social Policy,* ed. George Gerbner, Larry P. Gross, and William H. Melody, pp. 555–73. New York: John Wiley and Sons.
1973b   "Teacher Image in Mass Culture: Symbolic Functions of the 'Hidden Curriculum.' " In *Communications Technology and Social Policy,* ed. George Gerbner, Larry P. Gross, and William H. Melody, pp. 267–86. New York: John Wiley and Sons.
Gerbner, George, and Gross, Larry P.
1976   "Living with Television: The Violence Profile." *Journal of Communication* 26 (2):173–99.
Gernsheim, Helmut
1969   *The History of Photography.* New York: McGraw-Hill.
Goffman, Erving
1976   "Gender Advertisements." *Studies in the Anthropology of Visual Communication* 3:69–154.
Gordon, George N.
1977   *The Communications Revolution.* New York: Hastings House.
Gouldner, Alvin W.
1976   *The Dialectic of Ideology and Technology.* New York: Seabury Press.
Green, Frederick
1945   "Corporations as Persons, Citizens, and Possessors of Liberty." *University of Pennsylvania Law Review* 94:202–37.
Grimsted, David
1972   "Rioting in its Jacksonian Setting." *American Historical Review* 77 (2):361–97.
Gross, Larry P.
1973   "Modes of Communication and the Acquisition of Symbolic Competence." In *Communications Technology and Social Policy,* ed. George Gerbner, Larry P. Gross, and William H. Melody, pp. 189–208. New York: John Wiley and Sons.
Habermas, Jurgen
1971   *Knowledge and Human Interests.* Boston: Beacon Press.
1974   *Theory and Practice.* Boston: Beacon Press.

Hage, George S.
　1967　*Newspapers on the Minnesota Frontier 1849–1860.* Minneapolis: Minnesota Historical Society.
Halevy, Elie
　1955　*The Growth of Philosophic Radicalism.* Boston: Beacon Press.
Hall, Stuart; Critcher, Charles; Jefferson, Tony; Clarke, John; and Roberts, Brian
　1978　*Policing the Crisis.* London: Macmillan.
Halliday, M. A. K.
　1976　"Anti-Languages." *American Anthropologist* 78 (3):570–84.
Harris, David J.
　1966　*Socialist Origins in the United States: American Forerunners of Marx 1817–1832.* Assen: Van Gorcum.
Hill, Christopher
　1975　*The World Turned Upside Down.* Harmondsworth: Penguin.
Hindus, Michael Stephen
　1977　"The Contours of Crime and Justice in Massachusetts and South Carolina, 1767–1878." *American Journal of Legal History* 21 (3):212–37.
Hobbes, Thomas
　1968　*Leviathan.* Ed. C. B. Macpherson. Middlesex: Penguin. (First published 1651.)
Hobsbawm, Eric
　1975　*The Age of Capital 1848–1875.* New York: Charles Scribner's Sons.
Hofstadter, Richard
　1955　*The Age of Reform.* New York: Vintage Books.
Hohendahl, Peter Uwe
　1979　"Critical Theory, Public Sphere and Culture: Jurgen Habermas and His Critics." *New German Critique* 16 (Winter):89–118.
Hollis, Patricia
　1970　*The Pauper Press.* London: Oxford University Press.
Horlick, Allan Stanley
　1975　*Country Boys and Merchant Princes.* Lewisburg: Bucknell University Press.
Horwitz, Morton J.
　1977　*The Transformation of American Law, 1780–1860.* Cambridge, Mass.: Harvard University Press.
Hughes, Helen MacGill
　1940　*News and the Human Interest Story.* Chicago: University of Chicago Press.
　1942　"The Social Interpretation of News." *Annals of the American Academy of Political and Social Science* 219:11–17.
Hugins, Walter
　1960　*Jacksonian Democracy and the Working Class.* Stanford: Stanford University Press.
Hymes, Dell
　1974　*Foundations in Sociolinguistics.* Philadelphia: University of Pennsylvania Press.

Ivins, William M., Jr.

　1953　*Prints and Visual Communication.* Cambridge, Mass.: MIT Press.

Jenkins, Reese V.

　1975　*Images and Enterprise: Technology and the American Photographic Industry 1839 to 1925.* Baltimore: Johns Hopkins University Press.

Johnstone, John W. C.; Slawski, Edward J.; and Bowman, William W.

　1972　"The Professional Values of American Newsmen." *Public Opinion Quarterly* 36:522–40.

Jussim, Estelle

　1974　*Visual Communication and the Graphic Arts.* New York: R. R. Bowker.

Keller, Edward

　1980　"Television's Coverage of Nuclear Energy." Unpublished manuscript.

Kolb, Harold H., Jr.

　1969a　*The Illusion of Life.* Charlottesville: University Press of Virginia.

　1969b　"In Search of Definition: American Literary Realism and the Clichés." *American Literary Realism 1870–1910* 2 (2):165–73.

Kunzle, David

　1971　"Narrative Emphasis in Broadsheets of Private Crime." Paper read at the College Art Association Meeting at Chicago (28–30 January).

　1973　*The Early Comic Strip.* Berkeley: University of California Press.

Langbein, John H.

　1973　"The Origins of Public Prosecution at Common Law." *American Journal of Legal History* 17 (4):313–35.

Larson, Magali Sarfati

　1977　*The Rise of Professionalism: A Sociological Analysis.* Berkeley and Los Angeles: University of California Press.

Laurie, Bruce

　1974　" 'Nothing on Compulsion': Life Styles of Philadelphia Artisans, 1820–1850." *Labor History* 15 (3):337–66.

　1980　*Working People of Philadelphia 1800–1850.* Philadelphia: Temple University Press.

Lazarsfeld, Paul F., and Merton, Robert K.

　1971　"Mass Communication, Popular Taste, and Organized Social Action." In *The Processes and Effects of Mass Communication,* ed. Wilbur Schramm and Donald F. Roberts, pp. 554–78. Urbana: University of Illinois Press.

Leighten, Patricia D.

　1977–78　"Critical Attitudes toward Overtly Manipulated Photography in the 20th Century." *Art Journal* 37 (2):133–38.

Leiss, William

　1974　*The Domination of Nature.* Boston: Beacon Press.

Leith, James A.

　1968　*Media and Revolution.* Toronto: CBC Publications.

Lindquist-Cock, Elizabeth

　1977　*The Influence of Photography on American Landscape Painting, 1839–1880.* New York and London: Garland.

Lowenthal, Leo
    1968   "The Triumph of Mass Idols." In *Literature, Popular Culture and Society,* by Leo Lowenthal, pp. 109–40. Palo Alto: Pacific Books.

Lukacs, Georg
    1962   *The Historical Novel.* Harmondsworth: Penguin.

MacDougall, Curtis
    1958   *Hoaxes.* New York: Dover.

Macpherson, C. B.
    1962   *The Political Theory of Possessive Individualism.* London: Oxford University Press.

Matson, Floyd W.
    1966   *The Broken Image.* Garden City: Anchor Books.

Mayer, Stephen
    1978   "*People v. Fisher:* The Shoemakers' Strike of 1833." *New-York Historical Society Quarterly* 62 (1):6–21.

McMahon, Helen
    1973   *Criticism of Fiction in the Atlantic Monthly 1857–1898.* New York: Bookman Associates.

Meyers, Marvin
    1960   *The Jacksonian Persuasion.* Stanford: Stanford University Press.

Miller, Douglas T.
    1967   *Jacksonian Aristocracy: Class and Democracy in New York 1830–1860.* New York: Oxford University Press.
    1970   *The Birth of Modern America 1820–1850.* New York: Pegasus.

Miller, Wilbur R.
    1977   *Cops and Bobbies.* Chicago: University of Chicago Press.

Mills, C. Wright
    1967   *The Sociological Imagination.* London: Oxford University Press.

Molotch, Harvey, and Lester, Marilyn
    1974a   "Accidents, Scandals, and Routines: Resources for Insurgent Methodology." In *The TV Establishment,* ed. Gaye Tuchman, pp. 53–65. Englewood Cliffs, N.J.: Prentice-Hall.
    1974b   "News as Purposive Behavior: On the Strategic Use of Routine Events, Accidents, and Scandals." *American Sociological Review* 39:101–12.

Monkkonen, Eric H.
    1979   "Recent Historical Studies of Crime and Crime Control in the United States." *IASSIST Newsletter* 3 (Fall):14–22.

Montgomery, David
    1967   *Beyond Equality.* New York: Alfred A. Knopf.
    1968   "The Working Classes of the Pre-Industrial American City, 1780–1830." *Labor History* 9 (1):3–22.

Mott, Frank Luther
    1962   *American Journalism—A History: 1690–1960.* 3d ed. New York: Macmillan.
    1967   *A History of American Magazines.* 5 vols. Cambridge, Mass.: Harvard University Press.

Nash, Gary B.
  1979   *The Urban Crucible.* Cambridge, Mass.: Harvard University Press.
Navin, Thomas R.
  1970   "The 500 Largest American Industrials in 1917." *Business History Review* 44 (3):360–86.
Nelson, William
  1973   *Fact or Fiction: The Dilemma of the Renaissance Storyteller.* Cambridge, Mass.: Harvard University Press.
Nelson, William E.
  1975   *Americanization of the Common Law: The Impact of Legal Change on Massachusetts Society.* Cambridge, Mass.: Harvard University Press.
Newhall, Beaumont
  1976   *The Daguerreotype in America.* 3d ed. New York: Dover.
Nochlin, Linda
  1971   *Realism.* Harmondsworth: Penguin.
Nordin, Kenneth D.
  1977   "The Entertaining Press: Sensationalism in Eighteenth-Century Boston Newspapers." Paper submitted to History Division, Association for Education in Journalism Meeting at Madison, Wisconsin (August).
O'Boyle, Lenore
  1968   "The Image of the Journalist in France, Germany, and England, 1815–1848." *Comparative Studies in Society and History* 10 (3):290–317.
Perry, Louis B., and Perry, Richard S.
  1963   *A History of the Los Angeles Labor Movement, 1911–1941.* Berkeley and Los Angeles: University of California Press.
Pessen, Edward
  1973   *Riches, Class, and Power before the Civil War.* Lexington: D. C. Heath.
  1978   "Political Democracy and the Distribution of Power in Antebellum New York City." In *Essays in the History of New York City: A Memorial to Sidney Pomerantz,* ed. Irwin Yellowitz, pp. 21–42. Port Washington, N.Y.: Kennikat Press.
Peters, Marsha, and Mergen, Bernard
  1977   " 'Doing the Rest': The Uses of Photographs in American Studies." *American Quarterly* 29 (3):280–303.
Peterson, Ted
  1945   "British Crime Pamphleteers: Forgotten Journalists." *Journalism Quarterly* 22 (4):305–16.
  1950   "James Catnach: Master of Street Literature." *Journalism Quarterly* 27 (2):157–63.
Phillips, E. Barbara
  1977   "Approaches to Objectivity: Journalistic versus Social Science Perspectives." In *Strategies for Communication Research,* ed. Paul M. Hirsch, Peter V. Miller, and F. Gerald Kline, pp. 63–78. Beverly Hills: Sage Publications.
Pocock, J. G. A.
  1973   *Politics, Language and Time.* New York: Atheneum.

Polanyi, Michael
1962   *Personal Knowledge.* Chicago: University of Chicago Press.
Pred, Allan R.
1973   *Urban Growth and the Circulation of Information.* Cambridge, Mass.: Harvard University Press.
Pringle, Patrick
1955   *Hue and Cry.* New York: William Morrow.
Prothero, Iorworth J.
1979   *Artisans and Politics in Early Nineteenth-Century London.* Folkestone: Wm. Dawson & Son.
Raucher, Alan R.
1968   *Public Relations and Business 1900–1929.* Baltimore: Johns Hopkins Press.
Rediker, Marcus
1978   "The Discourse on Anglo-American Piracy 1713–1726." Unpublished manuscript.
Richardson, James F.
1970   *The New York Police.* New York: Oxford University Press.
Rock, Howard B.
1979   *Artisans of the New Republic.* New York: New York University Press.
Rogers, Daniel T.
1978   *The Work Ethic in Industrial America 1850–1920.* Chicago: University of Chicago Press.
Rosenberg, Charles
1962   *The Cholera Years.* Chicago: University of Chicago Press.
Rosten, Leo C.
1937   *The Washington Correspondents.* New York: Harcourt, Brace.
Rothman, David J.
1971   *The Discovery of the Asylum.* Boston: Little, Brown.
Rude, George
1962   *Wilkes and Liberty.* Oxford: Clarendon Press.
Rudisill, Richard
1971   *Mirror Image.* Albuquerque: University of New Mexico Press.
Ruud, Charles A.
1979   "Limits on the 'Freed' Press of 18th- and 19th-Century Europe." *Journalism Quarterly* 56 (3):521–30, 693.
Saxton, Alexander
1979   "George Wilkes: The Disintegration of a Radical Ideology." Paper presented to the Conference on Labor History, Walter Reuther Library of Labor and Urban Affairs and History Department, Wayne State University, Detroit (October).
Scharf, Aaron
1974   *Art and Photography.* Harmondsworth: Penguin.
Schiller, Dan
1976   "An Historical Investigation of the English Unstamped Press 1830–

1836: Institutions and Symbolic Content." Master's thesis, Annenberg School of Communications, University of Pennsylvania.

1977 "Realism, Photography and Journalistic Objectivity in 19th-Century America." *Studies in the Anthropology of Visual Communication* 4 (2):86–98.

1979 "An Historical Approach to Objectivity and Professionalism in American Newsgathering." *Journal of Communication* 29 (4):46–57.

1980 "From Rogues to the Rights of Men." *Media, Culture and Society,* forthcoming.

Schiller, Herbert I.

1973 *The Mind Managers.* Boston: Beacon Press.

Schneider, John C.

1978 "Public Order and the Geography of the City: Crime, Violence, and the Police in Detroit, 1845–1875." *Journal of Urban History* 4 (2):183–208.

Schudson, Michael

1978 *Discovering the News.* New York: Basic Books.

Seavoy, Ronald E.

1972 "Laws to Encourage Manufacturing: New York Policy and the 1811 General Incorporation Statute." *Business History Review* 46 (1):85–95.

Shaw, Donald L.

1967 "News Bias and the Telegraph: A Study of Historical Change." *Journalism Quarterly* 44 (1):3–12.

Siebert, Frederick Seaton

1952 *Freedom of the Press in England 1476–1776.* Urbana: University of Illinois Press.

Siebert, Fred S.; Peterson, Theodore; and Schramm, Wilbur

1963 *Four Theories of the Press.* Urbana: University of Illinois Press.

Sigal, Leon V.

1973 *Reporters and Officials.* Lexington: D. C. Heath.

Silver, Alan

1967 "The Demand for Order in Civil Society: A Review of Some Themes in the History of Urban Crime, Police, and Riot." In *The Police: Six Sociological Essays,* ed. David Bordua, pp. 1–24. New York: John Wiley and Sons.

Smith, Culver H.

1977 *The Press, Politics, and Patronage.* Athens: University of Georgia Press.

Steirer, William F., Jr.

1972 "Philadelphia Newspapers: Years of Revolution and Transition, 1764–1794." Ph.D. dissertation, University of Pennsylvania.

Sterling, Christopher H., and Haight, Timothy R.

1978 *The Mass Media: Aspen Institute Guide to Communication Industry Trends.* New York and London: Praeger.

Stewart, Donald H.

1969 *The Opposition Press of the Federalist Period.* Albany: State University of New York.

Taft, Robert
    1938   *Photography and the American Scene.* New York: Dover.
Taylor, Ian; Walton, Paul; and Young, Jock
    1973   *The New Criminology.* New York: Harper and Row.
Tebbel, John
    1974   *The Media in America.* New York: New American Library.
Thompson, E. P.
    1968   *The Making of the English Working Class.* Harmondsworth: Penguin.
Tuchman, Gaye
    1972   "Objectivity as Strategic Ritual: An Examination of Newsmen's Notions of Objectivity." *American Journal of Sociology* 77 (4):660–79.
    1978a   *Making News.* New York: The Free Press.
    1978b   "Professionalism as an Agent of Legitimation." *Journal of Communication* 28 (2):106–12.
    1980   "Facts of the Moment: The Study of News." *Symbolic Interaction,* forthcoming.
Turbayne, Colin Murray
    1970   *The Myth of Metaphor.* Columbia: University of South Carolina Press.
Van Every, Edward
    1930   *Sins of New York as 'Exposed' by the Police Gazette.* New York: Frederick A. Stokes.
    1931   *Sins of America as 'Exposed' by the Police Gazette.* New York: Frederick A. Stokes.
Van Tassel, David D.
    1960   *Recording America's Past.* Chicago: University of Chicago Press.
Walker, Samuel
    1976   "The Urban Police in American History: A Review of the Literature." *Journal of Police Science and Administration* 4 (3):252–60.
Wallace, Michael L.
    1973   "Ideologies of Party in the Ante-Bellum Republic." Ph.D. dissertation, Columbia University.
Ward, David
    1971   *Cities and Immigrants.* New York: Oxford University Press.
Watt, Ian
    1957   *The Rise of the Novel.* Berkeley: University of California Press.
Weinbaum, Paul O.
    1979   *Mobs and Demagogues.* n. p.: UMI Research Press.
Whisnant, David E.
    1972   "Selling the Gospel News; or, The Strange Career of Jimmy Brown the Newsboy." *Journal of Social History* 5 (3):269–309.
Wilentz, Robert Sean
    1980   "Class Conflict and the Rights of Man: Artisans and Radicalism in Antebellum New York." Ph.D. dissertation, Yale University.
Williams, Alden
    1975   "Unbiased Study of Television News Bias." *Journal of Communication* 25 (4):190–99.

Williams, Raymond
 1974 *Television Technology and Cultural Form.* London: Fontana.
 1976 "Developments in the Sociology of Culture." *Sociology* 10 (3):497–506.
Williamson, Chilton
 1960 *American Suffrage from Property to Democracy 1760–1860.* Princeton: Princeton University Press.
Wilsher, Ann
 1977 "Words in Camera." *History of Photography* 1 (1):84.
Winslow, Ola Elizabeth (ed.)
 1930 *American Broadside Verse from Imprints of the 17th and 18th Centuries.* New Haven: Yale University Press.
Wood, Gordon S.
 1969 *The Creation of the American Republic, 1776–1787.* New York: W. W. Norton.
Woodward, David (ed.)
 1975 *Five Centuries of Map Printing.* Chicago: University of Chicago Press.
Worth, Sol
 1976 "Doing Anthropology of Visual Communication." *Working Papers in Culture and Communication* 1 (2):2–21.
 1978 "Towards an Ethnographic Semiotic." Paper delivered to introduce the conference on "Utilisation de l'ethnologie par le Cinéma/Utilisation du Cinema par l'ethnologie," Paris, UNESCO (February 1977).
Zochert, Donald
 1976 "Science and the Common Man in Ante-Bellum America." In *Science in America since 1820,* ed. by Nathan Reingold, pp. 7–32. New York: Science History Publications.

INDEX

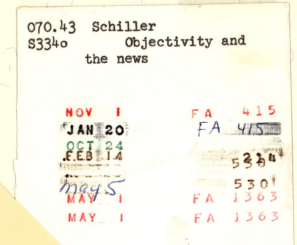